Teaching Mathematics

Teaching Mathematics

With emphasis on the diagnostic approach

Sam Adams
LOUISIANA STATE UNIVERSITY

Leslie Ellis
LIVINGSTON PARISH SCHOOLS, LOUISIANA

B. F. Beeson
LOUISIANA STATE UNIVERSITY

Harper & Row, Publishers
New York   Hagerstown   San Francisco   London

Sponsoring Editor: Wayne E. Schotanus
Project Editor: Richard T. Viggiano
Designer: Andrea C. Goodman
Production Supervisor: Kewal K. Sharma
Compositor: Progressive Typographers, Inc.
Printer and Binder: The Murray Printing Company
Art Studio: Vantage Art, Inc.

TEACHING MATHEMATICS: With Emphasis on the Diagnostic Approach

Library of Congress Cataloging in Publication Data

Adams, Sam, Date-
    Teaching mathematics.

    Includes index.
    1. Mathematics—Study and teaching (Elementary)
I. Ellis, Leslie, joint author. II. Beeson, B. F.,
joint author. III. Title.
QA135.5.A3   372.7   77-8652
ISBN 0-06-040164-8

contents

preface

This book is based on our composite experience of several decades in the area of elementary-school mathematics. That experience was garnered in our roles, at one time or another, as classroom teacher, elementary principal, elementary supervisor, teacher of college-level methods courses, and consultant to school systems. In deciding on the content of this text, our overriding concern was: How would something work in a classroom? Often the answer was arrived at by going into a classroom and trying it out.

Although much of the content of this book deals with standard methodology, special emphasis is placed on the diagnostic/prescriptive approach. In elementary mathematics there has been renewed interest recently in "the basics"—and what could be more basic than to teach students what they need to know? Yet this is impossible unless a teacher *knows* what students need to learn. Identifying needs and then meeting them is the heart of the diagnostic/prescriptive approach.

We feel that merely studying a method leads to an incomplete understanding. Hence, we encourage future teachers to work with a student while studying this book. Some might even prefer to participate in an actual case study like the ones reported in the Appendices of this text. Work in the area of mathematics methods will be more meaningful if it includes some contact with one or more students. This provides an opportunity to learn firsthand what methods work best in the classroom.

S.A
L.C.E.
B.F.B.

part I

an overview

This section deals with some of the fairly general aspects of teaching elementary-school mathematics. Included are some informal definitions of terms along with a broad look at methodology. Practically all of the concepts presented in this section will be encountered later as we move toward specific applications.

Why do we need an overview? Why do we not go directly and swiftly to the heart of the matter and develop a series of steps to good teaching? It simply does not work that way; there is no such series of steps. Perhaps after years in the teaching profession you will develop a fairly definite mode of operation that is useful to you. But your procedure will probably be useful to no one else, and you yourself will constantly adjust it to new situations.

Background

Arithmetic is so well established in today's elementary-school curriculum that it is difficult to imagine that it was not always given major emphasis in early-childhood education. However, the curriculum of most colonial American elementary schools included very little, if any, arithmetic. There were two reasons why little arithmetic was taught at the elementary level in colonial times. First, education in the common schools had as its basic purpose the preparing of young men for the ministry, and although some arithmetic was taught in grammar schools and colonial colleges, it was not emphasized. Second, arithmetic was considered a very difficult subject to teach. The schoolmaster who was an "arithmeticker" was in great demand, and pupils who knew their "sums" were the envy of other pupils.

During the colonial period arithmetic books were very scarce. The teacher usually possessed the only copy in the school. Instruction was dictated and copied as each pupil made his or her own written book of rules and solved problems. Arithmetic books came into use near the middle of the eighteenth century but only in the larger towns. The first arithmetic books used in colonial schools were by English authors. The earliest American textbook was written by Isaac Greenwood in 1729. A few others followed, but arithmetic was still considered a very difficult subject to teach and remained largely a college study prior to 1800.

A turning point in the teaching of arithmetic was reached in America in 1821. In that year Warren Colburn's *First Lessons in Arithmetic on the Plan of Pestalozzi* was published. At that time there was also a greater need for mathematics because the nation was becoming industrialized. Thus, as a result of pressing needs and the introduction of a new textbook, arithmetic became one of the major subjects of the common schools.

But, emphasis on mathematics in the elementary schools did not remain consistently high. Around the turn of the twentieth century many American educators were very much interested in the teachings of the German philosopher Johann Friedrich Herbart (1776–1841). Herbart introduced many principles and aims of education, among them that of developing in the child a "many-sided interest." This principle led to an emphasis on literature and history in the elementary schools, thus reducing the time allotted to the study of arithmetic. At about the same time William James published his *Principles of Psychology,* in which he denied that training is transferable. Since this was one rationale for the emphasis on memorization in arithmetic, the generous amount of time given the subject was criticized.

In line with these attacks on the arithmetic curriculum, the Committee of Fifteen recommended in 1895 that arithmetic instruction begin in the second year of school and end at the sixth year. The committee also suggested that the practice of teaching two daily lessons—a "mental" and a "written" one—be discontinued.

In 1935 the "meaning theory" was presented in the *Tenth Yearbook of the National Council of Teachers of Mathematics.* This theory maintains that students must understand the structure of the number system in order to perform number operations meaningfully. Accordingly, students must be encouraged to find rules inductively rather than "using" rules deductively. In classroom discussions students explored number relations and principles and were urged to apply mathematical knowledge creatively in solving social problems. Many of these ideas were developed a few years later in what has been called the "new math."

Emphasis since 1950

Since the mid-twentieth century mathematics at all levels has been in a state of what has been described by many as a revolution. As in any revolution there were those who seemed to be advocating the eradication of all that was traditional. On the other side there were some who refused to accept any of the new ideas. As is usually the case, however, there were those who looked at the problem realistically: they were willing to accept new and exciting concepts and practices while holding on to older, proven methods.

Causes for the revolution

Several reasons account for the sweeping changes that occurred in the practices of teaching and the content of the mathematics curriculum. First, many advances made in mathematics by researchers in the first half of the twentieth century had not, by 1950, found their way into the curricula of colleges and public schools. Second, automatic digital computers were becoming quite common in the 1950s. These machines dramatically increased speed and accuracy in calculations, thus releasing much time for the study of theory. A third cause for the revolution was the introduction of automation, that is, machines that control machines. Designing and developing such machines require extensive mathematical knowledge.

An immediate cause of the revolution in school mathematics was the pressure exerted by critics of school programs in general. These critics gained some credibility by the fact that the Soviet Union was able to place a satellite in orbit around the earth before the United States did. Because it seemed at the time that this country was losing the space race, the time was ripe for critics to point out the shortcomings of school curricula. The excitement generated by these critics forced many officials to place greater emphasis on school science and mathematics. Thus a great deal of financial aid was extended to groups engaged in efforts to improve the teaching of these subjects.

New mathematics programs

In the late 1950s and early 1960s many mathematics programs were developed for high schools, junior high schools, and elementary schools. A few of the major ones were:

> School Mathematics Study Group (SMSG)
> University of Illinois Curriculum Study in Mathematics (UICSM)
> Boston College Mathematics Institute
> Ball State Teachers College Experimental Program
> Madison Project (Syracuse University)
> University of Illinois Arithmetic Project

Of these programs, which differed considerably in size, the SMSG was the largest. The SMSG was funded by the National Science Foundation and was able to engage large, well-qualified writing teams. The material, which was used in pilot projects on a very large scale, influenced teachers over the entire country.

Unifying themes

Although the material developed by each of the groups had certain unique qualities, there were unifying themes. Some of these were:

> Sets—language and elementary theory
> Structure
> Systems of numeration
> Operations and their inverses
> Properties of numbers and the development of the real-number system
> Measurement
> Graphical representation
> Statistical inferences and probability
> Logical deduction
> Valid generalizations

Each of these topics is discussed at some point in the chapters that follow in this book.

Compromise and stabilization?

The mathematics programs for elementary schools developed in the early 1960s emphasize meaning. The structure of mathematics is stressed as is the principle of discovery. The elementary curriculum introduces new content while omitting other material. Much attention is given to vocabulary. There does not seem to be any general agreement on the role of drill. Some seem to feel that if understanding is developed, skill will follow automatically.

Recent studies have shown, however, that arithmetic skills are somewhat weak among our high-school graduates. A great deal of attention has been given to this situation by the media. Professional journals dedicate considerable space to the topic of developing greater skills in arithmetic in the elementary schools. Many educators feel that this is a healthy sign. If we can teach for understanding and at the same time see to the development of good skills, then surely the revolution will lead to improvement. The viewpoint of this text is that the diagnostic/prescriptive approach to teaching, discussed later, can play a major role in helping bring about improvement in skills without excessive drill. In using the diagnostic/prescriptive approach, the teacher identifies specific difficulties, then targets instruction on them.

Basic aims of an arithmetic program

Regardless of the prevailing philosophy and practice at any given time, elementary arithmetic has certain basic aims. It seems particularly appropriate that those aims be stressed at this time in our history. Teaching materials are so diverse today that teachers may be placed in a position of having to make decisions as to what is really pertinent and what is supplemental. Many modern textbooks contain topics appropriate only for advanced pupils. Under such circumstances we believe it is essential for students to:

1. Develop a wholesome attitude toward and appreciation of mathematics
2. Comprehend fundamental mathematical concepts
3. Master basic computational skills
4. Develop problem-solving ability

These aims are not listed in order of importance, for they are all important and should be developed simultaneously. We believe they are basic in the sense that they are appropriate aims for everyone capable of attaining them, not just those who would be mathematicians, scientists, engineers, or technicians.

Attitude and appreciations

If surveyed, a large percentage of students would not list mathematics among their favorite subjects. In fact, mathematics seems to be the subject most dreaded by students in general. Why is this? Is mathematics by its very nature more difficult than other school subjects? Is it dull and incapable of being made interesting? Surely, the answer to each of these questions is no. It is a fairly well-accepted fact that attitudes are learned, not inherited. Thus, the teacher is in a position to encourage the development of positive attitudes. There are no pedagogical remedies for curing all learning ailments; however, certain features of teaching arithmetic, if recognized, may help guide young teachers in the area of attitude and appreciations.

Teacher attitude Attitude is contagious. The teacher who displays enthusiasm will find that students are also enthusiastic. But, one may ask, "Suppose a teacher just doesn't like arithmetic?" By recognizing the immense importance of basic mathematics to each pupil, the teacher may gain respect for the subject. Also, by actively engaging in a study of the structure of our number system, teachers may lose certain fears they may have developed during childhood.

With fundamental knowledge of structure a teacher can present topics of arithmetic in a well-ordered sequence, thus making his or her job more pleasant. The diagnostic/prescriptive approach to teaching skills has been known to help some teachers in following an ordered sequence. This approach enables an individual to see and document progress toward goals and, very often, helps build good attitudes in teachers and students.

Unique nature of arithmetic Arithmetic is somewhat unique among school subjects in that pupils' efforts very often lead to an answer that appears to have no degrees of quality: it is either right or wrong. A child may have worked for some time on a set of exercises only to be told, "They are all wrong—work them over." We can hardly imagine a pupil who has labored over a creative-writing assignment being told that it is "all wrong." The least we would expect is for the teacher to carefully examine the work and try to balance the negative with the positive points as a means of encouragement. Certainly this approach may be somewhat more difficult in arithmetic, since the only visible evidence of a student's labor may be a single number—the answer. Thus, the point of difficulty very often must be discovered by close observation of individuals at work or perhaps by having the pupil express his or her thought patterns aloud. Once the exact point of difficulty is apparent, correction is usually fairly simple and quick. This may prevent frustration, a common cause of poor attitudes.

Proper sequencing The structure of our number system is such that the study of arithmetic can be rather well ordered. Learning a new topic very often depends upon mastery of a concept that precedes the topic in question. This is particularly true in the area of arithmetic skills. For example, we must learn the facts of addition before addition of two-digit numbers can be mastered. A student who has failed to achieve needed proficiency in a subtask is almost certain to "bog down" further along the sequence. Left uncorrected, the pupil will continue to have trouble, since the next step is dependent upon the one on which he or she is now blocked, and the cycle continues. The end result is often frustration. Evaluation of a diagnostic nature is of utmost importance at this point. Discovering the stage of development of individuals is a rather simple procedure if a teacher is aware of the hierarchy, or sequence, of components implicit in each arithmetic operation.

Comprehension of concepts

Although almost any list of objectives for elementary arithmetic would place understanding at or near the top, that term is a difficult one to define. A dictionary definition lists several synonyms such as comprehension, knowledge, and awareness, any one of which is as nebulous as understanding. College students are often bombarded with the term without being told what pupils should be able to do in order to demonstrate that they in fact understand a particular concept. To be measurable and teachable, objectives for understanding should be stated in terms of pupil performance.

It is not within the scope of this text either to list all possible concepts that elementary-school pupils should develop, or to attempt to define understanding. However, understanding in arithmetic is indicated to some degree when pupils are able to work problems that they have never seen but that are of the same general type encountered in previous experience.

In the past few years a controversy has arisen concerning teaching for understanding versus teaching for skill. Some argue that traditionally arithmetic teachers have placed the major emphasis on development of skills, leaving the development of understanding largely to the intuition of pupils. Others feel that new approaches to teaching arithmetic overemphasize understanding and lead to poor skills.

Neither view contains the whole truth. It is unlikely that students will develop good skills without some degree of understanding. One must understand why and how a rule works if the operation is to be applied to new situations. On the other hand, understanding is difficult to reach without reasonably good skills. If the learner is unable to perform basic operations, communication soon breaks down. The argument concerning the chicken or the egg seems appropriate here. We may never know which came first, but we do know that we are unlikely to have one without the other.

Basic computational skills

Those whose philosophies range from the most traditional to the most modern would surely be in agreement on one point, namely, that a basic task of elementary teachers is to see that pupils develop basic computational skills. By the time a child has completed the sixth grade, we would expect that he or she could add, subtract, multiply, and divide whole numbers, common fractions, and decimal fractions with considerable speed and efficiency. These skills are essential, hand calculators notwithstanding, to every consumer, citizen, and worker. They are necessary tools for the further development of mathematical understanding.

Developing speed and accuracy in the operations requires a certain amount of memorization. The facts of addition, subtraction, multiplication, and division must be committed to memory. Certainly understanding should precede memorization. For example, the child should know *why* 5 × 4 = 20, but once understanding is accomplished, memorization should be the next step. The child should not need to "figure out" why 5 × 4 = 20 each time that fact is needed; it should be automatic.

Arithmetic operations of addition, subtraction, multiplication, and division of numbers of more than one digit are accomplished by means of algorithms. An *algorithm* is a rule of procedure. Each rule is a shortcut that takes advantage of the structure of the number system. Teachers should take great care to assure that the reason for each step is understood. But, once the operations are understood, the steps should become automatic. In other words, the pupil learns the procedure and then gains skill in its use. The second phase, gaining skill, is usually accomplished through drill and application.

Problem solving

Ultimately all goals in mathematics point toward problem solving. Skills and understanding are gained to enable people to solve problems encountered in the world outside the classroom. Although some study mathematics esthetically, to the vast majority it is a tool. Mathematics is the language of many other specialties such as engineering, accounting, physics, and chemistry, all of which focus on problem solving. Yet many students readily admit that problem solving is the most difficult phase in their study of mathematics. So difficult is the task of teaching problem solving that, if care is not exercised, this very important phase may be somewhat neglected in favor of computation.

Content

2

Content refers to those topics of mathematics that are the vehicles for developing those abilities described in the list of basic aims included in Chapter 1. Unlike the school curricula of earlier years, modern curricula may vary considerably in content. There is, however, a fairly comprehensive list of broad topics that make up the core of the elementary-school mathematics curriculum. The most common topics are:

1. Sets
   Meaning of sets
   Comparing sets
   Subsets of sets
   Ordering sets
   Joining sets
   Associating sets and numbers
2. Whole numbers
   Counting—rote and rational
   Cardinality and order
   Facts and algorithms of addition, subtraction, multiplication, and division
   Factors
3. Common fractions (rational numbers)
   Concepts and interpretation
   Addition, subtraction, multiplication, and division
   Ratio and proportion
4. Decimal fractions
   Decimal notation of rational numbers

Addition, subtraction, multiplication, and division
Exponents
5. Geometry and measurement
Recognizing geometric figures
Comparing sizes and shapes
Linear measurement
Associating points on a line and numbers
Measuring areas
Measuring volumes
6. Real numbers

The remainder of this chapter is devoted to brief preliminary discussions of a number of these topics. With the exception of sets, most are developed in greater detail later in this book.

Sets

Sets entered programs of elementary mathematics as a topic in the so called new math of the early 1960s. Although some of the content introduced by writers of the new math has perhaps not proven as useful as predicted, set concepts seem to be a valuable tool, particularly at the early levels. Set concepts are basic vehicles in introducing many number concepts. Number properties, the unifying elements in building a number system, are natural outgrowths of set concepts.

Language of sets

One reason why set ideas are easily employed in the early stages of elementary mathematics is that children bring some set ideas to school. For example, most children belong to a family, which may be thought of as a set. Certain toys come in sets, for instance, a set of building blocks or a set of playing cards. Many children have heard references made to sets of dishes, silverware, or other household items. Upon entering school each child becomes a member of a very special set, his or her class. Each student is also well aware that he or she is a member of a subset of the class, that is, he is a member of the subset of boys and she, a member of the subset of girls. Thus, the language of sets, when properly used, can flow quite naturally from common collections to sets of other concrete objects or subjects, and from there to sets of abstract numbers. The key concepts of set theory usually included in an elementary program are (1) belonging, (2) matching, (3) nonequivalent sets, (4) symbolic representation, (5) the null set, (6) equality, and (7) subsets. A brief discussion of each of these should clarify their meaning.

Belonging Long before entering school, most children learn to recognize various items on the basis of physical characteristics such as color, shape, or size. As this ability progresses, each child finds his or her own way of sorting the objects and placing them into rather crude classification. In short, children learn the concept of *belonging*. They learn that some animals are cats, some are dogs, some are fish, and so on. They also learn classifications on the basis of relationships; for example, they know siblings, grandparents, uncles, and others.

This preschool knowledge serves as a lead-in for the teacher to begin acquainting pupils with the idea of belonging to a set of numbers. Pupils learn to classify objects that they have at their disposal. These objects may be buttons, chips, Popsicle sticks, or any other small objects (preferably those that would be difficult to swallow). Games may be played using these objects in classification exercises. For example, pupils may be instructed to place all of their yellow chips on top of their desks. Such exercises teach the pupils how to identify objects belonging to sets, a very early stage in developing number concepts. From there, they can be taught to identify objects belonging to the set of four, five, and so forth.

Matching sets As will be seen in Chapter 6, matching is a step in developing readiness for numeration. *Matching* is accomplished by asking pupils to form sets having as many or the same number of objects as some given set. Since it is unlikely that pupils at this early stage count rationally, most of them will develop a one-to-one correspondence.

Nonequivalent sets Any two sets one of which has more elements than the other are *nonequivalent sets*. The sets do not match, and, of course, they do not have the same number property. Employment of nonequivalent sets is very helpful in building general ideas of nonequivalence.

Symbolic representation The *symbolic representation* of a set may be by means of a capital letter or by means of a list of the elements enclosed in braces { }. For example, the set whose members are a, b, c, and d may be named set A, in which case we write:

$$A = \{a, b, c, d\}$$

We say that each element or member of the set belongs to the set named A; in fact, "belongs to" and "is a member of" are, in the language of sets, synonymous phrases. Many teachers use loops of yarn, rubber bands, and similar items to show sets using concrete objects.

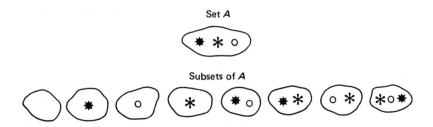

Figure 2-1. Yarn loops showing subsets

Null set A set may contain no elements, in which case we say that the set is empty or is a *null set*. This idea is symbolized by writing braces with no elements { } or by the symbol Ø. The cardinal number (number of elements) for the empty set is zero. The null set should not be confused with the set {0}, for this is the set whose element is the numeral zero and is therefore *not* empty.

Equality of sets A pair of sets are said to be *equal* only when they contain precisely the same elements. The phrase $A = B$, which is read as "Set A equals set B," means that set A contains the same elements as set B. The sets may be written with their elements in the same order or in a different order. For example, the set of elements {a, b, c} may be written:

{a, b, c}, {a, c, b}, {b, a, c}, {b, c, a}, {c, a, b}, or {c, b, a}

All of these sets are equal, since the only difference is in the arrangement of the elements.

Subsets The set B is a *subset* of set A if every element of set B is also an element of set A. If $B = \{a, b\}$ and $A = \{a, b, c\}$, then B is a subset of A. To symbolize the phrase "B is a subset of A," we write:

$B \subset A$

Subsets of a given set may be indicated by use of yarn loops as shown in Figure 2-1. Since the null set is common to all sets, it is a proper subset of any set.

Operations with sets

Certain operations on sets are fundamental in defining number sets such as the natural numbers. The two most basic operational ideas are union and intersection.

Union of sets The *union of* two *sets* A and B, is a set containing all elements in either A or B or both. This is symbolized by A ∪ B and is read, "The union of A and B." Thus, if A = {a, b, c} and B = {d, e, f}, then:

A ∪ B = {a, b, c, d, e, f}

In naming the union of two sets, common elements are not repeated. For example, if C = {1, 2, 3, 4} and D = {3, 4, 5, 6} then:

C ∪ D = {1, 2, 3, 4, 5, 6}

Notice that 3 and 4 are elements of both sets and are not repeated in the union of the two sets. Pupils may discover that C ∪ D is the same as D ∪ C, in other words, that the operation is *commutative*.

Intersection of sets The *intersection* of two sets C and D is the set containing elements in both C and D. The symbol for this operation is C ∩ D, which is read, "The intersection of C and D." Thus, if C = {1, 2, 3, 4} and D = {3, 4, 5, 6} then:

C ∩ D = {3, 4}

Notice that 3 and 4 are common to the two sets.

Sets with no elements in common are called *disjoint sets*. The union of disjoint sets is useful in introducing addition. Do you see why? The intersection of such sets is the null set. Thus, if A = {a, b, c} and B = {d, e, f} then:

A ∩ B = Ø

The operations union and intersection are very useful ideas in the study of geometry. Certain relationships such as the intersection of geometric figures may be better understood if pupils have an understanding of operations on sets. Another application of union and intersection is seen in determining greatest common factors and least common multiples of two or more numbers.

Relation between sets

Frequently, a set is designated as a general set and is called a *universal set* or simply the *universe*. This means that all sets under consideration would be subsets of the universe. Which set constitutes the universe is a matter of definition. For example, we may designate as a universal set the elements a, b, c, d, e, and f, which may be written:

U = {a, b, c, d, e, f}

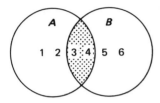

Figure 2-2. Intersection of sets

Any set to be considered must have as its elements the letters *a*, *b*, *c*, *d*, *e*, and *f* in some combination.

Venn diagrams

One interesting method of demonstrating sets is by designating the interior of geometric figures as sets. The figures may be circles, triangles, rectangles, or any other closed figures. Such designated figures are called *Venn diagrams*, named for the English mathematician, John Venn, who first made use of them. These diagrams are very good ways of illustrating relationships between sets. For example Figure 2-2 shows the intersection of two sets, *A* and *B*, where *A* = {1, 2, 3, 4} and *B* = {3, 4, 5, 6}. The interior of the circle on the left represents the set *A*, while the interior of the circle on the right represents set *B*. The two sets have common elements, 3 and 4, which are represented by the shaded portion of the circle and form a set called the "intersection of *A* and *B*." Symbolically, we would write this as:

$$A \cap B = \{3, 4\}$$

The union of the two sets is represented by the interiors of both circles, as shown in Figure 2-3. The shaded area is called the

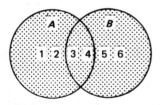

Figure 2-3. Union of sets

"union of sets A and B," symbolically designated as:

$A \cup B = \{1, 2, 3, 4, 5, 6\}$

Two sets may have no elements in common, in which case the Venn diagrams do not intersect. Suppose $C = \{1, 2, 3\}$ and $D = \{4, 5\}$. If the interiors of two circles do not intersect the intersection of the two sets form a null, or empty, set.

Number systems

The content of modern elementary-school mathematics differs considerably from that of two or three decades ago. Not only have many new concepts been introduced, but many concepts and skills have been pushed down into lower grades. Also, the language used to describe long-established concepts has been modernized considerably. A few years ago elementary children learned to count, add, subtract, multiply, and divide whole numbers, usually in the order listed. Once these skills were mastered, the class then moved into the four operations involving common fractions, decimal fractions, and application problems for all types.

Today's elementary-school arithmetic curricula look quite different. The introduction of the language of sets in the early 1960s led to an emphasis on a clearer definition of the types of numbers with which the pupils were working at any given time. Whether this has been an improvement or not is uncertain, but these changes have made teaching elementary arithmetic somewhat more complex.

The sets of numbers found in modern elementary-school curricula include:

1. Natural or counting numbers
2. Whole numbers
3. Integers
4. Rational numbers
5. Real numbers

As they are listed here, each set is a proper subset of the next set. A Venn diagram of the sets is shown in Figure 2-4.

Each of these sets of numbers, along with certain basic assumptions and laws, comprises a *number system*. Authors of modern arithmetic textbooks are generally concerned with the historical and logical development and structure of each of the number

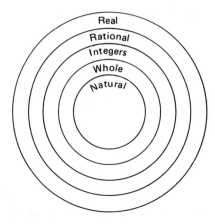

Figure 2-4. Sets of numbers
in our number system

systems. As each set or system is introduced, certain assumptions
are made and properties are investigated.

Natural numbers

The most familiar and simplest numbers are known as the *natural
numbers*, the set traditionally called "whole" numbers. The set of
natural numbers is designated as:

$$N = \{1, 2, \ldots, 10, 11, 12, \ldots, 100, 101, 102, \ldots\}$$

It forms an unending chain of consecutive numbers, any one of
which is less than all succeeding numbers. For example, 1 (the
least of the natural numbers) is less than each of the other numbers,
4 is less than 5, 5 is less than 6, and so on.

The set of natural numbers is also known as the set of counting
numbers and is the first set of numbers encountered by
elementary-school pupils. The idea of counting or enumerating is
probably almost as old as civilization. Primitive peoples surely
needed to know "how many" in reference to their flocks, children,
or subjects. Although the earliest method of counting was no doubt
some kind of tally system (which works on the principle of one-
to-one correspondence), research reveals that many primitive tribes
developed at least small-number concepts. Some tribes seemed to
have concepts of only the numbers 1 and 2 or perhaps 1, 2, 3, and
many.

There are two ways children count. One is called rote
counting; the other, rational counting. *Rote counting* is simply

saying the names in proper order. Many parents teach their children to count by rote before the children are of school age. Although many children enter kindergarten with the ability to "count up to 100," they may not be capable of *rational counting,* that is, specifying the number of a set of objects. Some teachers feel that learning to rote count prior to rational counting may retard learning the latter. While teachers should certainly teach rational counting from the outset, it is doubtful that having learned the names of numbers in proper order prior to entering school retards learning arithmetic concepts and skills.

Addition Young children, like primitive peoples, do most of their computation by counting. Sums of two or more sets are found by joining the sets and counting all of the elements of the sets. This is a time-consuming procedure. Addition is a shortcut to counting and makes possible operations on very large numbers with relative ease. Addition seems to be a very simple thing, yet teachers find that, even in the upper grades, many pupils cannot handle it.

Addition is fundamental to all other operations of arithmetic. Being able to add is not enough; one must understand addition. One must know the properties of addition with respect to natural-number systems.

There are two main stages of development through which children must pass in understanding addition. First, the 100 facts of addition must be learned, which requires memorization. The second stage involves what is called the *addition algorithm,* for the addition of numbers of two or more digits. A thorough study of place value must precede and accompany the development of addition algorithms. These and related topics are discussed in Chapter 7. Learning the fundamentals of addition will facilitate an understanding of many subsequent operations.

Subtraction The concept of subtraction is probably somewhat more complex than that of addition, yet it is introduced very early in the child's school life. As usually presented subtraction follows very closely after the teaching of addition. In fact, the two may be fused in such a way that students do not realize that a new operation is being introduced.

Whereas there is essentially only one addition situation, there are several basic subtraction situations. Some writers list four situations: (1) finding the remainder, (2) finding the difference, (3) finding how much more or less one group is than another group, and (4) finding a part of a group. Normally, in the early stages, only the general notion of "taking away" is presented.

It is important that addition and subtraction be seen as opposite processes, both built around the key concepts found in the study of groups. Whereas addition means combining two groups into one, subtraction basically involves converting a single group into two groups (which, you may notice, relates to subsets).

Like addition, subtraction is basically a two-phase learning experience. The basic facts of subtraction must be mastered and the subtraction algorithm must be learned. Each phase requires both understanding and memorization. The question might be raised, "To what degree should I expect mastery of the facts before progressing to the algorithm?" It would be unrealistic to expect total mastery of the 100 facts before teaching the algorithm. On the other hand it is reasonable to expect mastery of those facts useful to teaching the algorithm. The ultimate goal, of course, is complete mastery—mastery to the degree that the pupil sees $7 - 3$ and thinks 4. One of the greatest difficulties in arithmetic operations is that some pupils lack the mastery necessary to proceed with confidence.

Multiplication Multiplication of whole numbers is one of the most important elements in the content of elementary-school mathematics. Its importance stems from the fact that it is of itself a very practical operation in finding the sum of a number of sets having an equal number of members. For example, the total number of members in six sets of seven members each may be found by repeated addition, but a more efficient way is by multiplication. Multiplication is of great importance in relation to division. Since division is the inverse operation of multiplication, a certain degree of mastery of multiplication is prerequisite to division. An illustration of this is seen in the problem $18 \div 3$. The usual approach to this operation is to think, "What number multiplied by 3 yields a product of 18?"

Multiplication, like addition and subtraction, is taught in two phases—the basic facts and the algorithms. If there is one phrase concerning pupil weaknesses in arithmetic that is heard more than any other, it is probably, "They just don't know their multiplication tables." By this, of course, people mean that students have not mastered the basic facts of multiplying whole numbers.

The same principle expressed earlier concerning the facts of addition and subtraction applies to multiplication. Surely, understanding must precede memorization, but ultimately the facts must be learned to the point where the response is automatic. Some suggestions for accomplishing this task are found in Chapter 9.

Division The operation of division is of use in finding the number of equal subsets of a given set. For example, if 16 is divided by 2 the question is "How many sets of 2 members each can be found in the set of 16 members?" Since as we noted above, division is the inverse operation of multiplication and since we described multiplication as a convenient procedure for adding equal sets, then we may describe division as a convenient procedure for subtracting equal sets. Thus, it is necessary that the pupil master the subtraction algorithm before the division algorithm is introduced.

In many programs division and multiplication are taught as closely associated operations with many mutual learnings. It seems reasonable that pupils could learn that $6 \div 3 = 2$ and that $6 \div 2 = 3$ with a minimum of effort when they are learning that $3 \times 2 = 6$ and that $2 \times 3 = 6$. Teachers, of course, are then faced with the problem of keeping these two operations close enough together to use mutual learnings but far enough apart to minimize confusion. Some key terms in the teaching of both multiplication and division are factors, primes, and prime factors.

Factors The *factors* of any number a are those numbers that, when multiplied, yield a product a. For example, the factors of the number 6 are (1, 6) and (2, 3).

Primes A *prime number* is one having as its factors only itself and 1. Some prime numbers are 1, 2, 3, 5, 7, 11, 13, and 17. The number of primes to be found among the natural numbers is indefinite. In fact, it has been proven that there is no largest prime number among the natural numbers.

Prime Factors The *prime factors* of a number are those factors that are prime numbers. For example, 12 has several sets of factors—(12, 1), (6, 2), (3, 4)—but the prime factors of 12 are 3 and 2. Thus, if the objective is to factor 12 into its primes, we get $12 = 2 \cdot 2 \cdot 3$. This type of division can be very useful in some cases, for example, in the addition of fractions where we would like to find the least common denominator.

Fractions

The need for fractions arose out of inadequacies of natural numbers in measurement and division. No one knows exactly when, nor by whom, fractions were invented. Actually, they evolved rather than having been invented. We may see how this occurred by thinking of a hypothetical case. If we were attemping to determine the distance from one point to another, using only natural numbers, we would choose some appropriate standard unit and proceed in the usual manner. But, it is highly unlikely that the distance would be an exact multiple of our chosen unit. Let us suppose we find that the distance is greater than 4 but less than 5 units. We must then decide whether 4 or 5 is the better description of the distance. If we wish to be more precise, we must name a smaller unit, because the smaller the unit, the more precise the measure. More precision would require smaller and smaller units.

Division of natural numbers often suggests another inadequacy. Very often there is a need to divide one number by another number for which there is no natural-number quotient. For example, $5 \div 2$, $7 \div 3$, and $2 \div 4$, have no natural-number quotients. Such common operations as these could not be performed properly without the use of fractions.

Common fractions

The concept of fractions is introduced very early in modern school mathematics. The earliest fraction concept to be introduced is usually $\frac{1}{2}$. In fact, the term "half" may be familiar to pupils before they enter school; however, they may not know the exact meaning of the term. They may think that anything divided into two parts is halved. In fact, the "half" of the candy that a child shares with a friend may be considerably smaller than the "half" that he or she keeps. Thus, an early task for the teacher is to establish the idea that equal parts are one type of fractional parts.

The operations of addition, subtraction, multiplication, and division of fractions have traditionally been introduced in the order in which they are listed. In recent years, however, multiplication has been introduced before addition. The rationale for this switch in presentation is twofold. First, the operation of multiplication of common fractions is probably easier to learn than that of addition. Second, knowledge of multiplication may be very beneficial in learning the more difficult procedure of addition of unlike fractions.

Fractions extend our concept of the number system. Common proper fractions may be associated with many numbers (not all) located between 0 and 1. The numbers called *fractions* are expressed in the form a/b where a and b are natural numbers, b $\neq$ 0. All such numbers go to make up a set of numbers called the *rational numbers*. This term is very likely to be found in the elementary-arithmetic textbooks used in your school.

Decimal fractions

Decimal fractions, commonly called *decimals,* are a very convenient system for writing fractions in which the denominators are powers of ten (i.e., 10, 100, 1000, 10,000, etc.). Of course, the *whole numbers* are decimal numbers since they form a system of numbers whose base is ten (*deci* meaning "ten"). Generally, however, this is not stressed in elementary classrooms. Like common fractions decimal fractions extend our number system beyond natural numbers. All pure decimal fractions represent numbers between 0 and 1.

The decimal fractions have received increased attention in the last few years because the United States will convert to the metric system of measure in the near future. Since the metric system is based on ten, it fits perfectly into the decimal system of numbers. Also, our system of money builds upon decimal concepts.

The operations of addition, subtraction, multiplication, and division with decimal fractions are usually found to be somewhat easier than with common fractions. For instance, in column addition and subtraction of decimal numbers, the only rule to remember is to properly align numbers of equal place value. (This is sometimes referred to as "keeping the decimals in a line.") A more complete discussion of decimal fractions is found in Chapter 12.

Geometry

In the last few years elementary schools have started to emphasize the study of geometry. Geometry can offer a new and exciting dimension to the study of mathematics, because it is a tool for applying arithmetic skills. In the early stages, however, geometry should be intuitive and nonmetric.

As will be seen in Chapter 15, the principal aim in the primary grades is building vocabulary and association of names with shapes. When familiarity with basic figures is accomplished, certain elementary properties, such as the number of sides, may be introduced informally.

In the middle grades properties of geometric figures are investigated through discussion and discovery. Metric properties may be discussed in conjunction with the study of measurement.

Measurement

Methods of teaching measurement in the primary grades have changed considerably in recent years. Formerly, the study of measurement began with procedures for converting feet to inches, yards to feet, pounds to ounces, and other such measures. Converting from one unit to another is still an aspect of measurement, but the primary goals today center around relating measurement to the students themselves. Comparisons (all measurements are comparisons) are usually related to the student's body, such as height, length of arms, or hand span. Students, using "homemade" measuring sticks, measure familiar objects such as books and table tops in order to establish a need for fractional parts or smaller units.

Another important change in teaching measurement has been made necessary by the fact that the United States is moving toward metric measures. This makes it imperative that children entering school now be taught the metric system as a first system.

The topic of measurement is dealt with in detail in Chapter 14.

The real-number system

In the upper elementary grades the real-number system is introduced to many students. This is not to imply that all elementary students can profit from studying the real-number system. However, many seventh- and eighth-grade students are quite sophisticated in mathematics. For these students the real numbers help round out the system.

Ways
of teaching

3

Many students in teacher-education programs seek a definitive method of teaching mathematics. Some express amazement when they realize that teaching is not a matter of applying a predetermined series of steps. There are certain useful procedures, but the ways in which they are used has to be left to the individual teacher as he or she works in a specific setting with a specific group of students. Those procedures are the central concern of this chapter.

The material in this chapter is structured around (1) modes of teaching, (2) organizational patterns in teaching, and (3) some special situations.

Modes

In a generalized way we can identify a number of modes of teaching. Good teachers use all of them and on occasion develop some of their own. One of the traits of an effective teacher is that he or she can sense that it is time to use a different approach. The most common modes of teaching are exposition, inquiry, demonstration, and activity.

Exposition

The use of explanation in teaching is termed *exposition*. In college teaching it often takes the form of a lecture. With younger children this method must be used very carefully because such problems as short attention span cannot be ignored. Yet exposition does have a place, even with very young students.

Let us examine some situations in which the expository method might be useful in mathematics. An obvious one is when new material is being introduced. If this material is of interest to the entire class, then a very logical approach is to organize a session during which the new material is explained to all the students. Another situation in which exposition is useful is when some sort of culmination is needed, assuming that a block of content has been completed. Still another arises when certain students (not the entire class) show a need for more explanation on a particular phase of work. Some very good expository teaching is done with the teacher and a small group of students clustered at the board, working on a topic of concern to those students.

It is hard to imagine an expository session running to great length when young children are involved. Further, the students should have a role in the process—questioning, reacting, and in other ways. Anything approaching a formal lecture would be of doubtful value.

How does the diagnostic approach work in this mode? The diagnostic teacher is conditioned to be very observant of students. And students have ways of telling the teacher when a particular activity has run its course. (It may be useful for you to consider.) The important thing is that the teacher "get the message" and make the indicated changes.

Inquiry

This mode wears a variety of labels—the discovery approach, logical thinking, and others. However, one teacher who made very effective use of the *inquiry method* expressed it very simply: "I will not tell a student anything he can figure out for himself."

It is overly simple to identify the inquiry method with the asking and answering of questions. If the questions—and answers—are purely factual, based upon memorized material, very little discovery is likely to be involved.

Mathematics lends itself well to the use of the inquiry method, because there are innumerable situations for discovery. However, discovery is not just inviting the student to go off and find something. The teacher's role is more that of leader than teller, and the leadership must be exercised in a fairly subtle manner. Such expressions as, "What do you think we should do next?" "Why do you think this happens?" and others of this type are useful initiators of response.

A word of caution is in order relative to the inquiry approach. Some students simply are not discoverers by nature. If the teacher waits for such students to discover a concept, it is likely to be a long wait. But for those students who respond to this approach, the inquiry mode can be very effective and rewarding.

Demonstration

Demonstration involves a "show me" approach to teaching. Mathematics, with its major dependence on concrete materials, makes extensive use of demonstration. Can you imagine a teacher introducing the concept of addition without using sticks, books, or children to demonstrate the operation?

This mode is widely used in conjunction with others. For example, a demonstration of a process logically accompanies an explanation.

A common misconception of the demonstration mode is that only the teacher can use it. However, many good demonstrations are prepared and presented by students. Indeed, this is a good way to let certain students gain recognition from their peers.

Activity

The *activity mode* has undergone varying degrees of acceptance. Because of some inept usage, many people equate this mode with wasting time. More recently, however, as an alternative to a heavy dependence on books, activity seems to be returning to favor.

In an elementary-mathematics class there is often a great deal of activity. Students are involved in games, go back and forth to get materials, and check results with the teacher. However, carrying out major construction projects and other such undertakings are less likely to be encountered in a mathematics class than in some other areas.

This overview of some modes of instruction is not intended to be comprehensive. Indeed, when you are in your class with your own students, you are not likely to be unduly concerned with the type of effort in which you are engaged. Your prime concern is to use methods that work in your situation. A survey of the modes of teaching can serve as a point of departure for the more in-depth work on methodology that this text will discuss throughout.

Organization

A great deal of attention today is being given to ways of organizing the elementary school administratively. However, in this section we shall concentrate on organization within the elementary classroom, with specific applications to the mathematics area.

Total classes

One prevalent stereotype of the mathematics teacher is as a lecturer at the board, chalk in hand. In some respects lecturing seems to have been fairly effective. Certainly it is still in use in many classrooms.

One obvious problem with this procedure is that the teacher has to present the same material to the total group, regardless of varying needs. Further, there is little opportunity to differentiate students as to the rate of coverage of material. In short, there are built-in features of "same content" and "same rate of coverage" for all. The logical question is, "Who determines the rate of speed?" Some teachers lose contact altogether with class needs. Probably a more common practice is to pace the coverage in terms of the hypothetical average student. This, of course, is likely to lead to a pace that will both leave the lower-performance students behind and fail to challenge the higher-performance students.

Some teachers make good use of total-class instruction when introducing new material. Others use it mainly in games and related activities. But use of this procedure as *the* method, on a day-after-day basis, almost inevitably leads to problems.

Groups

Clustering students in groups within a class has long been a favorite procedure of many teachers. When properly used, the procedure can be very effective. However, grouping for the sake of grouping is pointless. The real merit of this approach is that it permits the targeting of instruction for specific student needs.

Stories are told about teachers who have grouped students on the basis of all sorts of criteria—even, unfortunately, on the basis of family socioeconomic status. One should not, of course, condemn a useful method because it has been misused.

Considerable attention is given to grouping throughout this book; hence, we will not give details on the subject at this point. But, when the students in a mathematics class are grouped according to need, when instruction is geared to that need, and when students move into and out of groups as needs are met, grouping can be a very effective method of teaching.

Individuals

Ideally, all teaching should be individualized because learning is an individual matter. Practically, however, few teachers have the organizational skills needed to work on a one-to-one basis with a class-sized group. Some school systems are reducing class size; others are increasing their use of teacher aides. These and other approaches are making individualized instruction more feasible.

Occasionally teachers manage to individualize instruction while dealing single-handedly with a class of 25 or 30. This is more common with middle and upper-elementary grades whose students have enough maturity to assume considerable responsibility for their own progress. Even granted this condition, the teachers of such classes are very busy people.

No one system of organization, including individualized teaching, can function in all situations. One trait of a good teacher is that he or she has developed a "feel" for matching organization to need—and making the system work after the matching is accomplished.

Some special situations

To a considerable degree the modes and organizational patterns described in this chapter are useful in many subject areas. However, there are certain problems and methods in mathematics that are somewhat unique to the field. We will examine a few of these.

The problem of mastery

We have long associated education with the process of "learning something." Yet the different subject areas vary widely as to the demands they make on students. An example in arithmetic is the need for the student to achieve mastery of, or memorize, a total of 390 basic facts—100 in addition, 100 in subtraction, 100 in multiplication, and 90 in division.

This mastery task is spread over a period of several years, and an effort is made to break it into manageable subtasks. But, whatever the method used, this is a formidable task in memorization. Still, it is a vital part of a student's work in arithmetic since all of the more advanced components of an operation, such as column addition or long division, build upon mastery of the facts.

Calculators

The development of small calculators has raised questions regarding the need to master the facts described above. Why learn that $4 \times 3 = 12$ if you can get the answer by punching buttons? A lower-elementary student, in asking for such a calculator, explained to his mother that if he had such an instrument, it would save him a great deal of brain power.

One observer has pointed out that any system of number usage that is dependent on gadgets (whether they are abacuses, calculators, or others) is an incomplete system. What happens, for instance, if a need for computation arises when a calculator is not at hand? And there is always the danger of a discharged battery. There is little evidence at hand to indicate that our need for mastery of the operations will cease to exist. Many teachers recall that the development of inexpensive tape recorders was once thought to have made the skill of reading unnecessary. Today the recorder has become a valuable tool in teaching the verbal skills, including reading.

What, then, is the role of the calculator in teaching arithmetic? A comprehensive answer will evolve over time. Some teachers let students use calculators to check their work, which seems to motivate some students. Other teachers allow students to use calculators in problem solving in the hope that students will be encouraged to give full attention to the process. Still other teachers are finding ways to team up with calculators. However, it appears that for the foreseeable future we will still be teaching for mastery, with the calculator a valuable tool in the process.

Tape recorders

Many students are fascinated by recorders and by recorded material. A teacher recently complained that she could say the same things that were on a cassette and not come close to getting the student response that was accorded the taped material.

Teachers are realizing that the recorder and recorded material have uses beyond language-arts classes. An illustration of one such use in arithmetic grew out of a situation in which substantial numbers of middle-elementary students had not mastered the multiplication facts. A cassette program was developed to incorporate the following features: (1) drill periods were short; (2) there was considerable repetition of facts; (3) a variety of the students' senses were involved; and (4) varying degrees of student involvement were included. A vital characteristic was that the facts were presented on cassette, and paced so that finger counting was not feasible. Usage of this program for as little as 20 minutes per week resulted in substantial gains in mastery of the facts, with a corresponding decline in dependency on finger counting.

Selected references

COPELAND, RICHARD W. *Mathematics and the Elementary Teacher.* Philadelphia: Saunders, 1976.

FEHER, HOWARD F., and PHILLIPS, JO MCKEEBY. *Teaching Modern Mathematics in the Elementary School.* Reading, Mass.: Addison-Wesley, 1972.

GRAHAM, MALCOLM. *Modern Elementary Mathematics.* New York: Harcourt Brace Jovanovich, 1975.

JAROLIMEK, JOHN, and FOSTER, CLIFFORD D. *Teaching and Learning in the Elementary School.* New York: Macmillan, 1976.

JUNGST, DALE G. *Elementary Mathematics Methods: Laboratory Manual.* Boston: Allyn & Bacon, 1975.

KENNEDY, LEONARD. *Guiding Children to Mathematical Discovery.* Belmont, Calif.: Wadsworth, 1975.

KRAMER, KLASS. *Elementary School Mathematics.* Boston: Allyn & Bacon, 1975.

National Council of Teachers of Mathematics. *An Analysis of New Mathematics Programs.* Washington, D.C.: National Council of Teachers of Mathematics, 1964.

WEBER, CUTHBERT G. *Mathematics for Elementary Teachers.* Reading, Mass.: Addison-Wesley, 1967.

part II

diagnosis

Diagnosis—or seeing the elements of a situation—is an important part of most kinds of teaching. What does this mean? As you will see it illustrated in this section, diagnosis means that the teacher is constantly looking for problem areas.

However, if you identify a problem but make no effort toward a solution, you will not make very much progress. Hence, throughout this book prescription is given careful attention as well. Basically, we are concerned here with methods of teaching mathematics, and an integral part of this methodology is the broad area of diagnosis and prescription as applied to teaching and learning mathematics.

The diagnostic approach: an overview

4

Let us set up a hypothetical class in elementary-school mathematics. In this class all of our students are at the same place, in terms of concept development, at the same time. As the teaching–learning process progresses, how long would it take for diversity to appear? Experienced teachers know that shortly some students would enjoy trouble-free progress while others would bog down and still others would be in between.

The diagnostic approach has little application insofar as the first group is concerned because these students are not encountering difficulty. However, regarding the other two groups, the teacher cannot be very helpful until he or she knows, for each student, such things as why the student is having trouble, at what point the trouble arose, and what concepts and/or skills are lacking. Once the teacher knows the answer to such questions, it is often fairly easy to apply corrective procedures. But how can the teacher function effectively until he or she *has* these answers? One means is by use of the *diagnostic approach*, which refers to a set of methods, materials, and procedures that are useful to teachers as they try to isolate and identify specific difficulties encountered by specific students.

Let us look at an actual case. Carey, a somewhat overgrown fifth grader, was still having trouble with subtraction. His teacher, knowing the area of difficulty but not knowing the specifics, had Carey work on subtraction generally. By using a simple diagnostic procedure, the teacher noted that, to Carey, $0 - 3 = 3$ or $0 - 9 = 9$. After the specific problem had been recognized, correction took only a few minutes. Yet this problem had been in existence, unrecognized, for several years.

There are those who might see in this approach an undue emphasis on skills, in contrast to understandings, of mathematical concepts. However, the two—skills and concepts—cannot be completely separated. Frequently the most efficient way to identify a misconception is through the skills. In the case of Carey, the child had a misunderstanding of a concept, which carried directly over into a skill.

Diagnostic teaching in the standard class

Although the term *standard class* can be variously interpreted, we use it to refer to any elementary-school mathematics class that is heterogeneous as to student performance, with a substantial number of the students functioning at or above grade level. Within this context a diagnostic approach does not constitute a total program. Rather, it is supplementary to the program as commonly implemented. If there are students who are not having problems, it would be a waste of time to try to improve their performance. They should be moving along to new material as rapidly as they can take it. If there are students who are having only nominal difficulty, we can usually identify and correct problems fairly easily. These students can then continue with grade-level material. If there are students who are having major trouble—and there usually will be—then much of their time and effort should logically be spent in the diagnostic and remedial phase, regardless of grade-level considerations.

There are two extreme patterns of instruction that may be used in the standard classroom. In the first the teacher instructs the class as a whole. This procedure assumes that all students are in the same place and are able to move along at the same pace. Usually, the teacher gears his or her instruction to the middle-performance group. The high-performance group is bored and unchallenged; the low-performance group is lost and frustrated. Behavior problems are the inevitable result.

The other extreme is the teacher who sets out to teach on an individualized basis. Although many efforts are being made to find procedures that will make this approach workable, it remains a very difficult task. The teacher is likely to be so rushed and pressured that his or her effectiveness suffers.

An in-between position is coming into considerable usage. Here, the teacher uses diagnostic procedures to locate specific difficulties. Then he or she groups students on the basis of these difficulties. Thus, if there are five who are having trouble with a certain phase of subtraction, these five constitute a group. Other groups are set up in the same way. With several such groups the teacher can work effectively without undue pressure. A vital part of this procedure is that, as individual students master the concept their group is working on, they join another group and work on another area, according to specific needs manifested. This means, of course, that the groups are loosely structured, with much inflow and outflow.

Diagnostic teaching in the remedial class

Many larger schools find it expedient to place those students who are performing at a relatively low level in mathematics in special sections. This simplifies the work of the teacher in some respects because he or she then deals with only a restricted span of performance. However, the group is still not homogeneous. (It has been said that a truly homogeneous group has only one person in it.) It is as true with the remedial group as it is with any other that each individual student will have his or her own set of problems. Hence, an early task of the teacher is to identify, in very specific terms, those operations or components of operations that give trouble.

Procedurally, the teacher could well use the method described earlier, the cycle of diagnosing and teaching in small groups. It should be noted that this *is* a cycle, or a recurring pattern. Diagnosis is not a one-time operation; rather, it should be continuous.

In a remedial class little attention should be given to the question of whether certain material is at grade level. In one instance we know of, a particular teacher, who was trying to teach his class some material on factors and primes because this material "was in the book," discovered that most of his class had not mastered the multiplication facts and hence could not possibly achieve success in the assigned work. Realistically, this teacher laid aside the book, went back as far as necessary, and moved his class in the direction of learning the basic multiplication facts. It would have served no purpose had the teacher held his class to grade-level material.

Components of diagnosis

There are two basic parts to the diagnostic approach in mathematics. One of these, which might at first seem nebulous, is teacher attitude. The other is diagnostic materials.

Teacher attitude

In order to use the diagnostic method successfully, the teacher must have a real desire to help students identify their own problems. Unless this attitude is present, no procedure will work. A proper attitude on the part of the teacher manifests itself in a number of ways.

Work methods We have long known the importance of good work methods on the part of the mathematics student. Let us look at a few situations and see what they tell us in this regard.

First, consider the finger counters. There are a variety of reasons why children count on their fingers. Kim, for example, counts on her "built-in abacus" in doing addition exercises. Close observation indicates that she really has to count because she does not know the basic facts. Andrew, on the other hand, counts as a "security blanket." He has mastered the facts but finds reassurance in checking them.

The diagnostic teacher may have to assume some unorthodox positions to locate finger counting. Some teachers pressure or even threaten their students who count fingers. The result is that the students "go underground" and devise all sorts of ways to keep their counting from being detected. Some move their hands under the desk. Some even substitute foot patting and other such devices.

Actually, finger counting as an isolated act is of little importance to us. But finger counting as a symptom of lack of mastery or lack of confidence can be very significant. The therapy for each case must be different.

Another work habit of interest is that of mumbling. This fairly common practice can, of course, be a major distraction to other students. Also, the practice often indicates that a student is somewhat insecure and needs to listen to his or her own voice for assurance.

One poor work habit that teachers sometimes ignore is sprawling over work. This is not necessarily a manifestation of poor posture. It often indicates that the student is lacking in confidence as to his or her work and is simply trying to hide it.

Other work methods could be described as to usual meaning. However, we have looked at enough of them to illustrate the point. The diagnostic teacher takes time to stand apart on occasion and watch students at work—not students generally, but each student individually. The information thus gained can be most helpful.

Work products Teachers must pay close attention to student output. An example will clearly show why. A teacher gives his students some exercises to be worked in class. Out of 25 exercises, Joe correctly works 20. Although the teacher—and Joe—may take pride in his percent of *correct* responses, it is really in the five he *missed* that Joe is crying for help. The diagnostically oriented teacher gives a second look at the scored paper to see which exercises Joe missed, what patterns of errors are to be observed, and what can be done to correct the situation. In part, this is again a matter of teacher attitude. While many teachers look only at "number right," the diagnostic teacher is even more concerned with number wrong, which ones, and why.

Work Aloud It sometimes happens that even the closest examination of an incorrect exercise will not convey to the teacher just what the thought patterns were. In such cases a very good diagnostic procedure is to ask the student to work the exercise aloud to the teacher, who listens carefully. Often, the erroneous concept comes to the surface almost instantly. Let us look at a case. Asked to multiply 3 times 28, Sally did the following:

$$\begin{array}{r} 2 \\ 28 \\ \times 3 \\ \hline 124 \end{array}$$

The teacher asked Sally to work this exercise aloud. What the teacher heard was, "Three 8s are 24; put down the 4 and carry the 2; 2 plus 2 is 4, 3 times 4 is 12." Sally added the carry number, then multiplied. Every isolated step was correct, but her sequencing, based on a misconception, was incorrect. By use of the work-aloud procedure, the teacher was able to locate the difficulty with a single exercise. Correction was a simple process.

Diagnostic materials

The efforts of the teacher and student in the area of diagnosis/remediation can yield results very early if there is help available in the form of structured instruments. While any piece of student work can serve a diagnostic purpose, a piecemeal approach is seldom adequate.

First, let us consider what a diagnostic instrument is. Many schools use a battery of standardized achievement tests once or twice a year. How do these tests differ from diagnostic tests? The achievement test is designed for breadth rather than depth. It seeks, by a limited number of exercises, to cover a broad spectrum of content. The test is designed to tell us, on an inventory basis, where a student is with respect to a norm group. But it tells little about specific difficulties experienced by students.

By way of contrast the diagnostic instrument is designed for depth. One such instrument breaks the operation of addition into twelve components or steps and includes some work at each step. When a teacher administers this test, he or she can easily check to see what parts of the operation of addition are giving trouble. Then the teacher is in a position to design correctional work for the student.

Whereas the standardized achievement-test battery is given only once or twice a year, and under carefully prescribed conditions, the diagnostic test can be given at any time that it might yield useful information. Since it is not usually normreferenced, the diagnostic instrument can be given in an informal, relaxed setting. Many students seem to appreciate the contrast.

The diagnostic approach: organizing a program

5

Regardless of the nature of the class—remedial, homogeneous, heterogeneous—the teacher needs to be aware of certain organizational matters relative to setting up a cycle of diagnosis and group teaching. This chapter will explore some of these matters.

Objectives

There can be a great waste of time and effort in the teaching–learning process unless the work is guided by a realistic sense of direction. Learning mathematics is not "doing what comes naturally." Careful attention must be given to such matters as structure and sequence. Readiness is an applicable concept. Teachers should also keep in mind that the broadly stated set of goals found in a teacher's edition of the text is usually inadequate.

Behavioral terms

One aspect of the diagnostic approach to teaching mathematics is the element of specificity. Many teachers recall the time when objectives were stated in terms of broad generalities. The broader the statement, the less likely it was to create problems. In recent years educators have come to realize that in order for an objective to function as a guide to the teaching–learning process, it must be quite specific in nature. Further, the statement must describe the behavior that indicates that the student has learned the objective. Some illustrations of such objectives are:

1. The student writes the multiplication facts in which 6 is a factor.
2. The student writes ten sentences to illustrate the commutative property in addition.

Specific statements

Objectives stated in broad terms can often serve as points of departure in the teaching–learning process. For example, we hope the student will develop an understanding of the process of multiplication—a general goal. However, how can you tell if this goal has been achieved? The obvious answer is that by observing the student as he or she carries out an assigned task or by examining the products resulting from his or her work on the task, we can gain an insight into the student's progress. Thus, we usually take a desired outcome as stated in general nonbehavioral terms and then bring it into focus by supporting it with specific, behavioral statements. One illustration might be the following:

General objective:
Student understands process of multiplication.

Behavioral objectives:
1. Student explains orally meaning of the process of multiplication.
2. From a group of problem situations the student selects those in which multiplication would be used.

Many of the desired outcomes of instruction are general in nature. However, only as we are able to fit specific behaviors to these general statements can we move forward with the teaching–learning process.

Emphasis on skills

The idea of diagnostic teaching—"doctoring the ailment"—is useful to teach many aspects of mathematics. However, it is apparent that the high-performance student will have relatively few ailments. Hence, from the practical point of view, this approach is most important for those students who are having problems. Even though the basic difficulty is in the area of concepts, the outward manifestation is likely to be at the skills level. Hence, the diagnostic approach puts heavy emphasis on learning skills. As applied to arithmetic, this means essentially the four operations (addition, subtraction, multiplication, and division) with whole numbers, fractions, and mixed numbers.

Materials

While objectives are important in the diagnostic approach, even the best set of objectives is futile unless there is proper implementation. This, of course, involves materials. However, no one set of materials is absolutely essential. Many types of materials are helpful—if they are used properly.

Textbooks

Those who view the diagnostic approach to the teaching of mathematics as something quite new and different are often surprised to learn that standard teaching materials—textbooks and workbooks, for example—are readily usable. However, the diagnostic approach uses such materials differently.

We often hear that the role of the text is to "serve, not dominate." This is true in the diagnostic method. Page-by-page coverage of the text seldom meets the needs of all the students in a class, especially if we are trying to give each student the type of work that meets his or her own unique needs. Obviously, in this type of teaching the teacher will draw from a variety of sources, including textbooks and workbooks. But the major concern is to use the material from these sources only when it is needed by the student. And this is obviously impossible unless the teacher knows what the needs are.

Another item of concern relative to the use of materials is that grade placement does not necessarily tell us a great deal about a student's level in mathematics. Hence, if teachers are drawing sources of material from textbooks, they need to have access to several grade levels of such books. A particular fifth grader might have a "point of entry" on a certain operation at third-grade level. In order to meet this need the teacher would ideally make use of a third-grade text.

Thus, if teachers are using texts and workbooks as sources in diagnostic teaching, they must be willing to (1) break away from any pattern of page-by-page coverage and (2) make use of texts designed for a variety of grade levels.

Diagnostic instruments

Although it is true that any test can function diagnostically, it is equally true that the best diagnostic instruments are designed for this specific purpose. What is unique about a diagnostic instrument? Basically, it is a test characterized by depth rather than breadth. Let us assume that there are five steps or stages of development in a particular process. A diagnostic instrument helps locate the point in this process at which the student meets difficulty. Hence the structure of the instrument must be such that (1) all five steps or components are represented and (2) the particular difficulty can be isolated. Obviously, special care must be taken in the design and development of an instrument if it is to be correctly classified as diagnostic in nature. There are several published diagnostic instruments available.

One publisher in this area is Adston Educational Enterprises (Drawer 18430B, University Station, Baton Rouge, Louisiana 70893). The series they publish, called Adston Diagnostic Instruments, begins with a test on readiness for operations. This instrument, nonverbal in nature, is designed to tell the teacher if a student has mastered the basic concepts so that the development of skill in the four basic arithmetic operations is feasible. If there are conceptual problems, the instrument is designed to help locate them. At a higher level this series includes a set of instruments based upon the four operations as used with whole numbers. Each operation is broken down into its components. By referring to the teachers' manual the teacher can interpret the work of the student on the diagnostic instruments. The motive, of course, is to pinpoint the component that is causing trouble. Once the specific difficulty is located, correction is often quite easy.

The California Test Bureau, which is now a division of McGraw-Hill, publishes Leo J. Brueckner's diagnostic series. Although this material is not new, it is still widely used. It includes screening tests, tests on basic facts, and tests on operations. The entire series consist of more than 20 separate tests. The accompanying manual gives good directions to the teacher on how to use these tests to maximum advantage. The emphasis is on skills.

The same publisher issued a "Prescriptive Mathematics Inventory" in 1971. This series is diagnostic in nature, comprehensive, and hence fairly long. Because it goes beyond the level of skills, many of the items on this inventory presuppose that the student reads fairly well.

Other diagnostic materials in mathematics are under continuous development. Hence, it is impossible to compile a complete list of such aids. The ones cited above are merely illustrative of the types of structured instruments that are available. Also, several kits and laboratories have diagnostic materials as components designed essentially for use with the supportive material in the kit.

Related material

Diagnosis has value only as it contributes to the teaching–learning process, and thus it is not unusual for publishers to issue support material for use in conjunction with diagnostic instruments.

The Adston Company has published a series of "prescriptive sets" to accompany some of their diagnostic instruments. These are so constructed that a student who has difficulty with a particular component of an operation found on a diagnostic instrument can go immediately to instructional and drill material. The material is designed to help the student with the specific troublesome component.

The Brueckner material, previously mentioned, includes "self-helps" along with the diagnostic tests. The self-help material is on the backs of the diagnostic tests, and thus the two are automatically keyed to each other. Although designed to give the student the lead role in his or her own diagnosis and prescription, these materials can be used in many ways.

A number of companies have issued kits, laboratories, or related materials for use in elementary-school mathematics. Others are appearing constantly. In most of these, diagnosis and prescription are closely coordinated. Many teachers are getting excellent results through the use of such kits.

Evaluation and Diagnosis

Not unexpectedly, diagnostic procedures vary somewhat among the several instruments available. However, it is important to keep in mind that these are not norm-referenced achievement tests. Rather, the diagnostic instruments are designed solely to help the teacher and pupil isolate and identify specific difficulties.

One characteristic of the diagnostic test is that it can be administered in an informal setting. Tests are generally not timed. If instructions are not clear, the teacher can explain them. The tests can be stopped at any convenient point, then resumed later. And all students do not necessarily take the same parts. For example, if a certain student is having no difficulty with subtraction, it would be a waste of time to have her take a diagnostic test in subtraction. The dominant concern throughout the process is student need.

After an instrument has been administered, the obvious next step is to score it. However, our interest is *not* in the number right, which is a common outcome of scoring. Rather, we are concerned with which ones are incorrect, what misconceptions or skill deficiencies led to the errors, and, ultimately, how corrective instruction can be used most effectively. In reality, the teacher is chiefly concerned with the patterns of the errors because these, in contrast to isolated errors, are likely to provide clues as to misconceptions. Most of the commercial diagnostic instruments provide ample help to the teacher in analyzing error patterns; it is important that the teacher make full use of this assistance.

Remediation

Key to remediation is the location of points of difficulty through diagnosis and the targeting of the remedial instruction and follow-up drill on these exact points. The remedial method is in complete contrast to the approach of the teacher who returns a paper to a student with the remark, "They are all wrong; do them again." In the absence of any more specific help, this student is likely to repeat the same set of errors.

The mechanics of remediation vary considerably. If every student in a class has the same difficulty, a most unlikely situation, then remedial instruction could be total-class instruction. If, on the other hand, individualized work is possible, targeting on the problem components for each student would be fairly straightforward. However, as has been mentioned earlier, if a teacher is working without an aide in a class of 30 or more students, he or she is in an extremely demanding position.

Grouping probably provides the best balance between feasibility and effectiveness. However, grouping should be based directly upon the needs of the students; that is, the groups should consist of students who share a common need. This, of course, is possible only when the teacher *knows* these needs, a type of knowledge provided by diagnosis. It is inherent in this approach that, as needs change, groups change.

If we assume that grouping is to be the basic approach, then the remedial cycle would probably be as follows: (1) On the basis of special diagnostic instruments, work-aloud procedures, observations of the student at work, and any other available sources, the teacher determines the specific areas of difficulty for each student. (2) Using this information, the teacher sets up groups on the basis of common need. (3) The teacher then instructs the group in order to eliminate misconceptions and draws upon any available sources for teaching helps. (4) As a final phase the teacher provides targeted drill material to fix skills in the area of concern. This phase, of course, can and should be on an individual basis.

Selected references

BRUECKNER, LEO J. *Diagnostic and Remedial Teaching in Arithmetic.* New York: Holt, Rinehart and Winston, 1930.

BRUECKNER, LEO J., and BOND, GUY L. *The Diagnosis and Treatment of Learning Difficulties.* Englewood Cliffs, N.J.: Prentice-Hall, 1955, chaps. 8, 9.

BUSWELL, GUY T., and JOHN, LENORE. *Diagnostic Studies in Arithmetic.* University of Chicago, 1926.

COPELAND, RICHARD W. *Mathematics and the Elementary Teacher.* Philadelphia: Saunders, 1976.

ELLIS, LESLIE C. "A Diagnostic Study of Whole Number Computations of Certain Elementary Students." Ed.D. dissertation, Louisiana State University, 1972.

GROSSNICKLE, FOSTER E., and RICKZEH, JOHN. *Discovering Meanings in Elementary School Mathematics.* New York: Holt, Rinehart and Winston, 1973, chap. 3, 20, 21.

National Council of Teachers of Mathematics. *The Slow Learner in Mathematics.* Thirty-fifth Yearbook. Washington, D.C.: National Council of Teachers of Mathematics, 1972, chap. 9.

OTTO, WAYNE, and MCMENEMY, RICHARD A. *Corrective and Remedial Teaching.* Boston: Houghton Mifflin, 1966, chap. 9.

REISMAN, FREDRICKA K. *A Guide to the Diagnostic Teaching of Arithmetic.* Columbus, Ohio: Merrill, 1972.

ROBERTS, GERHARD H. "The Failure Strategies of Third-Grade Arithmetic Pupils." *The Arithmetic Teacher* 15, 5 (1968): 442–446.

SMITH, ROBERT M., ed. *Teacher Diagnosis of Educational Difficulties.* Columbus, Ohio: Merrill, 1969, chap. 7.

TRUEBLOOD, CECIL R. "A Model for Using Diagnosis in Individualizing Mathematics Instruction in the Elementary School Classroom." *The Arithmetic Teacher* 18, 7 (1971) 505–512.

WEST, TOMMIE A. "Diagnosing Pupil Errors: Looking for Patterns," *The Arithmetic Teacher* 18, (1971): 467–469.

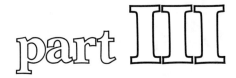
part III

whole-number operations

Traditionally, whole-number operations have occupied a prominent position in the elementary-school mathematics curriculum, although varying degrees of emphasis have been placed on this area. At times computational skills were stressed to the extreme. Exercises of enormous magnitude were given to students. The more capable became "human computers"; the less gifted were overwhelmed. Countering this extreme emphasis on basic whole-number operations was the new-math movement. With its emphasis on teaching for understanding, the discovery approach to learning, introducing new materials at an earlier age, and employing more exact terminology, the new math, according to many educators, de-emphasized basic skills in whole-number operations.

However, skills development remains a vital part of the elementary-mathematics program. Skills with whole numbers are important for several reasons. First, mastery of the fundamental computational skills is a worthy objective in itself. It is unlikely that the hand calculator will replace the need for computational skills. True, it may change the degree of emphasis but not the basic need for the skill. Second, whole-number operations are excellent vehicles through which the student learns about the number system. Certain basic elements of the nature of our number system must be taught before operational skills are introduced, but the theory is more fully developed, made more meaningful, and reinforced through development of the computational skills.

Readiness

The term "readiness" is variously interpreted, depending upon specific applications. However, as used here, *readiness* refers to those understandings and skills essential to student success in work with the operations of arithmetic. There is no such thing as a generally accepted list of readiness factors. However, those described in this chapter are considered to be of major importance.

Concepts

One-to-one correspondence

One aspect of readiness is the ability to deal with a very simple type of quantification, *one-to-one correspondence*. The ability requires of students that they match objects in one group to objects in another, without making any particular effort to associate number names with either group. Teaching the skill might involve such activities as giving a pencil to each student or matching books with cards. In many programs the student then moves to *one-to-one comparison*, still a rudimentary form of quantitative thinking. A student with this ability can determine whether there are enough balls for each student to have one or whether, on a worksheet, there are as many lollipops as children. Later, of course, the student will recognize this as a rudimentary form of subtraction. After learning this skill students would logically move to rational counting.

Rote and rational counting

Rote counting, the mere calling of number names, serves little purpose in a modern arithmetic program and hence is given minimum attention. From the first, however, children are given work in *rational counting*, that is the counting of objects. This ability is basic to further progress.

Number work is essentially abstract in nature, and we know enough of the learning processes of smaller children to realize that abstractions are difficult. Hence, in the earlier phases of number work, a great deal of attention is given to the use of concrete objects. Because rational counting involves counting things, most teachers make extensive use of the concrete in teaching this type of counting.

Although texts or teachers' manuals can suggest games or activities for students in which they work with concrete objects, essentially only the teacher is in a position to handle this phase of instruction. The very best the text can do is to provide pictorial and other semiconcrete representations of objects.

In the early phase of work on rational counting, teachers use many forms of materials—bottle caps, books, Popsicle sticks, bean-bags, and the children themselves. Many games and activities can be built around this type of work. Later, teachers usually guide youngsters into a slightly less concrete phase, where they count steps, handclaps, or something along this line. These, of course, can be experienced but cannot be touched or handled as concrete objects.

As rapidly as the students can progress, teachers lead them into rational counting of semiconcrete or pictorial materials. In this phase, texts, workbooks, worksheets, cards, and many other types of materials are available to help the student. The "twoness" of a pair of shoes is shown by pictures rather than the actual shoes.

Cardinal and ordinal numbers

Rational counting yields *cardinal numbers*, those numbers that answer the question, "How many?" Hence, cardinal numbers are taught along with rational counting. At the concrete level students are called upon to count out eight sheets of paper or twenty pencils. Semiconcretely, they are asked to tell how many monkeys are in the cage pictured in their book. Even less concrete would be the task of taking twelve steps forward. Most texts give many suggested activities for helping students with cardinal numbers.

Ordinal numbers describe a position in a sequence. Generally, we associate such terms as "first," or "third," or "tenth" with ordinals. There are exceptions, however. For example, when Susan gives her birthdate as March 14, 1970, she is using numbers in the ordinal sense.

It is usually accepted that ordinal usage is difficult for children. Many students who can count out twelve marbles cannot point out the seventh one counted.

One source of difficulty with ordinals is the names used. Although the relationship between "six" and "sixth" is fairly obvious, the relationship between "one" and "first" or "two" and "second" is somewhat obscure and hence difficult to comprehend.

Of course, teaching materials that can be used for any other type of counting activity can be used in working with ordinals as well. Also, many teachers find natural teaching situations to use, such as the lunchroom line. The usual competition to be first or second in line can be helpful. One little boy was told by his teacher that, because of misbehavior, he would have to go to the last place in line. In a moment, he was back to his old position, explaining brightly that he could not be last since that place was already taken.

Number structure

The study of number structure as applied to the numbers below ten appears to serve little purpose. True, there are certain legends regarding the origin of some of the number symbols ("2" evolving from "="); however, the actual study of number structure starts with the two-digit numbers.

One of the most widely used techniques for this study is place-value pockets. Many teachers make them, using such simple materials as 8″ × 11″ envelopes. These can be compartmentalized with staples, with the compartments labeled "ones" and "tens." They are readily mounted on a tack-board for class demonstration, as Figure 6-1 shows.

Some teachers get good results in number structure by having students outline a block marked "ones" and a block marked "tens" on their desks, using ordinary chalk. Students can follow at their desks the demonstration by the teacher if they have adequate supply of counters—pencils, Popsicle sticks, or other objects.

Many teachers introduce this phase of work by adding counters in the ones pocket until they reach ten. Then, through questioning, they lead the class to understand that this pocket is overcrowded.

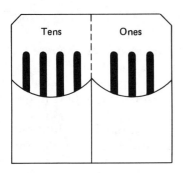

Figure 6-1. Place value pockets

Suggestions are invited as to solutions. Usually the class will provide the plan that some of the counters should go into the tens pocket. Some teachers make this a moment of drama by taking 10 ones and, grouping them by means of a rubber band, changing them to 1 ten. Obviously, the new group now belongs in the tens pocket.

Activities of various sorts can be built around the place-value pockets. For example, a student might volunteer to put 16 in the pockets. Having placed 1 ten and 6 ones in the appropriate pockets, she might "prove" her work by holding the pockets against the board and writing a description of this number. Because the tens pocket contains 1 ten, she writes a "1" above this compartment. Because the ones pocket contains 6, she writes a "6" above it. She has now described the contents of the pockets by writing 16 while seeing them visually. Many similar activities can be used.

As is generally true in number work, students are led forward from the concrete toward the abstract as rapidly as they can move. For example, after working with sticks in the place-value pockets—about as concrete as you can be—students are usually moved into semiconcrete work in the same area. For example, a student might be asked to draw 16 circles on the board. Then he is led, through class discussion, to see 1 ten and 6 ones in the number. Sometimes, the first ten circles will be enclosed in a box or compartment in order to bring out more clearly that this is 1 ten. It is of vital importance that students see the difference between 1 ten and 10 ones.

It is unfortunate that among the earlier two-digit numbers studied some depart in a rather illogical manner from the usual nomenclature. The fact that "eleven" is believed to signify "one left" while "twelve" means "two left" would normally not be presented to students. Even the teens are somewhat confusing, especially because the "teen" comes last. That is, one would logically expect that, in "14," the "4" would be written first, since it is first in the number name. Because there is little likelihood of any changes occurring in such terms, we have no choice but to teach them as they are.

Of course, after explanations, laboratory work, and other such activities, a certain amount of drill (frequently called by a more palatable term) is necessary in order to help youngsters master the concept that in 26, the symbol "2" describes the number of tens, and the "6" describes the number of ones composing the number.

Sets

Almost from the first teachers observe two different approaches that students use in working with sets. Some students look at five objects in a set or in a picture of a set and, without conscious effort, see it as a group of five. Others continue for months to operate at a much lower level by counting "one, two, three, four, five." Those who continue to see the individual members rather than the set will probably tend toward finger counting when they reach the study of addition.

There is no general agreement on the best methods of teaching set recognition. Indeed, many students make the transition—from seeing ones to seeing sets—without knowing just how it happened.

In some classrooms dominoes or domino cards are much used in teaching set recognition. One precaution needs to be observed here. A domino with five dots, for example, *always* has the same pattern. If this type of material is used repeatedly, there is danger that the student will come to recognize the pattern rather than the set. Hence, it is important that cards, charts, or other materials show sets in a variety of patterns as in Figure 6-2.

Concurrently with, or immediately after, the work on recognizing sets, students study how to make sets. This, of course, can be done by a variety of approaches. Some of these are: "Get enough pencils from the cabinet so that each child in your group will have one" (concrete); "Draw a circle around five goats in the picture" (semiconcrete); or "Draw a line under the set with four dots in

Figure 6-2.
Recognizing sets

it" (less concrete than pictures of animals). This type of activity leads logically and almost painlessly into work in addition and subtraction.

Another aspect of set work is counting by groups. Certain programs require that students develop some facility in counting by twos, fives, and tens. These are usually introduced concretely but go rather rapidly toward pictorial material. To many students counting by twos is the most difficult of these three types of group counting. Such natural pairing situations as counting ears, eyes, feet, or hands in a group of students can add interest to this operation. Also, such grouping devices as egg cartons are frequently used. Counting by fives and tens frequently makes use of coins (nickels and dimes) as a familiar group-counting situation.

Associating number names, symbols, and sets

A crackerbarrel philosopher once described how "impossible" arithmetic was to him by telling about how he had to learn it in three languages. He said that his first chore was to learn the word "two" and to learn where it fitted into a sequence of such words. Then, he said, the teacher suddenly confronted him with the same thing in another language by writing the numeral "2" on the board and insisting that he use it. Next, having learned the word and the numeral, he was told that he actually didn't know what 2 stood for until he counted out two objects. This particular individual insisted that he "knew he was licked" when this happened.

Frequently, it is difficult for adults to see the complexity just pointed out: the complexity of teaching names, symbols, and rational counting simultaneously. In most modern programs, however, all these approaches are so closely coordinated that students are not aware that they are doing several things at once. Many arithmetic programs start, almost from the very first day, by presenting pictures of sets along with the descriptive number word and the numeral. Many parallel aids, such as flash cards, charts, and assorted games, can be used to further this complex job of learning in three languages.

Of course, the first phases of this work are concerned with recognizing number names and numerals; usually, however, and as an integral operation, students are introduced to the task of writing the numerals. This is frequently troublesome because (1) there is no way for a student to figure out why the symbol "4" stands for the same thing as the word "four," and (2) some degree of muscular coordination is required.

Several different approaches are available to aid in this task.

For years, first-grade teachers have used commercially available charts for letters and numerals. These, in characters several inches high, are frequently mounted above the chalkboard, presumably to serve as models for the students. Also, of course, the teacher uses every opportunity to write the numerals on the board, pointing out how each is correctly written.

Certain first-grade teachers have developed or adapted verses, jingles, or songs to help students learn to write the numerals. These are usually built around the separate motions used in writing the symbols. For example, one such jingle describes, with much repetition and many accompanying motions, "A line straight down and that is all, to make the number 1." Two is described as "half around and straight across"; three is "half around and half around." Four is "down, across, and then straight down." Five is "across, down, and half around." Six is "a line straight down, then all around." When used, of course, such jingles are rapidly superseded. Conceivably, these could become a crutch, with a third or fourth grader still having to sing the jingle in order to write the symbol.

In order to involve the sense of touch in teaching students to write numerals, some first-grade teachers make extensive use of cardboard or wood cutouts of the numerals. Such numerals, made of Bakelite, are commercially available but can be improvised by teachers. Usually, the numerals are large, possibly up to 6 inches high. Youngsters who are having trouble in writing numerals frequently get a great deal of help by tracing such figures with their fingers. Variations of this technique might involve giving the figures a light cost of plastic material from a pressure can and sprinkling lightly with sand, or gluing sandpaper to them. Both techniques add more "feel" to the symbols and seem to increase their effectiveness as a teaching aid.

Tracing is a widely used approach in teaching children to write numerals. Many workbooks and worktexts use dotted symbols, usually with arrows showing the direction of motion for each part of the symbol. Many students will require supplemental practice on this type of work, usually provided by use of teacher-prepared worksheets or some other type of duplicated material. As was mentioned earlier, teachers must accept the fact that skill in writing these symbols comes slowly and hence is developed over a period of years.

Some numerals give much more trouble than others. For example, many students have trouble with the numeral 5. Despite their best efforts, it comes out looking like a capital "S". Probably even more troublesome is the 8. This symbol, of course, requires a downward stroke followed by an upward motion. Also, and frequently more of a problem, it has two separate and distinct segments. As a result youngsters tend to make it twice as large as the other numerals. Occasionally, a student will insist on reversing a symbol; 3 and 7 are common offenders in this respect. The correction of such difficulties usually requires additional practice under close supervision by the teacher. Sometimes it may be desirable to break down the difficult numeral into parts in order to help students develop the desired facility.

Diagnosis

At the readiness level, close observation on the part of the teacher is absolutely necessary in diagnosing problems. This observation applies to performance as well as product because each can give the teacher useful information.

As noted in Chapter 5, structured instruments are available to the teacher to use for diagnosis. However, it is a relatively simple process to develop diagnostic material when the need arises.

Many types of diagnostic activities are useful. Some of these activities are described below.

1. Can the student *put items in one-to-one correspondence?* Give the student a picture showing some balls and bats or other objects of interest. Let him or her draw lines connecting balls to bats to arrive at an answer to the question: Is there a bat for each ball?
2. Can he *see equivalency of sets without drawing lines?* Set up some cards with varying numbers of spots and have the student select matching cards for each—three to three, four to four, and others. The spots should vary as to pattern to avoid matching on the basis of pattern.
3. Can he match *sets with numerals?* This is somewhat like the activity described above except that the student matches the set as in Figure 6-3 with the numeral 4. Incidentally, this can be carried out with these items in opposite columns on a sheet. The student does the pairing by drawing lines.

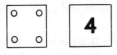

Figure 6-3. Matching
sets and numerals

4. Can he *identify numerals from the spoken name?* The student is given a strip bearing the numerals 1 through 9, in proper sequence. Then he or she is given oral directions to "put a ring around the 8," "put the 4 in a box," and so forth. The directions should take the numbers out of sequence.

5. Can he *write the numerals properly?* Here, the student is simply called upon to write numerals as called by the teacher. Close observation as to work habits and products is essential here. An unusual show of tension may indicate a problem spot. Also, a look at the paper may well disclose such difficulties as reversed 3s and 7s, an oversize 8, and others.

6. Can he *write numerals in proper sequence?* A few simple cases should suffice. These might include 1, 2, 3,☐; 7, 8,☐, 10; 6, 5, 4,☐; and one that is likely to give trouble, 3, 2, 1,☐.

Other, more sophisticated types of diagnostic testing can be carried out as part of readiness, but these will be obvious to the teacher who is attuned to the diagnostic point of view.

7 Addition

The student's first encounter with whole-number operations is with addition. Although addition is the least difficult of the four operations, it would be unwise to assume that it can be passed over lightly. Numerous studies have indicated that many students lack mastery of addition in the upper-elementary and junior-high-school grades. A well-planned and well-executed program that is diagnostically oriented can do much to help students overcome many difficulties.

Developing addition concepts and skills

Addition begins at a very early stage in a child's development of number concepts. Addition in an informal and intuitive manner is often an outgrowth of counting. Combining or joining small groups without the use of formal language or signs may be considered rudimentary addition.

In order to develop addition concepts and skills to their fullest, it is necessary to investigate the basic structure and content of the operation. This investigation will consider the nature or purpose of addition, its properties, the elements or content involved, and the relationships among these components.

Nature and purpose of addition

Addition involves combining or grouping two or more sets of objects into a single set. It is a frequently used operation in daily activities. In its abstract form addition uses numerals to represent the number of elements in the sets to be combined. The numbers to be combined are called *addends,* and the numeral representing the number of combined elements is called the *sum.* Therefore, addition may be viewed as addend plus addend equals sum (or addend + addend = sum). In the example $2 + 6 = 8$, 2 and 6 are addends and 8 is the sum.

Another characteristic of addition is that it is a *binary operation.* This means that two numbers are involved in the operation. A single number cannot be added: It would not be meaningful to ask someone to add five. Ask even a beginning student to perform such an operation and he or she would probably reply, "Add five and what?" Of even greater importance to the binary nature of addition is the fact that only two numbers are directly involved in the operation at a single time. In column addition with three or more addends, only two are involved at a time. Consider the exercise $5 + 4 + 7$. All three addends are not combined simultaneously. Two are combined, any two, to form a partial sum; this partial sum is then transformed mentally into an addend and combined with the other addend to determine the sum. No matter how proficient one becomes, this procedure is always followed.

Properties of addition

There are several properties of addition that govern its behavior. These properties are introduced at a very early point in the development of the concept and skills of addition. Formal names and definitions are not stressed in the early developmental stages, but the concepts are acquired and utilized by students at an early age.

The commutative property of addition is one of the first to be encountered by the student. The *commutative property* states that the order of the addends does not affect the sum. Consider the utility of this property. There are 100 basic addition facts which the student should master in order to become proficient in addition. Of these 100 facts, 10 consist of *like* addends such as $1 + 1, 2 + 2$, and so on. The remaining 90 are made up of addends such as $3 + 4$. Applying the commutative property, which states that $x + y = y + x$, where x and y represent 0 through 9, the number of remaining basic facts has been reduced from 90 to 45 for most purposes. True, the order of the addends may affect an individual's proficiency. Often one order is easier to learn than another; thus,

8 + 5 may be easier than 5 + 8. Yet, when such is the case, the student who understands the commutative property realizes that he or she can mentally change the order of the addends as an aid in computation.

Another valuable property that aids in the mastery of basic addition facts is the *identity element for addition:* The sum of 0 and any number is that number. To state this more formally, for any value of x, $x + 0 = 0 + x = x$. Knowing that zero is the identity element for addition is also most useful. There are 19 basic addition facts that include 0. Of the 55 basic facts remaining after applying the commutative property, 10 contain 0 as an addend. A student who understands and can apply the identity element, or zero property reduces the number of difficult addition facts to 45.

As students move beyond two-addend addition the associative property becomes important. The *associative property* states that for all x, y, and z, $x + (y + z) = (x + y) + z$. In other words, regrouping three addends, with order unchanged, does not affect the sum. This property allows flexibility in the operation of addition. A student may have an opportunity to select easier combinations. Consider the example $7 + (8 + 2)$. Many times a sum of 10 may be obtained in a particular grouping pattern; thus, $7 + (8 + 2) = 7 + 10 = 17$. It could have been grouped $(7 + 8) + 2 = 15 + 2 = 17$. But, many students would find the $7 + 8$ combination more difficult than either the $8 + 2$ or $7 + 10$ combinations.

The associative property does not provide for changing the order of the addends. As students more fully develop number concepts, they may combine several of the properties of addition in the process of computation. In column addition they may rearrange addends (the commutative property) to produce specific partial sums, such as groups of ten (the associative property) and eliminate zeros in the process (the identity element). This will not happen over a short period of time. But learning the basic concepts of addition and understanding of its properties, students can master this most basic mathematical skill.

Content of addition

In order to obtain a proper perspective on any area of study, one needs to stand far enough away to view the broad scope and sequence before examining the minute details. As elementary as addition is, there is a need to treat it in this manner. Children appear to learn addition in four phases, which involves (1) developing concepts, (2) learning the basic facts, (3) going through a transitional stage, and (4) coming to an understanding of the addition algorithm. A consideration of the basic skills absorbed in each of these phases will provide the broad base necessary for an examination of the details involved in the diagnostic teaching of addition.

Concept development The concept of addition is introduced early in the mathematics program. Kindergarten children work with this during their number-readiness development. At this level the work is with concrete objects without the abstract plus and equal signs. Working with sets of objects, the children bring together counting elements and combining groups to develop the concept of addition.

From this rudimentary beginning the concept is developed step by step to its completion. By the second stage of development, the abstract is evident. Young students need much work with concrete objects during the early developmental stages, but within this stage the plus and equality signs may be introduced. These signs can be made of flannelboard or other types of material that the child can manipulate. The sign itself may be concrete, but the symbolism is abstract. The concept is further developed through semiconcrete materials that represent groups or sets to be combined to form a single set. As a final step, the abstract symbols and numerals alone are utilized.

Throughout the entire process of concept development, the basic addition facts are introduced. Initially, little stress is placed on memorizing the specific combination that yields a given sum. This stage of development should emphasize the discovery approach to learning. Through a variety of experiences with concrete objects, children will discover for themselves many of the easier basic facts. A more direct approach to learning the facts follows this phase. Through the use of concrete and semiconcrete materials, the student begins to commit to memory the easier facts. This memorization is a very important part of the developmental process. A student cannot become proficient in addition until this is accomplished.

The goal is to have students work at the abstract level. Are all students who work with numerals working at the abstract level? Obviously, the answer is no. As long as students count to themselves, count fingers, or use other such devices, they are translating the abstract numeral into a simpler form that they can manipulate. Therefore, students who rely on such methods are not able to capitalize on the abstract nature of symbolism in mathematics and are severely handicapped.

Mastering facts A variety of methods and materials should be used in helping students master the basic addition facts. The role of concrete objects in joining sets has been mentioned. Audio, visual, and audio-visual formats are available for reinforcement and mastery after the basic foundation has been developed. There are many games that provide drill on the basic facts. Good judgment should always govern the type and amount given. As a rule, it is best to give small amounts over a long period of time. There should be variety in the types of practice in order to maintain interest.

Learning the basic facts is achieved in several stages. Sequencing allows the student to gain a degree of proficiency at one level before moving to a more difficult one. Three stages of learning can be discerned.

The first level includes exercises with sums through five. It may be advisable at this level to exclude zero as an addend. This is done because in developing number concepts, the empty set, which is utilized to teach zero, is abstract. Usually zero can be introduced as an addend after work has progressed through sums of five.

Students at the second level learn facts about sums through nine or ten. There are two possible approaches to take in teaching the facts at this level. By stopping at sums of nine, we have not gone beyond the one-digit numbers. Although students have seen the numeral 10 written, and could probably add sums of ten as easily as sums of nine, there is probably little understanding of the meaning of the two-digit numeral. For this reason it may be advisable to work with sums through nine and then introduce some basic place-value concepts related to two-digit numbers. Again, we are considering the synchronization of all strands of the curriculum. Sums of ten can be used as an introduction to two-digit numbers, and the student will feel a need for learning place value. Regardless of the line of reasoning, it is obvious that place-value concepts enter the program at this point.

At the final level of development the remaining facts with sums through 18 are taught. All steps in the development of the basic facts are cumulative. Previously learned facts should be reviewed as the student works with the newer group.

Some clarification Several basic considerations should be taken into account with regard to teaching the basic facts. They include the role of the discovery method and the properties of addition.

We suggested above that the discovery approach should be utilized in the early stages of development of the concept of addition and with the basic facts. To what extent should this method be relied upon? Should students be expected to "discover" each basic fact? This could result in a very time-consuming process if carried to an extreme. After students have experienced a number of discoveries related to addition and the basic facts, they can generally profit from a more direct approach. They may still need many experiences with concrete materials in order to visualize the operation, but this is done more to fix the fact in their minds than to discover something.

The properties of addition are incorporated into the process of concept development at a very early stage. Directly associated with the basic facts are the commutative property and the identity element of addition. As pointed out in the section on properties, the commutative property effectively reduces the number of basic facts as does the identity element. The name of these properties and their formal definitions are not important during the early stages of development, but an understanding of them is vital. The names and definitions of properties are not introduced in most cases until all the facts have been introduced and worked with for a period of time. The third or fourth year of school is the approximate time of formal introduction.

For the average student all basic facts in addition are introduced and learned to a degree of proficiency by the second school year. This does not mean that all students will have mastered the basic facts by that time. *Formal teaching of the basic facts should continue as long as there is evidence of a need.* Continuous diagnosis helps determine this need.

Transitional-stage learning Between the time that students learn the basic facts and the addition algorithm, they enter a *transitional phase.* Several types of exercises are used at this stage.

Adding by endings without bridging is one such exercise. The example, 12 + 6, may be used to illustrate the usefulness of this type of exercise. Students must move beyond the basic facts to arrive at the answer, but it is not necessary to go through the process of adding each column separately. The 2 in 12 should be the clue for students that the sum will have an 8 in the last place on the right. By utilizing their knowledge of the basic facts, students have increased their knowledge of number facts. This type of exercise is a natural lead-in to the simple algorithm, or rule, which involves no renaming.

Column addition of single-digit numbers is another transitional step. The first experiences in this area should involve three addends that involve only basic facts. For example, only basic facts are involved in the following:

$$
\begin{array}{r}
3 \\
2 \\
+4 \\
\hline
\end{array}
$$

If we proceed from the top, the unseen addend is 5. At this point work with an unseen addend is the most important aspect of the development. By working with exercises where the unseen addend and the final addend are basic-fact combinations, such as the 5 + 4 in the example above, students are not taxed by working with two difficult skills at the same time.

A step beyond either of the two operations above but within the transitional stage is adding by endings with bridging. This carries the earlier adding by endings one step farther. In the example 16 + 5, the same procedure is used to determine the sum; the clue is 6 + 5. Since 6 + 5 ends with 1 the sum of 16 + 5 must end with 1. The new feature is that a new decade (or set of ten) was entered, and we must go from one decade to another by bridging. Several approaches may be used to help the child determine when a decade has been bridged. In the exercise used above, it would not make sense for the sum to be in the same decade as the two-digit addend (i.e., the decade from 11 to 19) and still end in 1. (The sum would then have been 11.) The basic facts may also be called upon to furnish the clue. Because the endings that are to be added are always basic facts, any time that the endings have a two-digit sum, the sum of the complete exercise will be in the next decade, never two decades higher.

A step beyond adding by endings with bridging is column addition in which the unseen addend and the final addend are not basic-fact combinations. The following is an example:

$$
\begin{array}{r}
6 \\
5 \\
+4 \\
\hline
\end{array}
$$

After 6 + 5 have been added to get the unseen addend of 11, combining the 11 and 4 is an example of adding by endings without bridging. Because adding by endings with bridging has also been developed at this point, simple column addition can be extended to include an unseen addend and a final addend that will involve bridging (e.g., 7 + 6 + 8).

Addition algorithm development It is difficult to determine exactly when the development of the addition algorithm, the rule for adding multi-digit numbers, begins. Much intuitive work resembling work with the algorithm is done prior to the transitional work discussed above. When students work with basic facts such as 2 + 3 = 5, they intuitively grasp the idea that 200 + 300 = 500. Does this constitute work with the algorithm? Or, if they can work out that example in column form, is this algorithm work? At this stage the answer is probably no. For one reason, the algorithm involves set procedures. Students do not need to follow the algorithm procedures to get the correct sum. They could add the hundreds column first, which often happens, and get the correct answer.

Work with the algorithm may begin with very simple addition of two-digit and larger addends where no renaming is involved. When a student moves beyond multiples of 10 and 100 as addends, the development of the algorithm formally begins. Thus, $100 + 200 = 300$ may be considered intuitive, whereas $125 + 231 = 356$ is algorithm development, especially when it is written in column form and a column-by-column procedure is followed.

After procedures are established for adding columns correctly, the next major step involves renaming and carrying groups of ten to the next higher place. Students will pass through several stages of development in learning this procedure. Development should proceed from renaming ones as tens, to renaming at higher places, and then multiple renaming within the same exercise.

The addition algorithm is taken to its ultimate form in complex column addition. At this level students must integrate all their knowledge of the algorithm—column alignment, basic facts, adding by endings with and without bridging, unseen addends, regrouping, and carrying—in order to be successful.

It is evident that although addition of whole numbers is a relatively "simple" operation, several years are required for its development and even more time is needed for a student to become proficient.

A diagnostic approach in teaching addition

The diagnostic approach to teaching addition of whole numbers involves the systematic gathering of information concerning student performance that will pinpoint possible difficulties. It requires close observation of student performance of operations in addition arranged in order from least to most complex. The least complex are the basic facts, and the most complex is column addition involving several multi-digit numbers.

Addition facts

The basic addition facts are the foundation upon which the operation is built. Lack of mastery of the basic facts is often a major contributor to incorrect addition. In a study conducted by one of the authors, more than one-fourth of the errors in addition were attributed to incorrect combinations.

Diagnosis When diagnostic procedures are considered, teachers must always keep in mind the stage of development at which the student is working. The 100 basic addition facts are introduced and mastered over a span of several years. A logical division was previously described.

Diagnostic testing on the basic facts can yield some helpful findings. The test results can show the level of mastery best when the test is timed. Timing reduces instances of counting to acquire the answer. Given sufficient time, most children can use such aids as finger counting or tapping to get the answer. Several methods of pacing the test may be utilized. One method is to give each student a copy of the test and have him or her write in the answers as the exercises are read aloud by the teacher. The same procedure may be used substituting a tape recording of the teacher's questions. The second method gives the teacher a better opportunity to observe the actions of the students during the test. There are also filmstrips of the facts that may be projected at various speeds. With this presentation students are given numbered answer sheets upon which they record only the sums. Regardless of the method, proper pacing is important. It must be fast enough to eliminate most inefficient "crutches," and yet it must not be so fast that it frustrates students. It is a good idea for students to have some previous experience with the method before actual testing is undertaken.

Diagnostic testing is not concerned with the number of percentage of right or wrong answers. Rather the concern is with why some exercises were missed. The alert diagnostician should be aware of patterns of errors. A student may have his or her errors concentrated in relatively few areas. It may be that exercises in which one of the addends is 7 are the only ones missed. Or a student may have difficulty only with the most difficult facts or with sums of 13 or greater. If teachers pinpoint the problem area, the follow-up therapy will be more efficient and effective.

Therapy Once the area of difficulty has been determined, the teacher must initiate a plan of work aimed directly at overcoming the problem. Students with similar difficulties may be grouped together to facilitate instruction. Others may require individualized instruction.

What is the best method for remedial work? This question may be answered by considering the related issue of the best method of initial instruction. One of the first and most important lessons learned by a teacher is that no one method is best for all students or for the same student at all times. Good remedial or corrective teaching is similar to good initial teaching in that it adheres to basic principles of learning. The major difference between the two is that the scope of corrective teaching is narrowed and intensified in a particular area.

Armed with diagnostic test results and a knowledge of sound teaching procedures, the teacher can begin therapy. If no patterns of errors are apparent and most of the exercises are incorrect, the teacher should begin by determining if the student understands the meaning of addition. It may be helpful, or even necessary, to work with the student using concrete materials. After work at the concrete level the student can advance to work with graphic representations of sets. For example, Figure 7.1 pictures two sets of balls. A student might be presented with this figure and asked the following:

Set A has ____ balls. Set B has ____ balls.
Join Set A and Set B.
Call the new set, Set C.
Set C has ____ balls.

In answering these questions, the student not only moves away from actual manipulation of the members but grasps as well the more abstract concept of using a numeral to represent a given amount.

When a student understands the meaning of addition, he or she is ready to use numerals to represent numbers without the aid of visuals. After reaching this meaningful stage of development, the student can profit from practice or drill.

Mastery of the basic facts requires practice. The facts must be studied and memorized. The student should not develop the habits of counting on fingers, tapping, or relying on a number line. If certain facts are troublesome, he or she should concentrate on those. Student progress should be measured by checkups similar to the timed exercises presented in the diagnostic procedures.

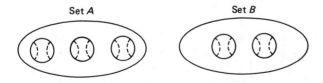

Figure 7-1. Joining sets

Two-digit addends, no renaming

Addition of two numbers with two digits is the first type of addition beyond the basic facts. Although this step is only slightly more difficult than the basic facts, several difficulties may appear. It is very important that potential difficulties be diagnosed and corrected at this early stage of development in order to assume the effective sequential development of addition.

Diagnosis The diagnostic procedure may take several forms, depending on the age and grade level of the students. For older students whose proficiency in addition is below expectations, a formal diagnostic test is a logical approach. Such a test would analyze addition into its developmental steps, enabling the teacher to determine the specific step at which difficulties become serious. For younger students who are just moving into the stage of combining two-digit numbers, *all* work should be approached from the diagnostic point of view. The diagnostic approach to teaching arithmetic implies that the teacher will be alert to indications of lack of understanding on the part of students. The teacher must circulate among students to observe their work and methods, question students concerning their work, and guide them in overcoming difficulties. This two-way approach—daily diagnostic teaching and formal diagnostic testing—should be used at all stages of development in all operations.

What are some of the difficulties that may occur at this level? As with all steps in addition, lack of mastery of the basic facts is a major source of errors. There are also certain procedural difficulties for which the teacher should be on the alert. Some students have a problem associated with place value of the two-digit numerals; they do not add each column independently. Another error, which does not result in an incorrect answer when no renaming is required, is adding from the left to the right. A teacher who relies solely on examination of written work after it is completed will not detect that practice until later when renaming is involved. By that time, however, the improper procedure has been reinforced and will be difficult to correct. This is only one example that emphasizes the necessity of observing students closely during work sessions.

Therapy Once the errors have been diagnosed, a plan of corrective work should be initiated. Addition combinations are a source of many errors, and thus a plan for reteaching the facts must be considered. Individual and small-group therapy will probably be the most effective. The work should be based on individual need as indicated by the diagnostic procedures.

Clarifying the basic procedural errors at this level centers on place value. A thorough development of the place-value concept is essential if addition of two-digit and larger numbers is to be meaningful. The three stages of development of a new concept—concrete, semiconcrete, and abstract manipulations—should be adhered to in the teaching–learning situation. Students should use materials such as place-value pockets in their initial encounter. After the student has had an opportunity to work extensively with manipulative materials, he or she should work with semiconcrete or representational materials. Pictures of single members and groups of tens and hundreds will convey the same message as concrete objects when the student's understanding matures. Finally, the student is ready to work with the abstract by having a numeral represent a given quantity.

Performing the actual additive operation with two-digit numbers should be approached in the same way. The student who experiences difficulty at this level probably will need help based on the lowest level of instruction. Manipulative materials should be used to enable the student to represent the quantities to be added. Then the student can advance to pictorial materials. Most textbooks and workbooks feature pictures of objects that may be combined to show addition. When a basic understanding of addition with place value has been developed with concrete and pictorial materials, the student can then advance to working with numerals. It may not be necessary to go back to the concrete stage with each problem; the important point is to go back to the level at which the student can work, then move forward from that point.

Between addition without renaming and addition with renaming there is an intermediate step where the final column has a two-digit sum. In the problem 52 + 76, written in column form, some students write a sum of 26. Was the error one of carelessness or a lack of understanding of place value? Diagnosis would have to include a work-aloud session or some similar type of communication between the student and teacher to establish the cause. This type of exercise is helpful in extending place value to the hundreds as well as establishing readiness for addition with renaming.

Adding by endings without bridging

Adding by endings without bridging involves horizontal addition of a two-digit addend and a one-digit addend, the sum being in the same decade as the two-digit addend. This operation is relatively simple if the teacher permits the student to rearrange the addends into columns. But such an approach is completely contrary to the reasoning behind the horizontal form of presentation, which may be viewed as an extension of the basic facts. The student should be able to see 13 + 5 = 18 without using the slower procedure of adding each column separately. The importance of this lies in the fact that he or she must be able to do exactly the same thing in column addition. Adding by endings is not an end in itself but a step toward column addition.

Diagnosis Because the solution to addition-by-endings exercises is easily attained when approached by an incorrect method, such as changing the form or counting up, diagnosis by written tests may not be completely satisfactory. Students should be proficient enough to give the answers orally at a steady pace.

Therapy The same type of remedial work as is used with the basic facts may be used. The basic facts are actually the cue for the correct procedure. In the exercise 13 + 5 the child should see the 5 + 3 = 8 as the key to the sum 18. When there is no bridging to the next decade, no other serious problem is encountered. Students should have sufficient practice with this type of work so that their responses will become as automatic as when working with the basic facts.

Adding by endings with bridging

A logical extension of addition is from addition by endings without bridging to addition by endings with bridging. There are two basic justifications for this stage. The first reason, the importance of this procedure to readiness for column addition, has been touched upon. Naturally, column addition cannot be carried far before partial sums in a column progress from one decade to the next, such as from the teens to the twenties and on until a final sum is reached. The second reason for adding by endings with bridging is that it is a natural lead-in to addition with renaming of ones or tens. When the student has experience with exercises such as 18 + 3 = 21, the more formal type of addition where the 8 ones and 3 ones are grouped as 1 ten and 1 one will be meaningful. This is similar to teaching reading by building a sight vocabulary of familiar words before the components are analyzed as to their sounds.

Diagnosis and therapy The technique for diagnosing and remedying problems in this area is very similar to that for addition without bridging. The basic facts are still the key to the solution. In

26 + 7 the student should see that the answer must have a 3 in the ones place because 6 + 7 = 13. Again the distinction should be made between adding each place separately, renaming, and carrying to the next column and adding the two addends as a unit. The major obstacle to overcome is that of bridging to the next decade. The basic fact will determine the ending, so that the question to answer is whether bridging has taken place. There are several means by which the student may reach a conclusion. One may be termed the "common sense" conclusion. If 26 + 7 must end with 3, it would not make sense to arrive at the answer 23. A second important point the student should discover is that even when bridging does take place, there will never be more than a one-decade advance with each addend. The largest addend to be dealt with in column addition at any time is 9. For that reason all work at this stage should involve a two-digit addend plus a one-digit addend, such as the examples given.

One other point should be considered when planning work in addition by endings. Results of a study by one of the authors indicated that students have more difficulty with higher-decade exercises. It was found that exercises such as 57 + 5 were missed more often than 17 + 5. If students had developed the method advocated, that of making the operation similar to a basic fact, there should have been no difference. Practice with both teens and higher-decade bridging would seem to be in order.

Simple column addition without bridging

As students progress toward mastery of addition, each stage of development serves as a readiness phase for the next step in the sequential program. Simple column addition with and without bridging is an important link between adding by endings with two addends and addition with renaming.

Diagnosis and therapy Diagnostic materials should include exercises where simple column addition requires no bridging. This would require exercises with three or four addends with a sum of nine or less, such as the following:

$$\begin{array}{r} 3 \\ 2 \\ +4 \\ \hline \end{array}$$

One study has shown that this particular type of exercise is not particularly difficult. The finding did not diminish the importance of the step in the developmental program. The high degree of accuracy students display on this type of exercise may be attributed to the fact that it is fairly easy to count up the sum with such small addends. The importance of the step lies in the need for students to be able to work with an unseen addend. In adding downward the student must add 3 and 2; then, because addition is a binary operation, the partial sum 5 becomes an unseen, or unrecorded, addend. Sufficient work with exercises of this type should be provided before the student moves into simple column addition with bridging.

Simple column addition with bridging

Closely related to adding by endings with bridging is simple column addition of one-digit numbers with bridging. This step is considerably more difficult than the previous step without bridging. Several factors contribute to its difficulty. To illustrate some areas of difficulty consider the following exercise:

$$
\begin{array}{r}
5 \\
8 \\
6 \\
7 \\
+\,8 \\
\hline
\end{array}
$$

With bridging the size of the addends is not limited. This may be overcome by purposely keeping the addends small, but eventually the student must be able to use all basic facts proficiently. Bridging itself is the major problem. Adding downward, one encounters the following:

1. The basic fact: $5 + 8 = 13$
2. Adding by endings without bridging: $13 + 6 = 19$
3. Adding by endings with bridging: $19 + 7 = 26$
4. More adding by endings with bridging: $26 + 8 = 34$.

After the first basic fact the student is working with unseen addends.

Diagnosis and therapy As work becomes more complex, the value of a well-constructed diagnostic test becomes evident. Often remedial work will consist of clarifying some procedural point once the specific problem area has been pinpointed. This is especially true after a basic understanding of the operation has been developed. It then becomes the teacher's responsibility to select material keyed to the specific problem area so that reteaching and practice are focused directly on the difficulty.

Addition with renaming ("carrying")

Up to this point addition with renaming in its formal sense has not been undertaken. Readiness for this stage has been gradually developed from the earliest two-digit sums of the basic facts through adding by endings and simple column addition with bridging.

Renaming in addition is a major concept that must be meaningfully developed if the student is to progress in his skills development. As previously noted, the development of computational skills cannot be separated from an understanding of the number system. The student needs to understand the properties of the number system and their relation to the computational skills. These two areas should complement one another.

Diagnosis There is an internal progression in renaming just as renaming in general is a phase in learning the operation of addition. Diagnostic instruments must take this internal progression into consideration. The first encounter with renaming should be with renaming ones as tens. After that tens should be renamed as hundreds and hundreds as thousands. Multiple renaming should be of no major difficulty if the earlier single-place renaming has been thoroughly developed. It may be wise to begin multiple renaming by renaming in the first two columns. From that point the progression could lead to various combinations that require some renaming in several consecutive places as well as renaming in alternate columns.

What are some errors that may be revealed through diagnosis of written work in this type addition? A recent study of 690 sixth-grade students revealed that over one-fifth of the errors in addition were directly associated with renaming or carrying. The most common error was failure to carry and add the renamed number to the next column. Some students reversed the digits, recorded the tens, and carried the ones. Others refused to be bothered with renaming and recorded both digits in each column. Carrying the wrong number and carrying unnecessarily were other sources of error. These were errors made by sixth-grade students who should have mastered addition by that time.

Therapy Helping to overcome the difficulties in renaming closely parallels good initial teaching. Regardless of the level of the student—a second grader with his or her first experiences with renaming or a sixth grader who does not understand—the three stages of development in instruction must be the basis for corrective work.

The basic concept of place value must be meaningfully developed at the concrete stage. Place-value materials and charts are very helpful. They should not be used exclusively for teacher demonstration; instead, each child should have many experiences with manipulating these materials. Place value and renaming cannot be separated if the latter is to be meaningful. Corrective work then may move on to the representative stage. There are many good exercises in textbooks, workbooks, and various educational games to help the teacher at this level. Work with abstract numerals can then follow. The important point at each stage is to select materials keyed to the specific need. Above all, the child should go as far back as necessary to get to the source of the problem. If a sixth-grade student needs work at the concrete-material stage, then that is where corrective work should begin.

Complex column addition

By far the greatest number of errors in addition occur in complex column addition. This is readily understandable for all the difficulties described to this point are found in this most difficult form of addition.

Diagnosis and therapy Because of its complexity, diagnosis of errors in column addition cannot rely solely on written work. The work-aloud method, which is useful at all levels, is necessary to locate sources of errors in columns. Naturally, this oral work is based on some structured written exercises.

If a student has progressed through the earlier steps of the addition sequence without major difficulty, he or she may be having difficulty putting it all together. Meaningful practice may be all that is necessary. If the diagnosis points to errors in a specific developmental skill, the teacher and student should work on that specific skill. For example, if a student skips around in a column to find easy combinations, the logical conclusion is that he or she needs to master the basic facts. Perhaps the trouble lies in bridging from one decade to the next; then, addition by endings may be the work needed. Every effort should be made to diagnose the source of error and plan corrective work to remedy the specific cause.

Subtraction

The concept of subtraction of whole numbers is relatively easy for children to understand, and yet subtraction skills cause considerable difficulty. At a very early preschool age the average child has had many experiences that involve "taking away" a portion of a set. This type of subtraction is generally the first type encountered in a structured learning situation.

Nature and purpose of subtraction

There are two basic characteristics of *subtraction* that need to be emphasized to make the operation meaningful. First, it is a process of separating. Readiness activities begin at an early age to develop the concept of subtraction through this approach.

Even this straightforward concept of subtraction is difficult for many students. One problem involves the various settings in which subtraction is utilized. In a directed activity in which students are guided through the operation of removing a subset from a set, the meaning of subtraction may be readily understood. But when asked to find the difference, remainder, or how much more is needed, students may experience difficulties in determining when to subtract. Although the concept of subtraction involves partition or separation, its use is not always easily determined because of its varied applications.

The second major characteristic of subtraction is that it is the inverse of addition. This relationship between addition and subtraction should be utilized in the development of subtraction from the initial concept to the most complex skills involving the algorithm.

Whole-number operations are so related that teaching an isolated skill is neither efficient nor effective. This is especially true with addition and subtraction. Although formal work with addition generally precedes subtraction, the two complement one another to such a degree that they can be learned as closely related operations. If addition is thought of as combining several groups or sets to make a single set, then subtraction may be looked upon as beginning with one set and separating it into two. Students should be led to discover the relationships among (1) the groups or sets put together in addition, (2) the single group formed by the combination, (3) the single group that is separated in subtraction, and (4) the two groups formed after the separation has been completed. This is what happens when students discover the related facts that $5 + 4 = 9$ and $9 - 5 = 4$. If they have discovered that addition is commutative, they have completed the set because $4 + 5$ is also 9.

Although addition and subtraction may be taught as related operations, not all addition and subtraction should be so developed. They must be undertaken as two distinct operations, each with its own laws and characteristics.

Content of subtraction

Subtraction, like addition, is learned sequentially. Children must learn the concept of subtraction and the basic facts before working with the subtraction algorithm.

The concept of subtraction has been considered earlier. Because of the varied settings in which subtraction is used, the development of the concept of subtraction will progress through several stages.

As with addition the basic subtraction facts are taught in several groups. The sequence followed in addition is recommended for subtraction. After a group of addition facts have been introduced, such as sums through five, the related subtraction facts are developed. Then the two operations can be carried forward almost simultaneously. The term "almost" is used to ensure that neither operation loses its identity. After both concepts are developed and some proficiency with the basic facts has been reached, the two operations can be taught together through the use of families of related facts. Through the use of this approach, both addition and subtraction facts should be developed over the same period of time.

Development of the subtraction algorithm is more complex than development of the addition algorithm because there are at least three different acceptable ways to teach the subtraction algorithm. They include the additive method, the equal-additions method, and the decomposition method.

Each method may bring a new dimension to the development of subtraction. The *additive method* capitalizes on the missing-addend approach to subtraction and the close relationship between addition and subtraction. This method is illustrated as follows:

$$
\begin{array}{r}
426 \\
-139 \\
\hline
287
\end{array}
\qquad
\begin{array}{l}
\text{9 and 7 are 16} \\
\text{4 and 8 are 12} \\
\text{2 and 2 are 4}
\end{array}
$$

The *equal-additions method* is based on the principle that when like quantities are added to the minuend (in column format, the top number) and the subtrahend (the bottom number), the difference between the two remains the same. This is illustrated as follows:

$$
\begin{array}{r}
621 \\
-458 \\
\hline
163
\end{array}
\qquad
\begin{array}{l}
\text{8 from 11 is 3} \\
\text{6 from 12 is 6} \\
\text{5 from 6 is 1}
\end{array}
$$

The decomposition method is illustrated as follows:

$$
\begin{array}{rrr}
5 & 13 & 11 \\
\not{6} & \not{4} & 1 \\
-4 & 7 & 3 \\
\hline
1 & 6 & 8
\end{array}
$$

In this exercise 1 ten in the minuend was renamed as 10 ones and placed in the ones column to give a total of 11 ones. The tens value in the minuend was reduced to 3, then 1 hundred was renamed as 10 tens and placed with the 3 tens for a total of 13 tens. The hundreds place then had a total of 5. From the renamed minuend, 5 hundreds + 13 tens + 11 ones, the 473 is subtracted.

Which method should be used as the basic approach to teaching the algorithm? Should more than one method be used? It is recommended that one method be used as the basic approach. The algorithm should be thoroughly developed, with emphasis on understanding its relation to the number system and not as a purely mechanical operation.

The *decomposition method* appears to be the most logical method to use, for two reasons. First, it is widely used. A student who moves from one school to another is more likely to be taught by this method than any other. Second, it is an approach that is deeply involved with an understanding of our number system. Therefore, the teaching of the number system and the algorithm complement one another.

Because the authors consider the decomposition method the preferred approach, the section on diagnosis is based on the use of this method. After the basic algorithm has been taught, other methods, such as the equal-additions method and the additive method, may be utilized to extend and enrich the operation.

The algorithm of subtraction can be developed in three steps. Each step may be taught by several specific types of exercises with varying degrees of difficulty. The more specific types will be dealt with in the diagnostic section of this chapter.

The first major step includes subtraction in which there is no renaming. The emphasis here is on place value and proper procedure in carrying out the operation. Work should progress from right to left, each column being named in the basic instruction. This is important even though the correct answer may be obtained without doing either of these. The first step is a readiness period for the more complex work to follow.

A major move into the algorithm is experienced in the second step when renaming becomes necessary. This is also a problem area for many students. The second stage of development should involve limited renaming—only one place—in order for the student to develop a good understanding of the process before more complex work is carried out.

The last step involves exercises in which there is multiple renaming. This is an especially troublesome area, particularly when several zeros are in the minuend.

Diagnosis in subtraction

Development of a clear understanding of the concept of subtraction is the foundation upon which the algorithm is built. Teachers should capitalize on the earlier experiences of children in developing the concept. Students should be given opportunities to work with many meaningful situations in which the take-away approach is utilized. Real situations in which some of the children are removed from the group can make subtraction meaningful to students. As with all new mathematical concepts, the learning should proceed from the concrete and semiconcrete to the abstract.

In order to strengthen students' understanding of groups and their function in subtraction, the teacher needs to help children realize that in the take-away approach to subtraction, the members taken away are conserved. When several students are removed as members of a given group, they still exist, but they no longer function as members of the original group. This idea of conservation has widespread implications. Many students have difficulty with renaming because they have not come to understand that in renaming, no quantity is discarded but is expressed in another form.

Basic facts

When students have an adequate understanding of subtraction, basic subtraction facts will be meaningful. The facts should be taught by means of real objects. Manipulative materials are a vital part of the developmental program. Each child should have many experiences in manipulating members of a group in subtractive situations. Addition and subtraction may be fused to some degree at this point in the program. Since addition is easier to comprehend, it should precede subtraction, and then subtraction may be built upon this foundation. Children may work with sums through five and then subtract with minuends of five or less. Next these facts may be worked with as families and the operations fused in a program stressing relationships and mastery. After these facts are mastered, students are ready to move to another basic group such as sums and minuends through ten. With each phase the basic pattern of addition followed by subtraction should be followed.

Subtraction facts must be mastered before students can compute with accuracy. Reasoning is very important in the initial development of learning basic facts. This is the rationale for stressing the use of manipulative materials and the discovery of relationships. However, a child is handicapped if he or she must continue to "reason out" each fact. The facts must be committed to memory for instant recall.

Diagnosis and therapy   Diagnosing problem areas in subtraction is very important. Through observation of students at work, the teacher may detect several symptoms. Often students rely on making marks for the minuend and crossing out the number representing the subtrahend. Counting fingers is another crutch used by some. Both these habits are time consuming, and it is necessary to consider speed as well as accuracy when working with basic facts at the abstract level. Timed exercises are needed to eliminate inefficient practices. The rate of speed will vary according to the level of maturity of the student. Good judgment on the part of the teacher must prevail at this point. Speed per se is not the goal. The major emphasis should be on eliminating poor work habits and committing the facts to memory.

It is also important to look for patterns of errors in order to administer the needed help. The whole diagnostic approach is keyed to locating the specific difficulty and attacking the problem head-on. Zero seems to contribute more than its share of difficulties. Some children simply refuse to deal with zero within an exercise. They must be led to see the true meaning of zero. Although there are some unique features about zero, we, often put it in a special class, to the detriment of future learning. Students begin to look upon zero as so different that they fail to see that it functions within our number system like any other number. In one study of sixth-grade students over one-fourth of the errors in subtraction were the result of some type of zero-related difficulty.

Students may work in pairs with fact cards, one showing the card and the other giving the answer. The difficult fact cards on which the student hesitates or misses could be placed aside for more study and practice. Groups may also work with facts presented on timed filmstrips or recorded practice sets. There are many commercially prepared games that may be used in reinforcing the child's knowledge of the basic facts. Milton Bradley Mathfacts Games is one example of material that is of interest to many students. Again it should be emphasized that there is no limit to the ingenuity of a good teacher in providing stimulating methods of practice.

Subtraction without renaming

Subtraction without renaming ordinarily causes little more difficulty than the basic facts. Most of the incorrect responses are due to basic fact errors because there is little else involved. The only new factors are subtracting each place correctly and knowing what to do when the minuend has more digits than the subtrahend.

Diagnosis The procedure is very simple and clear at this stage so that most diagnosis can be informal. The teacher should observe students at work for signs of lack of mastery of basic facts. The written work should be observed during the work sessions to make sure that children begin their work in the ones column and progress to the left. As in addition without renaming, inspection of the written work after completion will not reveal this error, which can cause much difficulty when renaming is encountered.

Therapy With the relatively low number of errors encountered at this level, practically all corrective work can be carried out on an individual basis at the first sign of difficulty. If the problem centers around properly subtracting each column, expanded notation may clarify the procedure. Children must understand the meaning of the two-digit and larger numbers, and this is an excellent time to reinforce the concept of place value before more complicated work involving renaming is undertaken. Place-value pockets can be used before expanded notation if students need work at a lower level.

Subtraction with renaming

When renaming is required in subtraction, the number of errors increases substantially. A recent study of errors of third- and fourth-grade students in subtraction of whole numbers found a positive correlation between performance on subtraction and understanding of place value in the decimal system.

From this level of subtraction onward, both diagnosis and therapy should become more formal and specific. Even if all basic facts have been mastered and the concept of subtraction is understood, there may still be many procedural difficulties confronting the student.

Diagnosis A well-constructed diagnostic test is an essential part of the teaching–learning process as students progress more deeply into the basic operations. At this particular phase of subtraction there should be various types of exercises with renaming in only one place. A logical sequence for renaming one place in the minuend would be renaming a ten as ones, a hundred as tens, and a thousand as hundreds. Some exercises with zero in the minuend should also be included because zero-related errors seem to be more numerous than errors with other numbers in the same type of exercises.

Renaming is vital to subtraction proficiency. It is helpful in detecting errors for students to show their renaming on their written work as an aid to diagnosis. However, the teacher should not require it on a diagnostic test. In many programs the ultimate goal is to move away from this practice. Therefore, it would be indefensible to require it for the teacher's convenience.

Therapy A major emphasis in remedial work is on place value and renaming. It is doubtful that lack of understanding of the subtraction algorithm is the cause of students' subtracting a smaller digit in the minuend from a larger one in the subtrahend, as in 345 − 168 = 223. Yet, this problem is widespread.

During the initial stages of learning to subtract where renaming is involved, students should be subjected to many experiences with concrete and semiconcrete materials that center upon place value and renaming. As stated earlier, the degree to which students develop a clear understanding of this work is related directly to their later success in subtraction. It is logical to assume that effective remedial techniques will attempt to clarify students' understanding of place value in the decimal system and its implications for renaming in subtraction. Many good suggestions are available from textbooks in which the concept is introduced and developed. Workbooks offer a variety of related activities to develop and reinforce specific skills. And, there are many commercially prepared materials that may aid the teacher.

The technique of having students rewrite the numeral as they rename the minuend is beneficial. This forces students to give more direct attention to the procedure in use, and it also helps the teacher locate the specific error. Certain precautions should be taken to make the renaming process meaningful rather than mechanical. In the decomposition method, when a number is renamed, such as 32 as 2 tens and 12 ones in the exercise 32 − 14, students should not follow the common practice of taking a 1 from the 3 and making a 12 out of the 2. Students should be led to see that they are not taking a 1 from the 3 but are instead taking a 10 and renaming it as 10 ones. The newly acquired ones should be added to the 2 already in the ones place. The newly obtained total in the ones column of 12 should be rewritten in its entirety above the original 2, which should be marked out. This method is recommended because it emphasizes the true meaning of renaming rather than reducing it to a mechanical process.

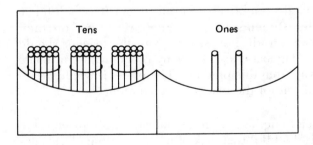

Figure 8-1. Number pockets

If students have difficulty understanding the explanation, the teacher can resort to concrete examples such as number pockets. In the exercise 32 − 14, the 3 tens would be represented by 3 bundles of sticks in the tens pocket and the 2 ones are represented by 2 individual sticks in the ones pocket, as shown in Figure 8-1. Since 4 ones must be subtracted from the ones pocket and there are only 2 sticks, one of the bundles of 10 must be untied and placed in the ones pocket. Now, there are 2 bundles of 10 sticks and 12 individual sticks, and the subtraction can be done. Students can subtract 4 ones from the 12 in the pocket and 1 bundle of 10 sticks leaving 1 bundle of 10 and 8 individual sticks, or 18 sticks.

Subtraction with multiple renaming

Subtraction errors continue to increase as renaming becomes more complex. Multiple renaming involves all the difficulties of single-digit renaming plus additional problems of its own.

Diagnosis Diagnosis of errors where multiple renaming occurs is similar to diagnosis of errors in single-digit renaming. A well-constructed diagnostic test is the basic tool utilized. The test should have several exercises of various types with multiple re-naming. There should be exercises involving (1) renaming of two consecutive digits without zeros, (2) renaming of three consecutive digits without zeros, (3) renaming of alternate digits with and without zeros, and (4) renaming of two or more consecutive digits of zeros. Much of the analysis can be done by the examination of the test results. In some cases it may be necessaary to have a student work the exercise aloud.

Diagnosis may reveal several major errors. One error is the failure to deduct from the minuend after renaming. Another common error is incorrect distribution of the renamed quantity throughout the minuend. This problem is especially acute in exercises where there are several consecutive zeros in the minuend. On one diagnostic test several students renamed 5 10 as 4 9 10. Such errors indicate that although students may realize that renaming is needed, many have not developed a clear understanding of the concept and are merely going through a mechanical process. For the type of student who lacks understanding multiple renaming greatly increases the chance of error. Lack of understanding of renaming may result in renaming the largest place in the minuend more than one time. For example, many students will say that 800 − 227 = 483. This indicates that each time borrowing occurs, these students reduce the 8 in the hundreds place.

Therapy At these most difficult levels of subtraction, diagnosis usually reveals major difficulties related to procedure, renaming, and zero. Even the procedural and zero errors seem to be centered on renaming difficulties. In a study by Leslie C. Ellis these three areas of difficulties produced 83 percent of the errors. Many of these errors could probably be eliminated if renaming were made meaningful, and this should be the primary goal of remedial work.

Multiplication 9

Multiplication is a natural outgrowth of addition, and many teachers capitalize on this fact. The transition from repeated addition to multiplication may be so subtle that children are not aware they are learning a new operation.

Nature and purpose of multiplication

Multiplication may be considered an operation that expedites addition of like addends. Addition of $5 + 5 + 5$ may not pose any greater challenge than multiplication of 3×5, but consider the difficulty people would encounter if 26×5 were attempted through addition.

Multiplication has a specific vocabulary to define its components. In one system the terms are labeled thus:

$$\begin{array}{rl} 25 & \text{Multiplicand} \\ \times 9 & \text{Multiplier} \\ \hline 225 & \text{Product} \end{array}$$

More commonly used today are these terms:

$$\begin{array}{rl} 25 & \text{Factor} \\ \times 9 & \text{Factor} \\ \hline 225 & \text{Product} \end{array}$$

This terminology carries over into other aspects of the mathematics program, such as work with prime and composite numbers.

Multiplication is also a binary operation. It is an operation on two numbers, the factors, to get a third number, the product. Like any binary operation, multiplication works with only two numbers at any one time.

Because multiplication is really an extension of the process of addition, repeated addition is used extensively in the introductory stages of multiplication development. But multiplication is also closely related to division; in fact, they are inverse operations. Whereas multiplication is an operation of combining multiples of like-number sets, division is an operation of separating a single set into a specific number of subsets or into subsets of a specific size. This relationship may be seen in the following illustration:

$$
\begin{array}{ll}
135 \longleftarrow \text{Factor} & \text{Quotient} \longrightarrow 135 \\
\underline{\times 4} \longleftarrow \text{Factor} & \text{Divisor} \longrightarrow 4\overline{)540} \\
\overline{540} \longleftarrow \text{Product} & \text{Dividend} \longrightarrow
\end{array}
$$

Properties of multiplication

Mathematics is often referred to as a highly structured discipline. This is true because certain laws or properties govern its functions. It is important that students understand the basic properties in order to successfully cope with new situations encountered in their studies and problem solving. Several properties of multiplication must be stressed in any mathematics program.

One of the first properties of multiplication encountered by the student is the *commutative property*. Because this property is concerned with the order of the factors, it is often referred to as the "order property." It may be symbolically expressed as $a \times b = b \times a$; $a \cdot b = b \cdot a$; or $ab = ba$. In other words, the order of factors does not affect the product.

The commutative property of multiplication is an important characteristic for several reasons. One reason is that it is a property common to addition and multiplication, thus reemphasizing the close relationship between these two operations. As was true for addition, the commutative property of multiplication has a very utilitarian function. The property may be used to aid in the mastery of the basic facts. When students apply this property and reason that $9 \times 6 = 6 \times 9$, they have learned two facts with minimum effort.

Zero also holds a very important position in multiplication. The *zero property* of multiplication dictates that $0 \times a = 0$. This one characteristic of multiplication is responsible for a large number of errors. Again, knowledge and understanding of this basic principle can expedite the learning of the basic multiplication facts. If any number multiplied by zero equals zero, then, in essence, 19 basic facts have been mastered. (It may be a useful exercise for you to try to list them.)

The *identity element* for multiplication is one. It may be stated as $x \times 1 = x$, or the product of any number and one is that number. How many basic facts will this property develop? It seems strange that something so seemingly simple can be a problem but many incorrect multiplication exercises contain errors such as $6 \times 1 = 7$.

The associative property of multiplication is similar to the same property described in relation to addition. Because multiplication is a binary operation involving only two numbers at a time, provision must be made for the situation in which more than two factors are involved. The *associative property* of multiplication states that for all a, b, and c, $a(bc) = (ab)c$. In other words, we can associate any two of three factors in order to perform the first step of the binary operation of multiplication without affecting the product. The associative property does not allow for the reordering of the factors.

A more advanced property is the *distributive property* of multiplication over addition (or simply, the distributive property of multiplication). This property states that for all a, b, and c, $a(b + c) = ab + ac$. That indicates that when one factor is expressed as two addends, as shown in the parentheses, the multiplication must be distributed over both addends. Consider the example 6×13. By using the distributive property, the exercise may be solved as $6 \times 10 + 6 \times 3$ or $60 + 18$. One important contribution made by this property is its role in preparing for development of the multiplication algorithm. Compound multiplication is made meaningful by expressing a large factor in expanded notation, which is a way of expressing the number as several addends and distributing the multiplication over each addend.

Another property that demonstrates the close relationship between addition and multiplication is *closure*. The set of whole numbers is closed with respect to both multiplication and addition. This means that if the addends or factors are in the set of whole numbers, then their sum or product will also be a member of the set of whole numbers.

Content of multiplication

Learning the content of multiplication involves learning the fundamental concepts, basic facts, and the multiplication algorithm.

Although the three strands are introduced in the order stated above, no single strand is developed in its entirety before another is introduced. At times, work in all three categories is carried out simultaneously.

Fundamental concepts

The concept of multiplication as repeated addition is introduced early in the mathematics experiences of students. One of the earliest type of activities leading into the multiplication concept is skip counting by 2s, 5s, and 10s. As students count 5, 10, 15, 20, they can be led to discover that it required 4 fives to reach 20. Addition of like addends is another premultiplication activity used to introduce the multiplication concept. The same example would be expressed as $5 + 5 + 5 + 5 = 20$. Again the child should be helped to discover that 4 fives make twenty.

Several types of materials are useful in the development of the concept. Concrete objects are needed by some of the less mature students in work involving addition of like addends. Most students need semiconcrete or representational materials such as pictures of objects before they can work with abstract numerals.

Rectangular arrays are most helpful in presenting multiplication in graphic form. The array may be presented concretely with materials such as pegs in a pegboard or loose objects such as discs or semiconcretely with pictures. The sheets of stamps distributed by many fund-raising organizations are well suited for use as rectangular arrays.

These basic types of activities may be used at the beginning of concept development in multiplication. As students mature, other elements of the mathematics program complete the development process. The properties of multiplication are important to an understanding of multiplication. Concept development is carried out over a period of several years, along with the other strands of the multiplication operation.

Basic facts

As with other operations, the basic facts of multiplication must be mastered if students are to become proficient. Although it is important for students to understand the meaning of the basic facts, it is not necessary for each fact to be discovered by the student. Facts should be committed to memory for instant recall when needed.

Learning the basic facts is spread over a period of several years. Facts should be introduced and mastered in several groups in order to facilitate the mastery process. The easier facts are introduced as part of the basic concept presentation. There are several natural groupings for presenting basic facts. One group may include facts with factors no greater than five. This would include the product of 25 in the fact $5 \times 5 = 25$ but would not include some products less than 25 in which there is a factor greater than 5, such as $4 \times 6 = 24$. After this group has been mastered, the facts with products of 25 or less, regardless of the factors, could form another group.

Another common grouping practice for basic facts is to learn those with a product of 45 and less, regardless of the factors involved. At this point students have progressed to a point with the basic facts that work with the algorithms of multiplication can be carried on.

Once the concept development is well underway and work with the algorithms is progressing, the remaining facts must be learned. The more difficult facts, those with products greater than 45, are mastered as a last group.

The properties of multiplication are most helpful in the mastery of the basic multiplication facts. The commutative property effectively reduces the work involved in mastering the facts because it is fairly easy to learn $6 \times 5 = 30$ and $5 \times 6 = 30$ together. Likewise, an understanding of the identity element and the property of zero takes care of two groups of facts. These two properties must not be taken lightly. A study of multiplication errors will indicate that many incorrect answers are due to faulty understanding of these ideas.

One property that is very important to the development of both concepts and basic facts is the distributive property of multiplication. This property is helpful in learning the more difficult facts by breaking them down into easier facts. Consider the following arrays:

```
      x x x x x   x x x x
      x x x x x   x x x x
  6   x x x x x   x x x x   6
      x x x x x   x x x x
      x x x x x   x x x x
      x x x x x   x x x x
         5    +    4
```

It may be difficult for the student to solve 6×9 as a single unit, but if 9 is named $5 + 4$ and the factor 6 is distributed over both addends, the exercise is more easily managed.

The distributive property allows the following:

$$6 \times (5 + 4) =$$
$$6 \times 5 + 6 \times 4 =$$
$$30 + 24 =$$
$$54$$

Not only is this a means for breaking down a large factor; it also provides a means of checking when there is doubt.

The multiplication algorithm

The basic multiplication algorithm is developed through several stages. Several years' work is required from the first introduction to most complex exercises involving the algorithm.

Proper alignment of columns of numerals becomes very important as students progress to more sophisticated multiplication exercises. This should be emphasized from the very beginning, even as students are working with basic facts in the vertical form, such as the following:

$$\begin{array}{r} 6 \\ \times 4 \\ \hline 24 \end{array}$$

Both factors, 6 and 4, are ones. The product, 24, is 2 tens and 4 ones. Therefore, the ones in the product should be written in the ones column, which includes both factors. In a sense, work with basic facts in this form is an introduction to the algorithm. Some students find it helpful at the beginning to work on ruled paper turned sideways because this gives columns for digit placement.

The students' first encounter with the algorithm usually involves multiplying multiples of 10 and 100. This is usually introduced in such a manner as to involve little difficulty beyond knowing the basic facts. The exercise 3×20 may be written as 3×2 tens or

$$\begin{array}{r} 2 \text{ tens} \\ \times 3 \\ \hline 6 \text{ tens} \end{array}$$

By building on their past number experiences, students can change the product from 6 tens to 60. Sufficient practice should be given with small multiples of ten in order to help students make the transition from the numeral-word product (e.g., 2 tens) to the simple numeral product (e.g., 20).

After this meaning of the concept and algorithm has been developed to a degree of reasonable understanding, the standard numeral approach to multiplication of multiples of tens should be developed. Because the numeral-word factor and product are familiar to the student, this approach should serve as a point of departure for the development of the standard form. A method such as the following might be used.

$$
\begin{array}{rcr}
2 \text{ tens} & = & 20 \\
\underline{\times 3} & & \underline{\times 3} \\
6 \text{ tens} & = & 60
\end{array}
$$

    The earliest stages of this development may be strictly intuitive. The recording of the factor 20 and the product 60 should be the result of translating the numeral-word form on the left. After working several exercises by this method, students might be asked to try and figure a way to complete the form on the right without help from the one on the left. This will provide student activity that should lead to the first formal steps in the multiplication algorithm. Through this approach students should discover that the factor 3 must first multiply the factor 0, with this product being recorded in the ones column; only then can the 3 multiply the factor 2 and the product be recorded in the tens column. A similar approach should be used to develop multiplication of multiples of 100.

    The next level of difficulty involves multiplication of a multidigit factor, other than multiples of 10 and 100, by a single-digit factor. By working with factors in which no renaming is necessary, students can extend the algorithm with little difficulty.

    Both approaches used earlier may be employed with this type of exercise. Thus:

$$
\begin{array}{rcr}
3 \text{ tens} + 2 & = \quad 30 + 2 \quad = & 32 \\
\underline{\times 3} & \underline{\times 3} & \underline{\times 3} \\
9 \text{ tens} + 6 & 90 + 6 & 96
\end{array}
$$

The relationships among these types may be easily studied in the above arrangement. This is also an excellent point at which to emphasize the distributive property of multiplication. The factor 3 must be distributed over each part of the 32 regardless of how it is named.

    The next form of the algorithm provides a means of carrying out the work without having to remember unseen parts of the product that must be carried to another column. The problem 734×6 may be displayed like this:

$$
\begin{array}{rl}
734 & \\
\underline{\times 6} & \\
24 & = 6 \times 4 \\
180 & = 6 \times 30 \\
\underline{4200} & = 6 \times 700 \\
4404 &
\end{array}
$$

At first students may need to write each partial factor as shown. Later they should be able to visualize each part of the composite factor without this aid.

A further stage of development is the use of the short form with certain aids. The same example as above may look like this:

ⓄⒶ
734
×6
4404

At this point students follow the same procedures they have learned in the earlier developmental stages. The major difference is that they must rename a two-digit partial product and carry the second digit to the next column. Most students find it necessary to record this carried number above the factor in the proper column, as shown above. Since $6 \times 4 = 24$, the 4 ones are recorded in the ones column and the 2 tens are carried over to be added to the tens after that digit has been multiplied. The 3 tens are now multiplied by 6 with a product of 18 tens plus the 2 tens carried earlier. This gives a total of 20 tens, therefore, the 0 is recorded in the tens places and the 2 hundreds, (20 tens equal 2 hundreds) are carried to be added to the hundreds. The exercise is completed when the 7 hundreds are multiplied by 6 for a product of 42 hundreds plus 2 hundreds carried, or 44 hundreds to be recorded.

The algorithm with one-digit multipliers is fully mastered when the student can work accurately without the aid of recording the carried number. Students should try to achieve this goal before they work with multi-digit multipliers because the work can get very confusing when too many carried numbers are recorded. However, many adults still write in the carried numbers.

The ultimate mastery of multiplication involves the ability to perform any multiplication operation, regardless of the size of the factors. Of course, this goal must be tempered with reality. No student should be burdened with the ordeal of carrying out an operation involving extremely large factors for several reasons. First, it is not practical. There are computers and calculators readily available for those whose work involves such large numbers. From the standpoint of understanding the algorithm, one who thoroughly understands the principles involved in multiplication has little to gain from going beyond three-digit multipliers.

Complex multiplication builds directly on the single-digit multiplication learned earlier. One major obstacle lies in the procedure for carrying out multiplication by the digits other than those in the ones column of the multiplier. A second procedural problem is what to do with the partial products, but this is not new since a similar task was undertaken in the use of the long form with single-digit multiplication. The long form used with single-digit multipliers may also be used with multi-digit multipliers:

$$
\begin{array}{r}
348 \\
\times 25 \\
\hline
\end{array}
$$

40	=	5 ones × 8 ones
200	=	5 ones × 4 tens
1500	=	5 ones × 3 hundreds
160	=	2 tens × 8 ones
800	=	2 tens × 4 tens
6000	=	2 tens × 3 hundreds
8700		

This is an excellent opportunity to reinforce some basic principles that will clarify and give meaning to the algorithm development to follow. The *principle of one* in multiplication states that one times any number will be that number. Is it applicable to ones in relation to place value? How can this help in determining where to record the first digit in a partial product when the short form is used? Observe the following patterns, using the last example:

Place in first factor (Multiplicand)	×	Place in second factor (Multiplier)	=	Record first digit of product	Basis
Ones (8)		Ones (5)	=	Ones	1 × 1 = 1
Tens (4)		Ones (5)	=	Tens	10 × 1 = 10
Hundreds (3)		Ones (5)	=	Hundreds	100 × 1 = 100
Ones (8)		Tens (2)	=	Tens	1 × 10 = 10
Tens (4)		Tens (2)	=	Hundreds	10 × 10 = 100
Hundreds (3)		Tens (2)	=	Thousands	100 × 10 = 1000

This provides the mathematical basis for the placement of the partial products in the short form, one of the major steps in development of the algorithm. From this basis students should be led to discover other principles that govern the algorithm. When students discover that each partial product will have its first digit in the same column as the multiplier for that product, they will have reduced the algorithm to a fairly simple operation; however, they will have developed the algorithm through a meaningful approach. The same general sequence used in the development of single-digit multiplication should be employed with multi-digit operations.

Diagnosis in multiplication

The transition from repeated addition to multiplication should be given ample time but it should be developed completely. The diagnostic teacher must be alert for signs of prolonged reliance on repeated addition.

One-digit multipliers

Work with one-digit multipliers is primarily of three types. First, the concept of multiplication is developed. In the second phase, which is interwoven with the first, the basic facts are introduced and mastered. Finally children learn to work confidently with the algorithm.

Concept of multiplication There are many opportunities to introduce the idea of multiplication to small children long before a formal introduction is undertaken. The direct relationship between addition of like addends and multiplication is a natural starting point. This intuitive introduction to multiplication can be developed through the teacher's incidental but positive interaction with students. Even when students are working at the concrete stage of addition, the method can be effective. As students combine two sets of objects, the teacher may remark, "Yes, 2 and 2 are 4; 2 twos are 4." There is no special attention called to the multiplicative form, only a subtle but consistent reminder. As children mature, the basic idea may be presented in a more formal manner. Students also have many opportunities to develop a better understanding of multiplication as they work in like-numbered groups or organize themselves in teams of the same numerical size. The opportunities are unlimited once the teacher becomes aware of the possibilities and capitalizes on them. If these opportunities are utilized to their greatest extent, the later formal teaching will be much more effective.

The use of arrays in concrete and semiconcrete form has proven a successful means of introducing multiplication. Work with the addition of like addends can also be closely linked to multiplication. Both help students see the economy of multiplication over repeated addition or counting.

The diagnostic teacher must be concerned with particular students' understanding of multiplication regardless of the students' age or grade placement. A student who needs help at this elementary stage must receive it if he or she is to progress. One cannot help the child by trying to blame failure on the program or teachers of an earlier level.

Basic facts When should the multiplication facts be taught? A direct answer to the question is that they should be and are taught from grade one through grade six in the elementary school. But there is often a need for teaching multiplication facts long after they were introduced in the basic program. Many studies indicate that a major difficulty in multiplication, even for students in the upper-elementary and junior-high-school grades, is the lack of mastery of the basic facts. One such study is summarized in the Appendices of this book.

Diagnosis in mastery phase Difficulties with multiplication facts are readily diagnosed by several means. Because students find it more difficult to use counting in multiplication than addition, lack of mastery becomes quite obvious. The teacher may observe unusually long delays by a student in recording a product. Often the result is an incorrect product. Although counting may be inefficient, many children cling to the method of skip counting or even writing the multiplicand as addends and adding. Both methods are useful in the readiness phase but students must be led beyond reliance on such cumbersome methods or else difficulty will arise at the level beyond the basic facts.

Diagnostic techniques may vary from casual observation to formal diagnostic testing. The diagnostic teacher is always a critical observer of students' work habits. Faulty and inefficient work habits such as counting and writing addends must be corrected. After students have worked with groups of facts they should be tested for mastery of the facts covered to that point. As with the basic facts in the other operations, both speed and accuracy should be stressed.

Indicated therapy in mastery phase By the time a need for specific therapy for difficulties with basic multiplication facts is observed, a student has had a considerable amount of exposure to the operation. At this point a teacher should not assume that the child understands even the most elementary concept of multiplication. It may be necessary in some cases to go all the way back to the rudimentary components, such as the meaning of multiplication, repeated addition of like addends, and skip counting.

It is helpful for students to visualize the results of their skip counting by writing the results in vertical form as shown below:

5	10	5	25	5	50
4	8	4	20	4	40
3	6	3	15	3	30
2	4	2	10	2	20
1	2	1	5	1	10
	2		5		10

Various forms of the technique may be used. The column on the left as well as the number below the right column, which indicates the number used in counting, may be filled in by the teacher. As a child counts, he or she fills in the right column. The student is then able to see that 2 twos are 4 and 4 twos are 8. It may be helpful for some of the right column to be completed before the exercise is given. One should vary the approach according to the amount of help required by particular students. As more difficult facts are learned, the numbers may be extended to 9 or even 12 in the left column.

The number line is widely used in helping students visualize multiplication. Individual number lines that may be marked on are most useful. Students can draw on the line the number of jumps of the same length it takes to arrive at various points. Multiplication by fours would look like this:

1 four 2 fours 3 fours   4 fours   5 fours

0 1 2 3 4 5 6 7 8 9 10 11 12 13 14 15 16 17 18 19 20 21 22 23 24 25 26

A transition from addition to multiplication is often accomplished through the use of arrays. Consider the following:

How many dots are in the array? There are several levels of sophistication at which children may solve this problem. They may take the most elementary method of counting each dot. Even if they choose a more advanced method, they may check their answer by counting. They could arrive at the answer by addition of either $4 + 4 + 4 + 4 + 4$ or $5 + 5 + 5 + 5$. Rather than writing the addends, they may elect the mental skip-counting method. Finally, they may reach the logical conclusion that 4 fives is another name for 20. The ultility of the use of arrays is obvious.

Remedial work should be prescribed to meet a specific need and should never be just more of the same. With basic facts, a teacher should have students work on those missed, but the work should concentrate on specific problem areas. Often the problem is approached more effectively by clarifying a mathematical principle than by drill on isolated facts. The multiplicative principles of one and zero are prime examples. It is much more effective to have students discover and understand the role of zero and one than to drill on all the facts in which they are factors. The commutative principle is one of the very important concepts of multiplication that drastically reduces the work involved in learning the facts.

The diagnostic teacher should look for patterns in incorrect responses. Most errors will probably be found with factors of 6 through 9. If that is the case, it is not necessary to give additional work on the ones already mastered.

The unique features of the decimal system aid older students in mastering the facts. Knowledge of even and odd numbers as factors is helpful to the student who is not sure of a product. If he or she is aware that two odd-number factors yield a product that is an odd number, an answer of 48 for 7 sevens is recognized as incorrect. Knowing that two factors, one an odd and one an even number, and that two factors both of which are even yield products that are even proves helpful to the student. Other features, such as that any product derived from a factor of 5 must end in 0 or 5, can be helpful.

How well should students know the basic facts? Ideally, one would want 100 percent accuracy at a reasonable rate of speed. Although the ideal must be compromised at times, both speed and accuracy should be stressed. Students should know the combinations in random order. Exercises that refine skills should take this approach. The exercises should be of various types and should include oral and written responses. The methods used in working with addition and subtraction facts are applicable to multiplication.

Multiplication without renaming

After the concept of multiplication has been developed and the basic facts have been mastered, the next step in the program is application of this knowledge in developing the multiplication algorithm. This is done at various stages even before all the basic facts are introduced. If students have worked with combinations through the factors of 5, they can begin work with exercises in which all factors are 5 or less. Generally, this step is of very little more difficulty than work with the basic facts.

Diagnostic procedures The apparent simplicity of multiplication without renaming must not lull the teacher into a less vigilant role than the situation demands. It is of the utmost importance that this initial work on the algorithm be carefully observed by the teacher. Faulty procedures are best corrected before they become established. Diagnostic work by the teacher should accompany the initial presentation. A student should not be assigned extensive work before the teacher has had the opportunity to observe his or her work and help clarify any incorrect procedure. Another method in diagnostic work at this level is to study all assigned exercises that could not be observed during the work session. There is a limited number of ways to err at this stage, and careful analysis of errors can usually pinpoint the problem.

Therapy When corrective work is undertaken, the sequence of the initial instruction is important. Multiplication by a one-digit multiplier without renaming is basically a two-step sequence.

Armed with knowledge of the basic facts, or with a specific subset of the facts, students can extend their knowledge to multiples of 10 and 100 without any great difficulty. One approach is to use a word name for a given multiple. Rather than have students multiply 4 × 10 we may have them work with 4 × 1 ten. They are then confronted with the simple fact of 4 × 1, with the answer being named tens. They can then be asked to give the common name for 4 tens. If they correctly identify the amount as 40, they can then write 40 in its most common form. Work with multiples of 100 is as easy as work with multiples of 10.

When students move into multiplicands other than multiples of 10 and 100, they should proceed through a series of small and familiar steps. In the exercise 3 × 231, the 231 could be expressed in the expanded form 200 + 30 + 1, then each part multiplied separately. Note that nothing new is required in this operation, only basic facts and multiples of 10 and 100. The only new step is to add the partial products. It may be necessary to go back to the form 2 hundreds + 3 tens + 1 in order to clarify the multiplication for some students. From this beginning students may progress to the form in which the multiplicand is mentally expanded and the partial products written in a column next to the exercise, thus:

$$
\begin{array}{r}
231 \\
\times 3 \\
\hline
3 = 3 \times 1 \\
90 = 3 \times 30 \\
600 = 3 \times 200 \\
\hline
693
\end{array}
$$

The next step is to move on to the final form in which each place is multiplied in order, from the ones through the hundreds place, and the product recorded on a single line.

Once the multiplication algorithm has been developed for this type of exercise, most of the difficulty is a direct result of lack of mastery of the basic facts. Work should continue on the facts on an individual basis according to the needs indicated by analysis of students' work.

Multiplication with single renaming

When multiplication is extended to include renaming, several new problem areas appear. Diagnostic teachers should be aware of the various types of errors that may occur within any operation, but especially when the operation becomes complex, as when renaming is introduced in multiplication.

Diagnosis A well-planned diagnostic instrument is the basic tool with which the teacher must work. The instrument need not be a highly sophisticated, commercially prepared test administered by someone who is an authority in measurement. Classroom teachers can prepare and administer their own diagnostic test if they follow some basic procedures. They should determine exactly what new skill or type of work is to be undertaken. At this point in multiplication, the concern is with renaming, specifically, renaming in only one place. Even after the work has been limited to single renaming, there are other considerations for a well-developed plan. In which place will renaming occur? Does it make a difference? Is one sequence more effective than the other?

A logical approach is to progress from the simple to the more difficult. The initial encounter should be limited to renaming ones as tens; then the diagnostic phase should extend into renaming tens as hundreds and hundreds as thousands. Often there is little difference in the level of difficulty among the exercises with renaming at the various places, but the sequence given above does provide a meaningful basis for developmental work.

Diagnosis through analysis of written work aids the teacher in grouping difficulties into broad categories. These categories generally include difficulties with combinations, renaming, and procedures of the algorithm. Through close examination the teacher can pinpoint many specific types of errors within each category. By individual work-aloud sessions with students, other difficulties not evident through visual analysis may be identified.

Therapy A continuing difficulty will be lack of mastery of basic facts. Work on this aspect of the program must be constant, but the emphasis will need to shift to developing the algorithm. Work with the basic facts should be on an individual basis at times when the student can work alone. It is not necessary for the student to have close guidance by the teacher as he or she works toward mastery.

Is there a place for fact tables at this level? Should students be allowed to use a multiplication table if they have not mastered the facts? A student may have learned many of the basic facts but some may still cause difficulties. He or she also may be slow in calling up known facts so that use of a card with the multiplication facts may be helpful. But how would you defend such an action? The justification is that, by eliminating one of the variables, knowledge of the basic facts, greater attention may be focused on the major concern of the lesson. Often a student may make seemingly unrelated errors due to the lack of mastery of the facts. Failure to carry a ten after renaming ones may seem unrelated to knowing basic facts, but if a child takes so long at arriving at the answer that he or she forgets what is carried, the relationship may be closer than it appears. There is also the argument that children will learn the facts as they use them in a meaningful way such as in the algorithm.

Renaming or carrying and procedures used in carrying out the multiplication algorithm present new challenges. Working with the multiplicand in an expanded form is one of the best ways to help students see and comprehend the "internal" functions of the algorithm. This technique is especially good in work with groups where several individual sources of errors may be clarified and other important points reinforced.

The exercise 3×327 could be solved in the following manner:

$$
\begin{array}{rr}
300 + 20 + 7 & 21 \\
\underline{\times 3} & 60 \\
900 + 60 + 21 & \underline{900} \\
& 981
\end{array}
$$

We write the multiplicand as $300 + 20 + 7$. The next step is to set up the exercise with the expanded multiplicand and the multiplier. We multiply each part of the multiplicand independently to get three separate products. The three partial products are then added to get the product. By placing the partial products in a column for addition there is less chance of addition errors, and the form is a natural step in the sequential development.

The second major step in developing the algorithm is to expand the multiplicand as in step one but to place the partial products in a column beneath the multipliers as follows:

$$
\begin{array}{r}
300 + 20 + 7 \\
\underline{\times 3} \\
21 \\
60 \\
\underline{900} \\
981
\end{array}
$$

This is the last stage of development wherein the student sees each place written in its complete form, such as three hundred being written 300 and not as a 3 in the hundreds place. The expanded form has made renaming and carrying unnecessary to this point.

Now the student should be ready for a modified conventional form, such as the following:

```
  327
 × 3
  21
  60
 900
 981
```

Again, only one new idea is introduced here. The student must read a numeral written in the conventional form and multiply each place. In multiplying the 2 tens, he or she must visualize the zero in the ones place, the same is true of the 3 hundreds.

On the basis of the above illustrations, it is apparent that diagnostic teachers must be very perceptive individuals. They must have a thorough working knowledge of the subject matter as well as an understanding of particular students' needs and capabilities. These perceptions must be developed to gain proficiency in diagnostic teaching. Individualized instruction is a key factor. The great variety of possible difficulties indicates that seldom will a whole class or large group need the same instruction. A teacher must work directly with the student to determine some of the more complex errors and misconceptions.

Complex multiplication

Paradoxically, as an operation becomes more complex, diagnosis of student difficulties may become more precise. This is often the case with complex multiplication because the work is divided into several very specific steps.

Diagnostic testing of complex multiplication should include a sequence similar to the following: (1) multipliers that are multiples of tens and hundreds without renaming, (2) other two-digit multipliers without renaming, (3) zero in multiplicand without renaming, (4) two-digit multipliers with renaming, and (5) multi-digit multipliers that include all previously developed stages.

In considering therapy for difficulties related to specific stages of complex multiplication, teachers should accept the findings of diagnostic testing and analysis of daily work for determining the appropriate point of initial remediation.

Multiples of tens and hundreds By beginning with multipliers of tens and hundreds as the introduction to complex multiplication, the teacher is capitalizing on the use of the familiar. The task at this point is to get students to relate their knowledge of the decimal system to the specific skill of using tens and hundreds as multipliers. Some students may need to review counting by tens and hundreds or work with multiples of ten as multiplicands with one-digit multipliers. At this point the commutative property should be stressed. This will indirectly bring about using a two-digit multiplier without any formal procedure. Students should be helped to see the relationship among exercises of the following type:

$$6 \times 10 = 60, \quad 10 \times 6 = 60, \qquad \begin{array}{r} 10 \\ \times\, 6 \\ \hline 60 \end{array} \quad \text{and} \quad \begin{array}{r} 6 \\ \times\, 10 \\ \hline 60 \end{array}$$

It is best to start with ten in the initial encounter with a two-digit multiplier. By using ten as the multiplier and a number in the teens as the multiplicand, very little unfamiliar work will be encountered. The exercise 10×16 can be solved at several levels of sophistication. The expanded form is very useful as a means of helping students understand the meaning of the operation. Thus:

$$\begin{array}{llll} 16 \text{ means} & 10 & & 6 \\ \underline{\times\,10} & \underline{\times\,10} & + & \underline{\times\,10} \\ & 100 & & 60 \end{array} = 160.$$

The work could be done in a second form as follows:

$$\begin{array}{rl} 16 & \\ \underline{\times\,10} & \\ 60 & (10 \times 6) \\ \underline{100} & (10 \times 10) \\ 160 & \end{array}$$

In this intermediate step the multiplier is considered as a unit and students think: 10 sixes are 60 and 10 tens are 100. They have not begun to work with a two-digit multiplier.

The point has been reached when students must use the two-digit multiplier. Because ten has been used to develop the two-digit multiplicand concept, it may be best to develop the two-digit multiplier concept in two steps. To continue with the original example, 10×16, the first step would be as follows:

$$\begin{array}{r} 16 \\ \underline{\times\,10} \\ 00 \\ \underline{160} \\ 160 \end{array}$$

Students should be guided to see that each digit in the multiplier must multiply each digit in the multiplicand. Initially the zero in the ones place is used as a multiplier, and the zero products are recorded. One of the most significant steps in complex multiplication is guiding the students to an understanding of the partial product obtained from the multiplication by the tens digit in the multiplier. The proper recording of this partial product should grow out of this understanding. As the 6 is multiplied by the 1 ten the student must be able to see that the product is 6 tens, not 6 ones. The product is tens because the multiplier is a 10. How can one show that the partial product is a 10? Place value is the only means: the 6 must be recorded in the tens column. At this point it may be wise to have students place a zero in the ones column so that each partial product may be complete. Once the proper position has been determined for the first digit of the partial product all the rest will fall into place.

Sufficient practice is needed to establish and reinforce the concept of proper position. One method is to have students determine only the first-digit position for each partial product. Vertically lined paper (regular writing paper turned on its side) with place value labels at the top is very helpful. The following examples are illustrative:

Hundreds	Tens	Ones		Hundreds	Tens	Ones
	2	0			3	4
×	1	0		×	1	2
		0				8
	0				4	

This exercise should be extended to include multiples other than ten in order to clarify the meaning of the partial products. Students should be able to visualize that the position of the multiplier determines the position of the first entry in the partial product.

After students have demonstrated an understanding of the procedure described, the short form of multiplying by multiples of tens and hundreds may be introduced. The original exercise of 10×16 may be used to illustrate the method. Set up the example in column form, thus:

$$\begin{array}{r} 16 \\ \times\, 10 \\ \hline 160 \end{array}$$

The steps are as follows:

1. Multiply the 6 by 0: $0 \times 6 = 0$.

2. Place the product under the multiplier.
3. It is not necessary to multiply the 1 by 0 because this place will be used when the multiplier 1 in the tens place is used.
4. Multiply the 6 by one 10 and place the product in the place under the multiplier: One $10 \times 6 =$ six 10s.
5. Multiply the one 10 in the multiplicand by the one 10 in the multiplier: one $10 \times$ one $10 =$ one $10 \times 10 =$ one 100.

The students should work with multiples of tens and hundreds as multipliers until they can demonstrate an understanding of the procedure.

Other two-digit multipliers without renaming Multiplication with two-digit multipliers other than multiples of tens and hundreds is similar to the work with tens and hundreds where the zeros are multiplied for each digit. Note the similarity between the following two exercises:

```
   231        231
 × 20       × 23
  000        693
 4620       4620
 4620       5313
```

In each exercise the multiplier in the ones place multiplies each place in the multiplicand. This should cause little difficulty if students relate this to multiplication with a one-digit multiplier. It was noted earlier that students may be taught to eliminate the unnecessary multiplication by zero where multiples of ten are used. If this proves difficult for some students to understand, they should be allowed to continue this practice until they discover the reasoning behind such a practice. Continuation of multiplication by zero may strengthen their understanding of the procedure used with multidigit multipliers. This is especially true when there is a zero in the middle position in the multiplier.

The position of the initial entry in the partial product derived from the tens multiplier has been introduced earlier. This concept should be retaught and reinforced as needed, with either small groups or individuals.

The final step is to obtain the product by adding the partial products. This relatively new step increases the possibility of errors. Addition, although a familiar skill, may contribute to the difficulty. The partial products must be arranged in their proper position in order for them to be meaningful. Orderly work becomes even more important as the procedure becomes more complex.

Paper with vertical lines is helpful in developing good work habits in this area.

Extending the algorithm   Once the basic algorithm has been introduced and mastered to a reasonable degree, the operation should be extended to its most complex forms. When a single multiplication exercise includes a multi-digit multiplier, renaming in multiplication and addition, zeros in the multiplier or multiplicand, and difficult basic facts, the chances of making mistakes are greatly increased.

The diagnostic teacher must be aware of the error possibilities and not overwhelm students with work beyond their level. Selecting and designing appropriate materials for diagnosis, instruction, and remediation are essential for carrying out a successful program. The materials should help the teacher locate the specific source of difficulty and also provide a basis for selecting material for reteaching.

10 Division

There is little doubt that division is the most difficult of the four whole-number operations. The length of time of the developmental program is one indication of its difficulty. In a graded school system division may be introduced in the second grade and developed through the fifth or sixth grades. Even after three or four years of sequential development, many sixth-grade students have not adequately mastered division. Contributing to the difficulty of division is the fact that its algorithm contains two other operations, subtraction and multiplication, which makes it the most complex of any of the whole-number algorithms. Also, in its final form division is the only whole-number operation that begins working on the left with the larger place-value numbers and progresses to the smaller ones on the right. Finally, the answer in a division exercise has a potential for difficulty not found in the other operations because the quotient may be complete in itself or there may be a remainder.

Division concepts and skills

Often division is best understood through its relationships with other, more familiar operations, namely, subtraction and multiplication. *Division* may be viewed as the operation of separating a large set into subsets of equal numbers of members. It answers the question, "How many subsets of a given number of members can be extracted from a specified set?" One method of determining an answer to this question is repeated subtraction. This is quite effective if the number with which one is working is small. In fact division is often introduced by this means. Just as multiplication is the repeated addition of like addends division is the repeated subtraction of like subtrahends.

Another characteristic of division is that it is the inverse operation of multiplication. Whereas multiplication and addition are involved with uniting or combining, division and subtraction are involved with separating. Subtraction may be approached as finding the missing addend in an addition problem; similarly, division may be viewed as a search for the missing factor in multiplication when one factor and the product are given, as can be seen from the following:

$$6 \times 5 = 30$$
$$30 \div 5 = 6$$

Properties

Unlike addition and multiplication, it is difficult to find direct property relationships with division. Division shares with subtraction the distinction of not being a closed operation with respect to the whole-number system. This means that one may not be able to arrive at an answer within the whole-number system when performing these operations with two whole numbers. Another example of division's close relationship with subtraction is that neither operation is commutative.

Although the commutative property does not apply to the operation of division, there is a relationship to this property that is very helpful in division. The factors in multiplication are covered by the commutative property, and, as noted above, division can be viewed as determining the missing factor. Learning the basic facts of division can be aided by knowledge of this fact. With regard to the example above, if $30 \div 5 = 6$, then $30 \div 6 = 5$.

Zero and one are important elements in the development of division concepts and skills. Because it is not realistic to attempt to determine how many subsets of no members can be taken from a given set, there is no operation with division by zero. Zero divided by another number is mathematically defined as zero. And, using the relationship between division and multiplication, the significance of one can be seen. Since $1 \times a = a$, then $a \times 1 = a$, and $a \div a = 1$, while $a \div 1 = a$.

Vocabulary

There is a special vocabulary for division as with the other operations. Division can also be written in several forms. The following examples illustrate these two features:

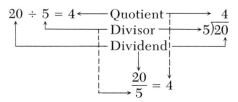

The relationship between exercises in division and multiplication may be thought of thus:

```
 7 ←——— Factor (Multiplicand) ——— Quotient ———→ 7
×5 ←——— Factor (Multiplier) ———— Divisor ———→5)35
35 ←——— Product ———————————— Dividend ———┘
```

Content

Like the other operations division involves three major strands —the concept, the basic facts, and the algorithm. The order of development of these strands is as listed; however, as work progresses, the three may be simultaneously developed strands.

The concept of division Division is introduced through sets. Although it is the last of the four fundamental operations with whole numbers to be taken up, most programs introduce the division concept by the third year of school. At this age the definitions of division have little meaning to the student. The initial development must begin with concrete materials. Students need to be provided with many opportunities to manipulate objects as they separate a set of objects into subsets of a given size.

A second stage of concept development utilizes pictorial and representational materials of a semi-concrete nature along with accompanying questions. Figure 10-1, for example, may be used with the following questions:

How many ice-cream cones in all?
How many cones in each set?
How many sets?
How many subsets of two elements are in a set of six elements?

The concept of division can be further developed in a more abstract manner through the use of arrays. This is more advanced than

Figure 10-1.
Division concept

a pictorial exercise, yet it is not as abstract as the use of numerals without representative materials. A line of questioning would also accompany an array like the following:

```
. . . . .
. . . . .
. . . . .
. . . . .
```

There is a fine line between where the emphasis on concept development ends and basic-facts development begins. Obviously, there is a degree of teaching basic facts in the concept development described above, although the main emphasis was on concepts.

Basic facts When students reach the more abstract level of manipulation of numbers, the emphasis shifts to the basic facts, along with refinement and extension of the concept. Concrete and semiconcrete materials are also used in this phase of work on division.

The concept of division is developed through extensive use of sets. Once the development of the basic facts gets underway, the emphasis shifts to the relationship between division and multiplication. It is an efficient procedure to teach groups of related multiplication and division facts together or in close proximity. As with addition and subtraction, multiplication is usually introduced and carried to a logical point and then the related division facts are introduced. Students then work on the two operations together. The work on the division facts parallels that of multiplication outlined earlier.

The division algorithm Developing the division algorithm requires four major stages. These stages include (1) readiness operations, (2) the subtractive method, (3) the intermediate method, and (4) the traditional algorithm.

As students move beyond the basic facts, there are several types of readiness activities that can prepare them for basic algorithm work. Uneven division is one such activity. Because division introduces the new difficulty of remainders, students should have a considerable amount of work with this type of exercise. Another type of readiness involves division that stresses relationships. An exercise such as, "$18 \div 9 = \square$; therefore, $180 \div 9 = \square$, may be used to develop an understanding of this relationship. The form $9\overline{)18}$ and $9\overline{)180}$ should also be used as a more direct transition to the algorithm.

The algorithm itself is generally introduced by the subtractive method, which emphasizes the concept of division as repeated subtraction. By using this method students are not under pressure to choose the exact partial quotient in each step. Another beneficial feature is that it allows students to progress to a more sophisticated level as their understanding of the concept and algorithm develops. The levels of development in working with the subtractive method may be illustrated by the following:

A	B	C
$\begin{array}{r} 83\ r\ 6 \\ 8\overline{)670} \\ \underline{160} \quad 20 \times 8 \\ 510 \\ \underline{160} \quad 20 \times 8 \\ 350 \\ \underline{160} \quad 20 \times 8 \\ 190 \\ \underline{160} \quad 20 \times 8 \\ 30 \\ \underline{24} \quad 3 \times 8 \\ 6 \quad 83 \end{array}$	$\begin{array}{r} 83\ r\ 6 \\ 8\overline{)670} \\ \underline{400} \quad 50 \times 8 \\ 270 \\ \underline{240} \quad 30 \times 8 \\ 30 \\ \underline{24} \quad 3 \times 8 \\ 6 \quad 83 \end{array}$	$\begin{array}{r} 83\ r\ 6 \\ 8\overline{)670} \\ \underline{640} \quad 80 \times 8 \\ 30 \\ \underline{24} \quad 3 \times 8 \\ 6 \quad 83 \end{array}$

The above illustrations show that, in dividing 670 by 8, several different patterns can evolve, and each be correct. In *A* eights were removed or subtracted in sets of 20, with four groups of 20 eights and one group of three eights as shown, for a total of 83 eights. The procedure is shortened in *B* and *C* by removing larger groups of eights at a time.

Note that in using this approach the meaning of the long-division algorithm can be thoroughly developed. Students can better visualize the quotient as the number of times the amount represented by the divisor can be removed from the dividend. Students can thus develop an understanding of the algorithm without having to select the exact partial quotient each time. They also develop this understanding gradually. Until they reach level *C* they will experience difficulty in using the conventional algorithm.

The final stage of development involves recording partial quotients without placing the zeros in the remaining places. Often this is developed in two stages, as shown in the following:

A	B
457 r 3	457 r 3
6)2745	6)2745
2400	24
345	34
300	30
45	45
42	42
3	3

In example *A*, the 4 in the quotient is thought of as 4 hundreds without the zeros being added. When the quotient is multiplied by the divisor, the 24 hundreds is recorded as 2400 for subtraction. The same procedure is followed when the 345 is divided by 6. The 34 tens are divided by 6 with a quotient of 5 tens. The 30 tens are written as 300 and subtracted from the 345. The final step involves dividing the 45 by 6. Example *B* is the most sophisticated level of the algorithm and eliminates all unnecessary recording of zeros.

The basic division algorithm can be developed with single-digit divisors. As students progress to multi-digit divisors, they may find it helpful to review the various stages of development of the algorithm. Ordinarily it will not require extensive work at each level because the basic algorithm has been thoroughly developed with single-digit divisors. The most difficult work with multi-digit divisors involves estimating the quotient. Estimation of quotients will be considered later in this chapter.

Diagnosis and therapy in division concepts

Most children encounter the concept of division at an early age, long before division is confronted as an entity of the mathematics program. Hence, we cannot say that diagnosis in this operation begins at a certain point or ends on a specified date.

Diagnosis

At the level of concept development diagnosis centers around several related questions. Can the child visualize subsets within a given set? Is he or she able to systematically remove these subsets until the whole set is used? Does he or she understand the relationships among the number of subsets removed, their size, and the original set? Given a set composed of members that are divisible by several numbers, can the child see and successfully remove all the possible multiples of the set and relate that to the concept of division?

With these basic questions as a guide, the diagnostic teacher may begin searching for initial division difficulties experienced by students. These specific questions as a basis for testing objectives allow the teacher to draw from several sources.

Formal readiness or diagnostic tests are available in two types. One type is developed independently of any particular textbook and is based on research in the area being tested. A second type is also based on research but is keyed to a specific textbook series and the procedure it uses in developing the topic. Materials used in the developmental program can be another source of diagnostic material. Since much corrective work closely parallels developmental procedures—the only difference being that the former is more intensified and individualized—it is logical to look to this material for help. Another source is often overlooked. Teacher-made tests and activities can add a new dimension to diagnostic teaching. This source can make two unique contributions to diagnostic teaching. It brings about the development of materials to fill a very specific need, and it involves the teacher personally in the process.

Therapy

The ability to visualize subsets within a set should be developed with manipulative materials in the initial stages. The readiness program for division emphasizes equivalent subsets. It should also concentrate on subsets with no remainders. Careful selection of exercises and guidance by the teacher are needed to avoid improper sequential development. Color may be used in the early stages to help children see the subsets of a set. For example, a set with nine members may have three red, three blue, and three green objects. Wooden discs of the type used on bingo cards make good manipulative materials for such a task. After children have used different colors long enough to know the meaning of subsets, they should work with like-colored objects and be allowed to manipulate them. Note that the teacher still gives close guidance by determining the membership of both the set and subsets with which children must work. The important concept developed at this stage is that a large group or set may be broken into or divided into smaller units without altering the original amount.

The process gradually moves to more complex exercises in developing the concept of division. The question as to how many of a given subset are in a set was not emphasized in the previous work. This may be a second phase in the development during which students are led to discover, in an intuitive manner, such a relationship. From this point on, the direct relationship of the concept of subsets within a set with division should be stressed but without the formal use of division. As students develop their understanding to the point where they can work exercises independently, they should be challenged with exercises in which only the number of the set is given and they must select and remove the subsets on their own. In each of the types of exercises suggested students should progress from manipulative materials to representational materials. There will be adequate opportunity for work at the abstract level later in the development of the basic facts and the algorithm.

Diagnosis and therapy in the basic facts

As with all whole-number operations mastery of the basic facts is an important phase in the development of the division process. The same general procedures for diagnosing difficulties and administering corrective measures that were used in the other operations are followed with division. The close relationship between the multiplication and division facts is a natural starting point for work in division. The two groups of facts can be effectively taught simultaneously as families.

Although the concept of division is introduced prior to the basic facts, once the introduction has been made and the concept developed in its rudimentary form, the facts become necessary for further development. The concept, the facts, and even the algorithm of division are all so interwoven that one cannot, and should not, attempt to complete one phase before moving into investigation of the next.

The students' final goal, relative to the division facts, is to commit them to memory for instant recall when needed. Practice and use of the facts will be necessary to develop proficiency. Mastery of the facts is especially important in division because the size of some of the numbers under consideration makes crutch-type activities very cumbersome and ineffective. Timed exercises should be used in the latter stage of work with the facts. This should be done only after the facts have been presented in a meaningful manner with real and representational materials as needed by individual students.

Therapy should focus on the specific difficulty identified through diagnostic testing of the basic facts. Patterns of errors may indicate that only a small portion of the facts are causing the major part of the errors. Concentrating on these specific facts and relating them to the multiplication facts can then help the student fix them in mind.

It is not necessary, or even wise, to expect complete mastery of the facts before moving into the development of the algorithm. In the first place, the facts are introduced over a long period of time and waiting would unduly delay development of the algorithm. Also, work with the algorithm gives meaning to the facts and is a means to further develop them. For this reason it may be advisable to allow some students to use tables of the basic facts in the early development of the algorithm. This practice provides one means of diagnosing to determine whether the difficulty lies with the facts or the procedure.

Diagnosis in the algorithm

Development of the division algorithm requires a considerable amount of time—several years to reach the most advanced understanding. Therefore, it is necessary to develop an orderly sequence to present each of the various levels of advancement. Development of the division algorithm may be accomplished in two steps—division with one-digit divisors and division with multi-digit divisors. Each of these major steps will follow a specific sequence, established by the curriculum guide used in the initial development. There may be some variation in the sequence of different programs. We have found the sequence given here to be effective in initial presentation and in diagnostic procedures. The important point to remember is that developmental procedures and diagnostic procedures must be compatible. A diagnostic test that does not follow the developmental sequence is of limited value unless the one administering the test is aware of the discrepancy and makes allowance for the differences.

One-digit divisors

We have found that in diagnostic work in simple division the following sequence has been useful:

1. Basic facts with remainders
2. Dividends of multiples of 10 and 100 without remainders
3. Two-digit quotients without remainders

4. Two-digit quotients with remainders
5. Three-digit dividends with hundreds not divisible
6. Larger dividends with zeros in the quotient

As stated previously the sequence may vary or may be divided into a greater or lesser number of identifiable steps. A diagnostic test designed to give each step adequate representation can help the teacher pinpoint the specific area of difficulty. Help may then be focused on the problem area rather than going through the whole process.

Let us consider the steps identified above and some implications for diagnostic teaching.

1. The basic facts with remainders provide a natural introduction to the division algorithm. Because remainders are a unique characteristic of division, they should be given thorough consideration. Children must be helped to gain a clear understanding of the meaning of remainder. By working with objects, children can remove subsets of a predetermined number until there are fewer than that number remaining. By actually manipulating the objects, they can see that the remainder is made up of single objects, whereas the quotient represents groups of a certain size. Even when students are working at a more sophisticated level, they must be aware of this difference—the singleness of the remainder and the grouplike quality of the quotient.

The use of basic facts with remainders is a means by which the division algorithm may be introduced without stressing the formal procedure. The exercise $6\overline{)28}$ may be used as an example. First, students must determine how many groups of 6 may be taken from 28. Using their knowledge of the basic facts, they will answer that 4 is the largest number, because 5 sixes would be 30. Students can then show the number of sixes in 28 by recording it above the 8 in the dividend as follows:

$$\frac{4}{6\overline{)28}}$$

By questioning the students and using real or representational materials, they can be led to discover that 4 sets of sixes are not all of the 28. By relating this to the multiplication facts, they will see that 4 sixes are 24. We then introduce a way of keeping an account of this amount by using the next step in the agorithm, thus:

$$\frac{4}{6\overline{)28}}\\ \underline{24}$$

This should lead into the meaning of the remainder. Has all the 28 been used? What is left? How can one determine what is left?

A variation to this approach is to give the correct quotient with the exercise and have students complete the remaining steps. Needless to say, this work cannot be mastered with a brief introduction and a few practice exercises. Individual and small-group work sessions will be necessary to ensure success for many students.

2. Dividends that are multiples of tens and hundreds may cause difficulties because of the zeros in the quotient. At this point the close relationship between subtraction and division may be utilized to make the division process clearer. By using the subtractive form of division, students can discover for themselves the internal procedure of the algorithm without the pressure of selecting the exact quotient. Consider the following:

$$
\begin{array}{ll}
5\overline{)600} & \\
\underline{500} & 100 \times 5 \\
100 & \\
\underline{\;50} & 10 \times 5 \\
\;50 & \\
\underline{\;50} & \underline{10 \times 5} \\
\;\;0 & 120
\end{array}
\qquad
\begin{array}{ll}
5\overline{)600} & \\
\underline{500} & 100 \times 5 \\
100 & \\
\underline{100} & \underline{20 \times 5} \\
\;\;0 & 120
\end{array}
$$

Because division is repeated subtraction, students are at liberty to subtract any amount of which they are certain in the form above. In their search for the number of fives in 600, the rather simple fact of $5 \times 100 = 500$ will help them realize that there are at least 100 fives in 600. They must be led to see the reason for the 500 and its subtraction from 600. This operation should be compared with the simpler operation in which the basic facts with remainders were used. The next step is new and must be thoroughly developed. Why must the remaining 100 be divided again? Why can it not be left as a remainder? Notice the two exercises at this point. One required two additional steps for completion while the other used only one. This is one of the advantages of the procedure: a student can progress at his or her own rate.

The teacher should never assume that students understand the meaning of the operation as a whole. Each step must be adequately developed. Even the partial quotients can cause difficulty. When they are added and a complete quotient obtained, it is a good idea to have students write the quotient in the conventional form above the dividend, thus stressing placement the quotient in its proper place-value position from the very beginning. This will help students overcome many problems with value as the algorithm becomes more formal and complex.

   3. The two types of division exercises that follow, two-digit quotients without and with remainders, are deceptively simple. They are simple in that a high percentage of students will respond with correct answers and deceptive in that many students do not adequately understand the processes involved. These types of exercises provide an excellent medium through which the conventional division algorithm may be introduced.

   To illustrate these points, consider the example $4\overline{)48}$. Most students readily arrive at a quotient of 12 by dividing 4 into 4 and 4 into 8. The answer is correct, although often adequate understanding is missing. If students work through each step of this example, they will be introduced to a higher level of the process, namely, bringing down the second digit to set up a new dividend after the first digit has been divided. After they have worked with similar exercises where there is no remainder, they should undertake exercises with remainders.

   When exercises such as $4\overline{)57}$ are introduced, students will be working with the complete algorithm in a very simple form. The numbers with which they are working are small enough to be understood. They can even check their answer with the use of concrete and semiconcrete materials if that is needed.

   4. Exercises with dividends of three digits with the third digit not divisible, such as $8\overline{)653}$, may cause difficulty for some students. Working with the conventional algorithm should not pose a problem in this type of exercise. The fact that the hundreds place cannot be divided by the divisor means only that the quotient will be less than 100. When this happens, students should be given an opportunity to reason out the next step. The solution, of course, involves dividing the first two digits. If they have difficulty with this point, they can work the same exercise by the subtractive method, paying special attention to the place value of the quotient. Once students master this point of determining the first partial dividend, the remainder of the exercise is repetition of previously learned procedures. The teacher should emphasize placing the initial term of the quotient in the proper place over the dividend and continuing until all places, from the initial entry to the ones place, have an entry in the quotient. The best means of determining the location of the initial entry in the quotient is to ask, "How many places into the dividend was it necessary to go in order to get a divisible partial dividend?" In the exercise $8\overline{)653}$, it was necessary to go two places;

therefore, the first entry must be above the 5, which was the second place.

5. The success of diagnosis depends upon the diagnostician's ability to take a complex operation and break it down into identifiable components. Each step in the process should differ from the preceding one and build upon it. This point is clearly brought out as one moves into division where zeros are found in the middle positions of the quotient. In the preceding step students learned what to do when the first digit of the dividend was not divisible. Building upon that knowledge, students will have some basis for dealing with the following example:

$$
\begin{array}{r}
306 \\
7\overline{)2142} \\
\underline{21} \\
42 \\
\underline{42}
\end{array}
$$

The difficulty may arise at the point where students bring down the 4 to set up the new dividend. They must show that the 7 could not divide the 4. Students encountered a similar situation earlier, but they did not have to record a zero in the far left position of the quotient. If students do not discover for themselves the need to bring down the 2 to complete the new dividend, they should review what they did earlier when one number was too small to be divided. The main lesson is that each place in the dividend must be divided, either alone or in combination with an adjoining one.

Multi-digit divisors

Division with two-digit and larger divisors is by far the most difficult of the whole-number operations. Several factors have already been noted that contribute to the difficulty of division in general. Another will be considered below in relation to difficulties with multi-digit divisors.

The following types of exercises have been used in developmental and remedial work with complex division:

1. Divisors that are multiples of ten with the dividend ending in zero
2. Other two-digit divisors with one- and two-place quotients
3. Four-digit dividends with two-digit quotients that are difficult to estimate because the divisor is near the center of a decade
4. Three-digit quotients with zeros in the dividend

5. Quotients with zeros in middle positions
6. Three-digit divisors

Results of a study by one of the authors indicated that the sequence as shown is a logical one.

A major difficulty in division involving multi-digit divisors is that of quotient estimation. Some continue to use the subtractive method in which an exact quotient never has to be estimated. Although some students become very proficient with this method, it is no solution if the goal is to develop proficiency in using the conventional division algorithm. The best method seems to be one in which students use the first number in the divisor as a divisor to estimate the real quotient. In the initial work with two-digit divisors, the apparent quotient should be the real quotient. Thus, in the exercise $24\overline{)78}$, students can divide 2 into 7, rather than 24 into 78, and obtain both the apparent and real quotient. This would not be true with $24\overline{)71}$. Students should be given sufficient time to work with the former type of exercise in order to refine their procedures and develop confidence before moving into more difficult estimations.

A more difficult type of estimation involves rounding off either the divisor, the dividend, or both. When $29\overline{)92}$ is encountered, the method used earlier is not sufficient because 9 divided by 2 would yield a quotient of 4 when the real quotient is 3. Students must see that 29 is so near 30 that 9 divided by 3 is a better estimation.

As divisors and dividends become more complex, the problem of correct quotient estimation increases. Even the best reasoning on the part of students may result in an incorrect estimation. How can they be helped in this situation? One way is to prepare them in advance for such a time. They should be made to see that sooner or later they will confront this kind of situation and that there is no reason to be upset or discouraged. An understanding teacher is a great help. A more positive defense is to develop understanding of the procedure so that students will be able to handle the situation.

Consider the following example:

```
        27
29)813
    58
   233
   203
    30
```

A reasonable approach would be to round 29 to 30 and divide 8 by 3 for the first partial quotient. With the new dividend of 233 the apparent quotient could be found by again rounding 29 to 30 and using 3 as the divisor. The 233 would be rounded back one place. Since the 3 in the ones place was less than half way through the decade, the dividend would be 23. By dividing 23 by 3 the apparent quotient is 7. In using 7 as the quotient, however, the end result would be a remainder of 30, which is larger than the divisor. This should indicate to students that their estimate is incorrect. Most errors in estimation will be detected if students understand the procedure and carefully check each step. Overestimation of the quotient seems to be an even greater difficulty for some students because they are more prone to overlook an error in subtraction than one of a remainder that is too large.

In addition to errors associated with quotient estimation, complex division is subject to all the other possible sources of errors found in division with a single-digit divisor. It is easy to see why division is such a difficult operation for many students. By diagnosing the particular problem and pinpointing therapy, the diagnostic teacher can be instrumental in helping all students come closer to fulfilling their potential.

Selected references

COPELAND, RICHARD W. *How Children Learn Mathematics.* New York: Macmillan, 1974, chap. 6.

GREEN, GEORGE F. *Elementary School Mathematics Activities and Materials.* Lexington, Mass.: Heath, 1974, chap. 4.

MARKS, JOHN L., PURDY, RICHARD C., KINNEY, LUCIEN B., and HIATT, ARTHUR A. *Teaching Elementary School Mathematics for Understanding.* New York: McGraw-Hill, 1975, chap. 4.

REISMAN, FREDRICKA K. *A Guide to the Diagnostic Teaching of Arithmetic.* Columbus, Ohio: Merrill, 1972.

STEFFE, LESLIE P. *Research on Mathematical Thinking of Young Children.* Washington, D. C.: National Council of Teachers of Mathematics, 1975.

SWENSON, ESTHER J. *Teaching Mathematics To Children.* New York: Macmillan, 1973, chap. 1.

UNDERHILL, ROBERT. *Teaching Elementary School Mathematics.* Columbus, Ohio: Merrill, 1972, chaps. 7, 8, 11.

part IV

fractions

In many ways working with fractions is very much like working with whole numbers. We perform the same operations in the same way. However, there are some difficulties in fractions, often because we have to deal with new terms (such as numerator and denominator).

Hence, from the standpoint of concepts, there is a great deal of carry-over from whole numbers to fractions. They look somewhat different, and often fractions require an extra step or two (finding a common denominator, for example). As a result, work with fractions is dealt with separately. Again, general methodology is closely allied with diagnosis and prescription.

Common fractions

One characteristic of a good number system is that it has the capability to describe any quantity, including quantities less than one. The developers of the Hindu-Arabic system met this requirement through our system of common fractions. Much later, this was supplemented by decimal fractions.

Role of common fractions in elementary-school mathematics

Although children's early contacts with our number system are restricted to whole numbers, common fractions also come up very early, although in an incidental way. Even in kindergarten, some simple fraction work is often included, with emphasis on one-half of an object. Indeed, many young children use the term "one-half," most commonly with respect to money (half a dollar) and time (half an hour). There is a steady expansion of concepts as students advance up the grade scale or through the phases of a continuous-progress program.

Mental disciplinists' view

During the era when mental discipline was viewed as a vital component in education, a great deal of content was included in mathematics programs solely because it was difficult. Fractions were ideal for this purpose because there is no ceiling on the level of difficulty that can be built into a fraction exercise. For example, students might have a task such as $\frac{1287}{2243} + \frac{1697}{1746}$. Assuming that they ultimately complete this, a third addend can begin the whole operation again.

There are actual cases recorded by educational historians that illustrate this point. For example, one assigned task was to change 0.821437437 to a common fraction. (For those who have misplaced their calculator, the answer is $\frac{102577}{124875}$.

Another aspect of mental discipline often stressed was "mental arithmetic," which frequently complicated a problem by using fractions. For example, children were presented the problem, "A lady, being asked the hour of the day, replied that $\frac{2}{3}$ of the time past noon equaled $\frac{4}{5}$ of the time to midnight; what was the time?" Considering that such problems were to be solved without paper and pencil, one can appreciate the unhappy lot of a student during the era of mental discipline.

For many years, as shown by the above illustrations, practicality received essentially no consideration in arithmetic programs. As a result, seldom-used fractions such as $\frac{5}{7}$ or $\frac{9}{13}$ received just as much attention as did fractions like $\frac{1}{2}$ or $\frac{3}{4}$.

Impact of the social criterion

It was well into the twentieth century before leaders in mathematics education, in part because of pressure from students, began to express concern about teaching meaningful fractions. Questions were raised as to whether certain fractions met the "social criterion," that is, whether such fractions functioned in the lives of students.

This concern led to the question, "Which fractions are useful?" Extensive research was carried out to identify those fractions that had practical meaning to students at varying age levels. Predictably, halves, thirds, fourths, and eighths were found more useful than, for example, elevenths and ninths. Subsequent programs in elementary-school mathematics gave special attention to those fractions that met the social criterion.

Impact of metric usage

For many years elementary-mathematics programs have treated common fractions and decimal fractions as parallel, and approximately equal, topics. However, this situation is changing, for a variety of reasons.

One reason has been the rapid development of computers and miniature calculators. Both of these, as a first step, convert common fractions to decimal fractions prior to any sort of processing.

However, the move away from common fractions encountered opposition because of our traditional system of measurements. For example, a ruler is divided into half-inch, quarter-inch, and smaller segments, depending upon the accuracy of the ruler. These divisions do not fit logically into a scheme of decimal fractions.

Today, the movement toward metric measures is causing a swing away from common fractions because ten or powers of ten serve as built-in conversion factors within the metric system. This system is thus well adapted to decimal-fraction usage and constitutes a further threat to the common-fraction method of describing quantities.

We should not assume, however, that common fractions are becoming obsolete. Some types of measurements, such as time, are not affected by the changes described above. Also, in many aspects of geometry, we will continue to use common-fraction concepts (for example, in bisecting a line).

Teaching the concepts

As with other aspects of work with numbers, understanding of concepts ideally should precede work in the skills area in the case of fractions. Obviously, it would be self-defeating to try to teach a student how to add $\frac{1}{2}$ and $\frac{1}{4}$ before the basic meanings of the terms have been cleared up.

Terminology

Adults sometimes overlook the fact that, to a literal young mind, writing one numeral above another violates certain concepts. Specifically, in our work with whole numbers, we read from left to right; for example, 225 is read as "two hundred twenty-five." In common fractions, however, we read from top to bottom, so that $\frac{2}{3}$ is read "two-thirds."

Some textbooks mention that the word "fraction" is related to "fracture." This can add meaning to the term if students have had contact with the latter term. Perhaps easier for students to understand is the idea of breaking something into two or more *equal* parts. After all, many young children are past masters at breaking things.

The use of "top number" and "bottom number" in describing the terms of fractions is difficult to avoid. However, as rapidly as is feasible, students should move toward usage of "numerator" and "denominator." The special function of each is worthy of emphasis. The numerator (counter) answers the question "How many?" and the denominator (namer) answers the question, "What kind?"

There are many types of teaching materials available for use in helping students to form concepts about fractions. Some of these are described elsewhere in this book. Others are cited in teachers' editions of most textbooks. Also, the catalogs issued by school-supply companies describe a wide variety of aids. Incidentally, the teacher who has no funds available for ordering such material can frequently get some good ideas for teacher-made or student-made aids by browsing through catalogs.

Teaching simple fractions

Probably the easiest fraction is one-half because the term, although not necessarily its meaning, is probably familiar to many young children. Conceptually, its meaning ("one of the two equal parts") is easy to demonstrate and to visualize. It should be noted that initially a teacher should use half of an object rather than half of a set of objects.

Moving from $\frac{1}{2}$ into work with other unit fractions—that is, fractions with one as the numerator—is a logical and easy process. In some programs the concepts of halves, thirds, and fourths are all taken up at the kindergarten level. Other programs concentrate on halves and fourths because these are related to each other in an easy and logical manner.

In work with fractions, as in work with whole numbers, it is important to move from the concrete to the abstract in fraction material. All sorts of fraction material—notably, plastic fruits and pies—are commercially available. Also, paper folding offers many opportunities for student activities. Students can work as well with rulers and scissors, using an assortment of index cards or even irregularly shaped pieces of paper or cardboard. As usual, better results are obtained if students are participants rather than mere observers.

Expansion of concepts

As students move toward higher levels of work with fractions, concepts expand in a variety of directions.

More Complex Denominators The sequence of halves to fourths to eighths is a logical one. For example, one additional folding of a sheet of paper can make the transition from halves to fourths or from fourths to eighths. However, thirds, fifths, and higher denominators—to the extent that they are used—are a sometimes fairly complex departure from the earlier sequence. The most important concept for the learner is the proper role of the denominator, which involves providing a name for the fraction. The denominator indicates into how many equal parts the object under consideration has been divided. This concept applies, regardless of the size of the denominator.

Larger numerators Although unit fractions are dominant in early work with fractions, teachers can move away from this type fairly rapidly. Basically, there are no new concepts involved in this progression. Students who see that $\frac{1}{3}$ refers to one of the three equal parts into which an object has been divided encounter little new in considering two such parts, that is, $\frac{2}{3}$. Many potential stumbling blocks in this area can be circumvented if students come to an early understanding of the role of the numerator and denominator.

Associating symbols with pictorial material Traditionally, students work with numbers by moving from concrete material to semiconcrete, or pictorial, material before manipulating abstract symbols. The same progression is widely used in learning fractions. Specifically, students work extensively with pictures of objects, parts of which have been made to stand out (by shading or a contrasting color). The task is to associate the pictorial representation with the fraction that describes it.

A variety of geometric shapes should be used in this work. For example, the circle and the square which are fairly easy to prepare, should be emphasized. But rectangles, triangles, and other types of figures (possibly some that defy normal categories) should also be used.

Activities with these figures can be carried on a variety of levels. At an elementary level, children might be assigned a matching exercise, as shown in Figure 11-1. At a slightly higher level students might be asked to (1) write symbols describing shaded parts of given figures or (2) shade figures to conform to given fractions.

Associating equal fractions A further step in the expansion of concepts is that of associating equal fractions such as $\frac{1}{2}$ and $\frac{4}{8}$. This can be illustrated at the concrete level by various types of linear or circular cutouts in which eighths are physically measured against something representing a half until equivalency is reached. Then

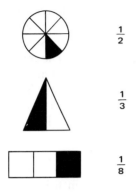

$\frac{1}{2}$

$\frac{1}{3}$

$\frac{1}{8}$

Figure 11-1. Matching
symbols and concepts

students simply count the number of eighths required in the matching. However, by the time this topic becomes meaningful, most students should be ready to deal with it in terms of abstract symbols.

Frequently, students raise questions about the logic of writing the same fractional quantity in more than one way. The teacher should point out that we do the same thing with whole numbers. We write the numeral 4, for example, in a number of different ways ($8 \div 2$, $5 - 1$, $3 + 1$, etc.). An application of this whole-number usage is in borrowing. To subtract 28 from 46, we rename the latter (from $40 + 6$ to $30 + 16$) in order to facilitate the process. Exactly the same reason explains why we, on occasion, need to change $\frac{1}{2}$ to $\frac{3}{6}$ or $\frac{4}{8}$ or something else.

Renaming As a continuation of the procedure described above, it is sometimes necessary to rename more than one fraction. Consider the analogy of adding or subtracting 47 cents, 2 dollars, and a 10 dollar bill. To do this the quantities must be renamed in order to describe all of them in the same terms. Similarly, preparing fractions for these same operations requires that they be described in the same way. For this purpose, $\frac{1}{2}$ and $\frac{1}{3}$ must be converted to the same family of sixths, $\frac{1}{3}$ and $\frac{1}{4}$ to the family of twelfths, and so on.

Fractional parts of sets In most programs concept development regarding fractions centers around fractional parts of a single object or of a single geometric figure. However, as an expansion of the basic ideas, teachers may have students begin to work with fractional parts of sets. They might start with concrete materials again

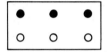

Figure 11-2. Fractional
parts of a set

(e.g., apportioning half a bag of marbles), but they would move rapidly toward the semiconcrete. At that level they would work with
an assortment of diagrams such as the one shown in Figure 11-2.
Students viewing this diagram might be asked, "What fractional
part of this set of spots is shaded?"

The experience of many students has indicated that the transition from parts of an object to parts of a set of objects is a potential
trouble spot. However, those who truly understand the concept of
fractional parts of an object generally take this transition in stride.
In most programs this expansion of fractional concepts occurs at the
second- or third-grade level.

Teaching the operations

There is merit in having students understand the concepts of fractions, but this does not constitute the end of the process. Operations
with fractions are also important. However, meaningful work in
operations is possible only to the extent that students have a basic
understanding of fraction concepts.

Addition

The process of addition as used with fractions has the same basic
meaning ("putting together") that it has with whole numbers. Also,
the operations evolve in a way that is somewhat parallel to the way
whole numbers are learned.

No renaming In many classrooms students' first contact with
addition of fractions is such that they do not see anything new about
the process. For example, students who know that 1 book + 1
book = 2 books, or that 1 dollar + 1 dollar = 2 dollars, will readily
move to 1 fourth + 1 fourth = 2 fourths. This is a simple case of
adding denominate numbers, and it is the same whether the
denominator ("namer") is books, dollars, or fourths. Obviously,
nothing new is involved in changing our method of writing from

one-fourth to $\frac{1}{4}$. Therefore, students who see 1 fourth + 1 fourth = 2 fourths should be able to make the transition to $\frac{1}{4} + \frac{1}{4} = \frac{2}{4}$. This approach also helps clarify our reason for adding only numerators. But, despite the best effort of the teacher, many students see $\frac{1}{4} + \frac{1}{4} = \frac{2}{8}$.

There are many teaching aids available at this level, including circular cutouts and matching strips. Even a sheet of paper folded and cut into fourths, with sections labeled, can serve a useful purpose for those students who need to use concrete materials.

Renaming Many people recall the glib references, made very early in their work with fractions, to "finding a common denominator." In many cases this process was carried out in a mechanical manner. The terminology about finding a common denominator has not changed, but it is usually used in a more meaningful way and related to giving the quantities the same name.

Probably the simplest case would involve two fractions, one of which needs to be renamed. For example, in $\frac{1}{2} + \frac{1}{4}$, only the first fraction needs renaming. By matching fourths against halves (using fraction strips, circular cutouts, folded paper), students can demonstrate to themselves that $\frac{1}{2} = \frac{2}{4}$. They are now ready to rewrite the exercise $\frac{1}{2} + \frac{1}{4}$ as $\frac{2}{4} + \frac{1}{4}$. At this point they can complete the exercise by performing the operation.

After students have mastered the procedure of renaming once they can proceed to the case of two fractional addends, each of which requires renaming. (In a graded program, this would probably be taken up around the fourth or fifth grade.) Several approaches are used in helping students decide how to rename in cases such as $\frac{1}{3} + \frac{1}{4}$. One widely used system is to concentrate on the larger denominator, in this case, 4. Doubling it produces 8, which is not divisible by 3. Therefore, it must continue to be multiplied—by 3, 4, 5, and so forth—until a multiple of 4 that is divisible by 3 is found.

One observant student noted that he could save time by multiplying the two denominators together to start the process. This, of course, will always identify *a* common denominator but not necessarily the *least* common denominator. For example, in the example $\frac{1}{6} + \frac{1}{8}$, this procedure would result in renaming both fractions as forty-eighths, despite the fact that twenty-fourths is a more usable denominator.

A junior-high teacher was surprised to note that one of her lower-performance students came up with almost instant answers on exercises like $\frac{1}{3} + \frac{1}{4}$. She had him work aloud and found that he was saying, "$3 + 4 = 7$; $3 \times 4 = 12$, so the answer is $\frac{7}{12}$."

Adding with multiple addends The transition to three or more addends does not involve any basically new concepts, although the inclusion of each additional addend is likely to further complicate the renaming process. In order to avoid undue complication, sometimes it is best to start with three (or more) addends that have the same denominator, as in $\frac{1}{5} + \frac{1}{5} + \frac{2}{5}$. From here, several levels can be identified. These might include:

1. $\frac{1}{5} + \frac{2}{5} + \frac{1}{12}$

2. $\frac{1}{3} + \frac{1}{4} + \frac{5}{12}$

3. $\frac{1}{4} + \frac{1}{5} + \frac{3}{10}$

All of the above require some degree of renaming, but the problem of renaming becomes increasingly complex in proceeding down the sequence.

In some programs considerable time and effort go into breaking each denominator into a set of prime factors, then synthesizing the least common multiple from the primes. Other programs use less sophisticated methods. One procedure parallels the one we examined earlier that concentrates on the largest number among the denominators. For example, in case (3) above, students would first check to see if 10 is divisible by 4 and 5. Because it is not, they would double the 10 and apply the same test, continuing as far as necessary.

A slightly different mechanism, applying the same general pattern of thinking described above, involves listing multiples of each denominator. For example, in $\frac{1}{4} + \frac{1}{5} + \frac{3}{10}$, multiples of 4, 5, and 10 would be listed as follows:

4	8	12	16	20
5	10	15	20	
10	20			

It is relatively easy to identify 20 as the new denominator. The student would then rewrite the exercise as $\frac{5}{20} + \frac{4}{20} + \frac{6}{20}$ and carry it through the final phase.

Adding mixed numbers There are no new concepts applied in adding mixed numbers. Often, this phase of work is introduced by adding a whole number to a mixed number, as in:

$$\begin{array}{r} 3 \\ +2\frac{1}{5} \\ \hline 5\frac{1}{5} \end{array}$$

It is obvious that this example involves a form of place value again, just as was the case in two-digit whole numbers.

A second phase might involve two mixed numbers with like fractions, such as:

$$3\frac{1}{4}$$
$$+2\frac{1}{4}$$
$$\overline{5\frac{2}{4}}$$

This frequently leads to carrying. For example:

$$\overset{\textcircled{1}}{4}\frac{3}{4}$$
$$+3\frac{3}{4}$$
$$\overline{8\frac{2}{4}}$$

The pattern of thinking students would employ is, "$\frac{3}{4} + \frac{3}{4} = \frac{6}{4}$ or $1\frac{2}{4}$, so we put down the $\frac{2}{4}$ and carry $\frac{4}{4}$, or 1, to ones place.

Many students, of course, would need to break this operation into several substeps in order to arrive at the correct solution.

As work with mixed numbers evolves, more complex denominators, or combinations of denominators, are used. More than two addends might also be included in exercises.

Many people recall a very mechanical operation in which mixed addends are rewritten as improper fractions. For example, $3\frac{1}{4}$ is translated as "4 threes are 12 plus 1 equals 13 fourths." Each addend is processed the same way, and then renaming is done. This time-honored system works, but teachers should try to make it a meaningful, rather than a mechanical, operation.

Subtraction

Students who are making satisfactory progress in adding fractions usually have no trouble with subtracting fractions. This is to be expected because the two operations involve the same procedures up to the very last step.

Because the operations of addition and subtraction of fractions are so similar, they are usually introduced and developed in parallel stages. As a result, the patterns of addition described earlier are equally applicable to subtraction and are not repeated here.

Subtraction of common fractions is usually introduced at the middle-elementary level and developed over a period of several years. In the earlier phases concrete materials are important. The same materials that are used in addition can be used in subtraction.

Multiplication

When introducing this operation, many teachers are accused by their students of being inconsistent: "But, Teacher, in addition you would not let us add the denominators; now you tell us that we should multiply them." Sometimes this is followed by a muttered, "I wish you'd make up your mind!"

Conceptually, the key to this apparent inconsistency lies in the unique character of denominate numbers. A number named two-fifths has many of the characteristics of a number named 2 feet or 2 meters. *Adding* 2 feet and 2 feet yields 4 feet, the name (feet) being unchanged. Exactly the same principle applies in adding 2 fifths and 2 fifths: the sum is still named fifths.

If multiplying, however, some different concepts apply. For example, 2 feet times 2 feet equals 4 *square* feet. In effect, we have "multiplied the names" and have produced a new unit that measures something quite different from that which is measured by feet. Essentially, this is what is done with other denominate numbers. Multiplying 2 fifths by 2 fifths results in the mathematical expression $2 \times 2 = 4$, but the 4 is associated with a new unit arrived at by "multiplying the names," in this case, fifths by fifths to get twenty-fifths. Thus, in the expression $\frac{2}{5} \times \frac{2}{5} = \frac{4}{25}$, we are multiplying the counters together (2×2), and arriving at the new name by multiplying the names together (5×5).

Multiplying a fraction by a whole number   Many teachers like to introduce the work in multiplying fractions by using a whole number as one of the factors. For example, $\frac{1}{4} \times 3$ can be related directly to earlier work with whole numbers. You will recall that multiplication has been described as a short form of addition dealing with equal addends. The expression $4 + 4 + 4$ is equivalent to three 4s or 4×3 ("four taken three times"). Exactly the same logic applies in $\frac{1}{4} \times 3$. It can be seen as $\frac{1}{4} + \frac{1}{4} + \frac{1}{4}$, or $\frac{3}{4}$. Hence, $\frac{1}{4} \times 3 = \frac{3}{4}$. Some students, incidentally, would probably write this as $\frac{1}{4} \times \frac{3}{1}$. There is no reason to object to this practice if it helps students in dealing with the algorithm.

Multiplying a fraction by a fraction   Students must make several adjustments as they start work on this phase of fractions. Many of them find it especially confusing that in contrast to the comparable operation with whole numbers, the product is smaller than the factors. Another confusion arises from nomenclature. With whole numbers many teachers describe 4 × 3 as "three fours" rather than "three times four." Indeed, there are some good reasons for using the former expression. In working with fractions, however, it would be very confusing to refer to "one half three fourths" for $\frac{3}{4} \times \frac{1}{2}$. The term "times" or some similar one is essential at this point.

The algorithm for multiplying numerators and multiplying denominators is fairly simple. However, this procedure should evolve from an understanding of the process. Teachers can use numerous methods to promote such understanding. One of the more direct ones is based on simple geometric figures. For example, let us take the case of $\frac{1}{2} \times \frac{3}{4}$, as shown in Figure 11-3. Teachers can reconstruct this figure by first dividing the area of the rectangle into halves (by means of a horizontal line). Then the rectangle can be divided into fourths by the vertical lines. The rectangle now has eight cells. By using different shadings for the areas representing $\frac{1}{2}$ and $\frac{3}{4}$, it is obvious that three of the eight cells, overlap in shading, thus demonstrating that $\frac{1}{2} \times \frac{3}{4} = \frac{3}{8}$. As the algorithm takes on meaning, of course, students outgrow the need for drawing figures to illustrate the process.

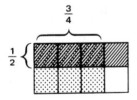

Figure 11-3. Multiplying
$\frac{1}{2} \times \frac{3}{4}$

Discussions of multiplying fractions by fractions usually devote a good deal of time to the process formerly called "cancellation." For example, before multiplying $\frac{3}{8} \times \frac{4}{9}$, we "cancel" the 3 into the 9 and the 4 into the 8 as follows:

$$\frac{\overset{1}{\cancel{3}}}{\underset{2}{\cancel{8}}} \times \frac{\overset{1}{\cancel{4}}}{\underset{3}{\cancel{9}}} = \frac{1}{6}$$

Because the term "cancel" basically means to wipe something out totally, and because nothing is wiped out here, the term is actually not descriptive of the process. This operation actually amounts to reducing before, rather than after, carrying out the operation. The procedure has merit in that it permits working with smaller numbers. Hence, the objections that some have raised center on the term "cancel" rather than on the operation itself.

Multiplying mixed numbers If students are clear on the process described above, they will encounter nothing that is essentially new in multiplying mixed numbers. However, in some programs the process is made to look quite complex. For example, in order to relate mixed-number work to comparable procedures using whole numbers, a teacher might use the following:

$$
\begin{array}{r}
3\frac{1}{2} \\[4pt]
\times 2\frac{2}{3} \\
\hline
\frac{2}{6}\left(\frac{2}{3}\times\frac{1}{2}\right) \\[6pt]
2\left(\frac{2}{3}\times 3\right) \\[6pt]
1\left(2\times\frac{1}{2}\right) \\[6pt]
6\ (2\times 3) \\
\hline
9\frac{2}{6}=9\frac{1}{3}
\end{array}
$$

Although the above might add meaning to the operation for certain students, it would probably be very confusing to most. Certainly as an algorithm, it has little to offer.

The more widely used system is to rewrite each factor as an improper fraction, then multiply in the usual way. This would yield the following:

$$3\frac{1}{2}=\frac{7}{2}$$
$$2\frac{2}{3}=\frac{8}{3}$$
$$\frac{7}{2}\times\frac{8}{3}=\frac{56}{6}=\frac{28}{3}=9\frac{1}{3}$$

Of course, in this illustration, the 2 and the 8 could have been reduced prior to multiplication if students prefer doing it that way.

Division

The algorithm for division of common fractions is like that for multiplication to a considerable extent. However, division adheres to the time-honored rule, "Invert the terms of the divisor and proceed as in multiplication." This procedure has been cited by some educators as the classic illustration of a mechanical application of a rule. Students should, at some point, consider the basis for this rule.

Why is the divisor inverted before multiplying? The rule is based on the fact that one is the identity element in division; thus, any quantity divided by one yields the original quantity. One is therefore the easiest of all divisors to use. The "invert and multiply" procedure is followed in order to multiply both dividend and divisor by the same number. The multiplier is selected so that, when multiplied by the divisor, the product is 1. It is easy to see that any number, when multiplied by its inverse or reciprocal, equals one.

By way of illustration, consider $\frac{4}{9} \div \frac{2}{3}$. The reciprocal of $\frac{2}{3}$ is $\frac{3}{2}$. Multiplying both dividend and divisor by $\frac{3}{2}$ yields $(\frac{4}{9} \times \frac{3}{2}) \div (\frac{2}{3} \times \frac{3}{2})$. Hence, we have (1) inverted the divisor ($\frac{2}{3}$ to $\frac{3}{2}$) and (2) moved from the operation of division to that of multiplication. However, throughout this sequence, the purpose for rewriting was to be able to use a divisor of 1.

A student recently asked his teacher this question: "When we were multiplying fractions, we multiplied numerators, then we multiplied denominators. Why don't we, in division, divide numerators, then divide denominators?" Let us examine his question as it would apply to the exercise $\frac{4}{9} \div \frac{2}{3}$. Following the student's proposed procedure, we would have $(4 \div 2)/(9 \div 3) = \frac{2}{3}$, which is a correct answer. So the answer to this student's question is that it is possible to divide numerators, then divide denominators. However, in many cases, this procedure would complicate rather than clarify. For example, in the example $\frac{4}{5} \div \frac{3}{4}$, the expression $(4 \div 3)/(5 \div 4)$ does not constitute progress toward a useful solution.

Again, division with mixed numbers does not present anything new conceptually. In the problem $2\frac{2}{3} \div 2\frac{4}{5}$, students should simply convert each to an improper fraction ($\frac{8}{3} \div \frac{19}{5}$), then invert and multiply in the usual way.

Diagnosis and prescription

The teaching and learning of fractions is a spiral process, with each new idea based upon earlier material. The diagnostic approach is vital because it is the means whereby missing concepts can be identified. Correction is frequently quite simple after the trouble has been brought into clear focus.

The general approach to diagnosis in common fractions resembles closely that involved in work with whole numbers. Hence, in this section, the material is not as detailed as in earlier chapters.

Fraction concepts

Obviously, if students are to succeed in work with fractions, they must understand the basic meanings of fractions. Thus, a beginning point for diagnosis in fractions is to explore students' background on concepts.

Associating symbols with pictorial form A common approach here is to have a set of circles and/or rectangles in which parts are shaded, as in Figure 11-4. It is important that the figures be quite clear as to the fractional parts shaded. Students are then asked to match these parts with a set of symbols, such as $\frac{1}{4}$, $\frac{2}{3}$, $\frac{1}{2}$. The figures and symbols should not always follow the same sequence.

A student who has trouble here may well be unclear as to the meaning of the terms in a written fraction. For example, he or she may not know that $\frac{2}{3}$ means 2 of the 3 equal parts of a figure. For practice work many circular cutout figures for use on felt boards and in other ways are available. To prepare such material from scratch, it might be easier to use rectangles. Conceptually, they would be equally effective.

Writing fractions to describe figures The next stage of development of fraction concepts involves writing fractions. In this process, instead of *associating* a symbol with a figure, students are shown a set of figures and they *write* the appropriate symbol for each. Figure 11-5 shows some representative figures. The task of students viewing such figures, is to write $\frac{1}{2}$, $\frac{1}{3}$, $\frac{3}{4}$, and so forth. This task is related to the first task described of associating, but students in this case operate at a somewhat higher level.

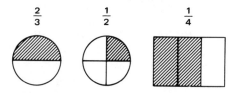

Figure 11-4. Associating symbols and
fractional parts

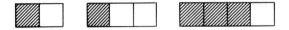

Figure 11-5. Writing symbols for figures

A student who has trouble here probably has two basic needs: he or she must learn the meaning of the denominator ("the namer") and the numerator ("the counter") and then practice writing the symbols for a variety of figures. Some teachers prepare sets of cards with such figures and shadings for use in this situation.

Conceptualizing the size of a fraction Many students have trouble in conceptualizing size. They have known with a high degree of assurance that 4 is greater than 3, but when confronted with the idea that $\frac{1}{4}$ is *less than* $\frac{1}{3}$, they see an apparent inconsistency.

The diagnostic work on this concept can be carried out at two different levels. The most basic would make use of pairs of fractions such as $\frac{1}{3}$ and $\frac{2}{3}$, $\frac{1}{2}$ and $\frac{2}{3}$, $\frac{2}{3}$ and $\frac{3}{4}$. The students' task is to select from each pair the larger fraction. The second level involves sets of four fractions written in random order. Illustrations are ($\frac{1}{2}$, $\frac{2}{3}$, $\frac{4}{5}$, $\frac{3}{4}$) or ($\frac{1}{4}$, $\frac{1}{3}$, $\frac{1}{6}$, $\frac{1}{5}$). Here students must rewrite each set in a prescribed order—smallest to largest or vice versa. The observant teacher can frequently locate a single type of fraction (thirds, for example) that is giving special trouble.

A good teaching device for students who have trouble with sizes of fractions is a set of 12-inch strips, some of which have been cut into halves (each 6 inches long), some into thirds (4 inches long), others into fourths (3 inches long), and possibly some in sixths and twelfths. In the metric system 12 centimeters or a convenient multiple could be used. With these concrete materials students can demonstrate for themselves, by physically matching parts, that $\frac{1}{3}$ is larger than $\frac{1}{4}$. (Incidentally, these same materials are useful in many situations involving fractions.) Ordering a set of fractions is a vital concept, and pupil progress is often quite slow, with many repeated errors. However, it is a basic concept, worthy of considerable effort on the part of teacher and students.

Associating symbols for equivalent fractions There are innumerable ways to describe the whole number 4, including $3 + 1$, $5 - 1$, $1004 - 1000$. Similarly, there are many ways to describe the shaded part of the rectangle in Figure 11-6—$\frac{1}{4}$, $\frac{2}{8}$, $\frac{3}{12}$, and others to numerous to mention. Furthermore, in some situations a fraction needs to be written in more than one form. Hence, the concept of equivalent fractions is worthy of attention.

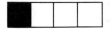

Figure 11-6. Ways in which
$\frac{1}{4}$ can be symbolized

Diagnosis can take a variety of forms. A basic one might include two columns of fractions like these:

$\frac{1}{2}$	$\frac{2}{12}$
$\frac{2}{3}$	$\frac{5}{10}$
$\frac{1}{6}$	$\frac{8}{12}$
$\frac{4}{5}$	$\frac{8}{10}$

The task of students is to associate $\frac{1}{2}$ with $\frac{5}{10}$, $\frac{2}{3}$ with $\frac{8}{12}$, and so on. At another level students might be given a set of fractions like $\frac{1}{6}$, $\frac{2}{3}$, $\frac{1}{4}$, and $\frac{1}{2}$ and instructed to rewrite each as twelfths. In our experience, the first system shown above, using the two columns, seems to be more effective.

For students who have trouble with this concept, a good corrective practice involves use of the 12-inch segments described earlier. Label a 12-inch segment as "1," 6-inch segments as "$\frac{1}{2}$," 4-inch segments as "$\frac{1}{3}$," 3-inch segments as "$\frac{1}{4}$," 2-inch segments as "$\frac{1}{6}$," and 1-inch segments as "$\frac{1}{12}$." Students can then demonstrate to themselves, by physically matching parts, that $\frac{1}{6} = \frac{2}{12}$, $\frac{2}{3} = \frac{8}{12}$, and so on. Of course, students should be encouraged to use the abstract symbols as rapidly as possible.

Associating symbols with fractional parts of sets   In their earliest work with fractions, students are usually presented with fractional parts of a single object, rather than parts of a set, because the former is a simpler concept. For example, half an apple is easier to envision than half a dozen apples. Yet students must understand both of these situations before they work very far with fractions.

A common diagnostic procedure makes use of sets of figures, some of which are shaded while others are not. Figure 11-7 provides an illustration. The figures should avoid patterns because these can provide clues. The task of students, of course, is to identify what fractional part of each set is shaded.

One correctional approach makes use of a familiar container

Figure 11-7. Fractional parts of a set

such as an egg carton. Students working individually or in small groups, place varying numbers of objects (not eggs!) in the pockets and then determine, by counting if necessary, what fractional part of 12 they have filled up.

Rewriting fractions

Rewriting or renaming is a widely used technique in number work. The purpose of rewriting is to make an exercise more workable. Renaming fractions also makes a problem more manageable. However, many students have become confused because they were rushed into processes such as finding a common denominator before they thoroughly understood the why and how.

Finding the greatest common factor Many teachers feel that students cannot engage in meaningful work in renaming fractions until they can isolate the greatest common factor for a pair of numbers. Hence, we will briefly examine this process.

The diagnosis consists of having students "write the largest number that will divide evenly into both numbers of this pair," thereby avoiding use of the phrase "greatest common factor." The pairs may be 6 and 4, 12 and 3, 6 and 8, and others as needed.

Corrective work can take a variety of directions. Some modern mathematics programs go rather deeply into set usage at this point. However, many teachers take a very simple approach by concentrating on the smaller number in the pair. Is the larger number divisible by the smaller? Then, the smaller is the greatest common factor. If the larger is not divisible by the smaller, then students try one-half the smaller, one-third of it, one-fourth of it, and so on. Many teachers would criticize this method as involving too much guessing. However, once most students are clear as to what they are seeking, they can work rather efficiently with this process.

Finding the lowest common multiple If students are to rewrite a fraction in terms of another fraction (i.e., find a common denominator), they must be able to determine, with a minimum of effort, the smallest number into which both denominators will divide evenly. This is the lowest (or least) common multiple.

Diagnosing the problem requires presenting the student with

pairs of numbers such as 6 and 3, 12 and 8, 7 and 4. Their task, of course, is to find the smallest number that is divisible by both. If a particular student seems to be unusually slow in arriving at his or her answer, the teacher should have the student work aloud. In that way the teacher, giving careful attention to what is said, can spot faulty work habits and correct them.

For those students who have trouble with this concept, there are several valid approaches. However, the procedure should not be so elaborate as to overshadow the purpose. One rather simple procedure involves checking first to see if the smaller number divides evenly into the larger. If it does, then the larger number is the least common multiple. If the larger number is not divisible by the smaller, then the larger number should be multiplied by 2, 3, 4, or larger numbers until the multiple that is divisible by the smaller is found. That number is the least common multiple for the pair of numbers. Of course, students need not be limited to just two numbers in this work; they can be called upon to find the least common multiple for three or even more numbers. However, the basic procedure described above is usable in all such cases.

Writing fractions in lower terms   Many teachers do not consider that an exercise in fractions is satisfactorily completed until the answer has been reduced to lowest terms, which involves rewriting or renaming again. The merit of such a position is debatable because in many types of work unreduced fractions are quite common. A machinist would be satisfied with a measure of $\frac{16}{32}$ or $\frac{8}{64}$ in just that form. And, who would think of referring to 40 cents as $\frac{2}{5}$ of a dollar? However, because reducing to lowest terms is a point of emphasis in many programs, it deserves some attention.

Diagnosis can proceed on two levels here. At one level the teacher would simply list a variety of unreduced fractions—$\frac{4}{10}, \frac{5}{20}, \frac{6}{16}$, and so on—and students would reduce these to lowest terms. It should be reemphasized that our motive is not merely to give some exercises to see "how well a student can do." Our concern is: Does the student have trouble on this operation? If so, what is the specific difficulty involved? And, what steps must be taken to correct the situation?

At another diagnostic level, teachers can supply students with incomplete statements such as $\frac{6}{8} = \frac{3}{\square}$ and $\frac{10}{20} = \frac{\square}{2}$ or $\frac{5}{\square}$. This approach may have some advantages over the other because the unknown can appear in any of the four positions. In short, it might yield more specific information than would the more generalized form described earlier.

The therapy for difficulties in this area is somewhat more general than for other types of problems. Basically, the task of the teacher is to (1) pinpoint the exact source of difficulty by use of the work-aloud procedure, (2) guide the student in clearing up misconceptions and gaps in requisite skills, and (3) give the student an ample but not overwhelming volume of practice work for skill development.

Writing fractions in higher terms As a result of the previously cited emphasis on writing fractions in their lowest terms, much time is spent on "reducing" fractions. However, the inverse procedure, writing fractions in higher terms is also a useful skill to have. For example, finding the common denominator in the example $\frac{1}{2} + \frac{1}{3}$ involves rewriting each fraction in higher terms, that is, $\frac{3}{6}$ and $\frac{2}{6}$. Hence, an equal amount of emphasis should be placed on this skill.

Diagnosis in this area, once again, can occur at two levels. The first involves a set of fractions all to be renamed the same way. For example, students might to asked to rename $\frac{1}{2}$, $\frac{2}{3}$, and $\frac{4}{9}$ as eighteenths. The other approach asks students to provide the missing term in statements such as $\frac{1}{2} = \frac{\square}{10}$, $\frac{7}{8} = \frac{\square}{14}$, and $\frac{1}{3} = \frac{8}{\square}$. Many students respond well to the second approach because it looks less like another set of exercises.

Students who have difficulty with the process of renaming in higher terms may well have misconceptions regarding the equivalency of fractions. Some may even need to revert to using the manipulative materials described earlier, thereby demonstrating for themselves the equivalency between $\frac{1}{3}$ and $\frac{4}{12}$, and $\frac{3}{4}$ and $\frac{9}{12}$, and so on.

Some teachers may be inclined to use a shortcut at this point and teach students the process of cross-multiplying. Using this system to find the missing term in $\frac{3}{4} = \frac{9}{\square}$, students arrive at $3 \,\square\, = 36$. By dividing 36 by 3, they come up with $\frac{3}{4} = \frac{9}{12}$. Obviously, this system yields a correct answer. However, to many students it would be a meaningless procedure. Probably a better approach is to relate this process to reducing a fraction, in which each term of a fraction is divided by the same number. This procedure is the inverse of reducing, and hence each term of the fraction is multiplied by the same number. In the above exercise, $\frac{3}{4} = \frac{9}{\square}$, the numerator (3) was multiplied by 3 in order to get 9. Hence, the denominator (4) should also be multiplied by 3, so that $\square = 12$. The terms of a fraction can be multiplied or divided by the same number without changing the value of the fraction because of the identity principle.

Writing improper fractions as mixed numbers Many operations with fractions yield quantities written in fractions that are greater than 1. For example, $\frac{3}{4} + \frac{3}{4} = \frac{6}{4}$. There is nothing incorrect with the answer $\frac{6}{4}$, although it would probably have more meaning if rewritten as $1\frac{2}{4}$ or $1\frac{1}{2}$.

Diagnostic material to uncover difficulties may consist of a variety of improper fractions, such as $\frac{5}{3}$, $\frac{9}{4}$, and $\frac{18}{5}$, to be rewritten as mixed numbers. If there are indications of trouble, a work-aloud procedure would be helpful because there are many approaches that work in the conversion. Although some of these could yield correct results, they may make use of highly inefficient procedures. Work-aloud sessions will bring such practices to the fore very easily.

Corrective work on this concept can make use of concrete materials if necessary. For example, using the familiar circular cut-outs, teachers can show that $\frac{3}{3}$ equals a complete circle, or $\frac{3}{3}$, with $\frac{2}{3}$ of a circle left over. Hence, $\frac{5}{3} = 1\frac{2}{3}$. Once concepts are clear, students should move to a more abstract procedure, such as $\frac{9}{4} = 9 \div 4 = 2\frac{1}{4}$. In keeping with the modern approach, this procedure should be a culminating rather than a starting point.

Writing mixed numbers as improper fractions The inverse of the procedure described above is also useful, especially in work with multiplication and division using common fractions.

In diagnosis teachers can use a set of mixed numbers, such as $1\frac{3}{7}$, $3\frac{1}{2}$, and $2\frac{3}{4}$, to be rewritten as improper fractions. Again, work-aloud sessions are useful to isolate work patterns.

In correctional work it is important that students see what they are doing. For example, in rewriting $1\frac{3}{7}$ as an improper fraction, they should think first of the 1 as $\frac{7}{7}$. Then they can add to this the fraction $\frac{3}{7}$, for a total of $\frac{10}{7}$. Only after the process has become meaningful should youngsters take the familiar route of "$7 \times 1 = 7$; $7 + 3 = 10$, so we have $\frac{10}{7}$."

Adding fractions

As noted above, we can add two fractions only if they are named alike, (e.g., 1 fifth plus 2 fifths equals 3 fifths). Because the denominator is the namer, $\frac{1}{5}$ and $\frac{2}{5}$ can be added. Of course, to add two unlike fractions, such as $\frac{1}{5}$ and $\frac{1}{3}$, the fractions would have to be renamed.

Adding two like fractions, no simplifying needed Probably the simplest operation in the use of fractions is adding two like fractions where the answer requires no further simplification. The diagnosis involves use of sets of exercises such as $\frac{1}{3} + \frac{1}{3}$, $\frac{3}{8} + \frac{2}{8}$, and $\frac{1}{5} + \frac{2}{5}$. Again, any evidence of confusion should lead the teacher to use a work-aloud procedure because this process reveals thought patterns by students.

How should a teacher react to the student who finds $\frac{1}{5} + \frac{2}{5} = \frac{3}{10}$? This student is not clear on the role of the denominator as the namer. It might help to write the exercise like this:

$$
\begin{array}{r}
1 \text{ fifth} \\
+\,2 \text{ fifths} \\
\hline
3 \text{ fifths}
\end{array}
$$

In writing it thus, the "fifths" are clearly identified as namers, as would be the case with pounds or gallons.

For those who need concrete help, fraction cutouts could be used, at least transitionally, to help students see that $\frac{1}{3} + \frac{1}{3} = \frac{2}{3}$.

Adding two like fractions, simplifying needed This case is quite similar to the one described above, with an additional step involved. For diagnostic purposes exercises such as $\frac{2}{6} + \frac{1}{6} = \frac{3}{6}$ and $\frac{3}{8} + \frac{3}{8} = \frac{6}{8}$ can be used. Because this is a case of adding fractions with like denominators, no renaming is needed prior to addition. However, the sum is not in lowest terms so that renaming or reducing the sum is required. The technique for doing this was covered earlier.

Adding two fractions, one to be rewritten A slightly more advanced case which builds on the concepts just described, is that of two fractions with different denominators. The diagnosis consists of having students work a set of exercises such as $\frac{1}{10} + \frac{3}{5}$ or $\frac{1}{8} + \frac{3}{4}$. In each case only one of the addends must be renamed. It is potentially very helpful if the teacher watches students rather closely as they work in the diagnostic phase because certain faulty work habits, such counting or extensive "self-discussion" (mumbling), are easily isolated by this procedure.

Corrective work for the student who has trouble with this concept usually lies in one or more of the following areas: (1) a review of the fact that the fractions $\frac{1}{8}$ and $\frac{3}{4}$ cannot be added as they are because they are named differently (are not like quantities); (2) a review of the process of renaming; and (3) a further look at the process of addition as it applies to these fractions after the $\frac{3}{4}$ has been renamed as $\frac{6}{8}$. The latter step may require a review of the fact that the correct procedure is to add numerators, not denominators—and why this is true.

Adding two fractions, both to be rewritten Diagnosis in this phase involves having the student work sets of exercises such as

$\frac{1}{2} + \frac{1}{3}$ and $\frac{1}{4} + \frac{2}{3}$. Many students have trouble with this type, and the work-aloud procedure is especially useful. Some students who ultimately arrive at a correct answer to so by highly inefficient methods; these are readily identified by having students vocalize their methods.

Therapy at this point may well involve a review of the renaming approach, why and when it is used. Most textbooks at the appropriate grade level offer some help in cases where both fractions must be renamed. Some of these present a rather theoretical approach to arriving at the least common multiple. A very practical method is to concentrate on the greater denominator. For example, in working with $\frac{1}{4} + \frac{2}{3}$, it is obvious that 3 does not "go into" 4. In doubling 4, 8 is still not divisible by 3. Only by going to 12, which 12 is divisible by 3, is the proper denominator to use in renaming identified. By changing $\frac{1}{4} + \frac{2}{3}$ to $\frac{3}{12} + \frac{8}{12}$, the usual addition procedures can be followed.

Adding more than two fractions, some rewriting needed All of the earlier work has used two fractions because for the concepts involved, two is usually enough. However, many situations require addition of three or more addends. Diagnosis here is based on such exercises as $\frac{3}{4} + \frac{1}{6} + \frac{1}{3}$ and $\frac{2}{5} + \frac{3}{10} + \frac{1}{2}$. One or two exercises in which all three fractions need renaming, such as $\frac{1}{2} + \frac{1}{3} + \frac{2}{5}$, can be used as well if they seem to be needed.

Therapy dealing with this concept can be carried on at several levels. We will consider only two of these. In working with an exercise like $\frac{1}{4} + \frac{1}{6} + \frac{1}{3}$, children should first try to see if the largest denominator, 6, could serve as a common denominator. Although 6 is divisible by 3, it is not by 4. Consequently 6 should be doubled to get 12. Because 12 is divisible by both 3 and 4, the exercise can be rewritten $\frac{3}{12} + \frac{2}{12} + \frac{4}{12}$.

Some students may observe that one can always arrive at *a* common denominator by finding the product of all the denominators. For example, in $\frac{1}{2} + \frac{1}{3} + \frac{1}{4}$, students could use 24 (i.e., $2 \times 3 \times 4$) as their common denominator. This procedure will always work, but it frequently requires the use of larger numbers. In $\frac{1}{2} + \frac{1}{5} + \frac{1}{10}$, it would surely be easier to use a common denominator of 10 rather than of 100 (the product of the three denominators).

Adding a whole number and a fraction It is fairly rare to find a student who has problems with this concept. However, this does happen occasionally so that $3 + \frac{3}{4}$ comes out as $\frac{6}{4}$. The basic concept that is misunderstood is that of place value. Frequently, students become clear on the concept when the exercise is written as:

$$3$$
$$+\frac{3}{4}$$

Misconceptions in this operation are usually easy to clear up once they have been identified. Again, a work-aloud session can be very helpful as a diagnostic procedure.

Adding involving mixed numbers There are at least eight types or levels of operations in adding mixed numbers. Because the diagnostic and correctional procedures grow directly out of the concepts discussed earlier, the work with mixed numbers will be restricted primarily to identification of types. The types include:

1. *Adding a mixed number and a whole number:* In cases such as $6\frac{3}{4} + 7$, place value is again of major importance.

2. *Adding mixed numbers, no renaming:* This involves work on two levels. In first-level work, such as with $3\frac{1}{5} + 2\frac{2}{5}$, the sum requires no simplification. In second-level work, such as with $5\frac{3}{8} + 3\frac{3}{8}$, the sum can be reduced to lower terms.

3. *Adding a mixed number and a fraction, no renaming:* Such exercises as $8\frac{1}{4} + \frac{1}{4}$ are involved here. Again, place value is a key concept. Some sums require reducing; some do not.

4. *Adding a mixed number and a fraction, one to be renamed:* In an exercise such as $3\frac{1}{12} + \frac{3}{4}$, the fraction $\frac{3}{4}$ must be renamed. In this case simplification is necessary.

5. *Adding a mixed number and fraction, both to be renamed:* An example of this case is $3\frac{3}{4} + \frac{1}{6}$. The fractions must be renamed so that they have a common denominator, preferably 12. Thus, $3\frac{3}{4} + \frac{1}{6} = 3\frac{9}{12} + \frac{2}{12} = 3\frac{11}{12}$. Of course, there could be further complications, for example, adding a mixed number and a fraction such as $4\frac{2}{3} + \frac{1}{2}$. In this exercise both $\frac{2}{3}$ and $\frac{1}{2}$ must be renamed. Thus, $4\frac{2}{3} + \frac{1}{2} = 4\frac{4}{6} + \frac{3}{6} = 4\frac{7}{6}$. Now, in order to simplify, $\frac{7}{6}$ must be renamed $1\frac{1}{6}$, resulting in $4\frac{7}{6} = 4 + 1\frac{1}{6} = 5\frac{1}{6}$.

6. *Adding two mixed numbers, one to be renamed:* This again involves two levels. At the first level one addend requires renaming but the sum requires no simplifying such as in $4\frac{7}{10} + 3\frac{1}{5}$. At the other level, one addend is renamed and the sum is an improper fraction, such as in $3\frac{5}{8} + 2\frac{3}{4}$, which turns out to be $\frac{11}{8}$. Many teachers treat this as a "carrying" situation; thus, $\frac{8}{8}$ is carried to ones place, leaving $\frac{3}{8}$.

7. *Adding two mixed numbers, both to be renamed:* This is an extension of the concept described above, using such exercises as $4\frac{7}{9} + 2\frac{5}{6}$.

8. *Adding more than two mixed numbers:* This is the culminating phase of work with adding fractions. It uses exercises such as $10\frac{5}{8} + 13\frac{7}{12} + 2\frac{5}{8}$. Some or all of the denominators require renaming, and often the sum is an improper fraction that requires simplification. Conceptually, both of these situations have been discussed earlier.

Subtracting fractions

Many teachers, in working with whole numbers, maintain a close relationship between the processes of addition and subtraction, which often reduces the student effort required to master certain types of content. For example, students can probably learn $3 + 2 = 5$, $2 + 3 = 5$, $5 - 2 = 3$, and $5 - 3 = 2$ (a "family" of facts) with less trouble than would be the case if they studied each fact in isolation.

Subtraction of common fractions requires that the fractions involved be named alike (have a common denominator). This is also true in adding common fractions. Hence, students who have mastered the addition process are familiar with all of the preliminary phases of subtraction. The two operations differ only in the final step, where the actual addition—or subtraction—occurs. As a result, there is not a great deal of "new" content in the subtraction operation.

Subtracting one fraction from another, like denominators Diagnostic works of this very elementary procedure should include exercises such as $\frac{7}{8} - \frac{1}{8}$ and $\frac{4}{5} - \frac{2}{5}$. Because it looks more like subtraction, some teachers prefer to write this type of exercise vertically. Students who have difficulty here might profit by reverting to the system used earlier and writing:

> 7 eighths
> $-$ 1 eighth

This, of course, should be used only to help establish the concept; it would be quite awkward as a regular procedure.

Subtracting one fraction from another, one to be renamed To diagnose problems in this phase, exercises of the type $\frac{7}{8} - \frac{1}{2}$ and

$\frac{15}{16} - \frac{1}{8}$ should be used. If a student is clear on the subtraction concept, renaming is about the only source of trouble. Corrective instruction on this aspect was discussed earlier in this chapter.

Subtracting one fraction from another, both to be renamed This operation includes such exercises as $\frac{3}{4} - \frac{1}{3}$ and $\frac{4}{5} - \frac{1}{2}$. Again, the likely source of difficulty is renaming because the procedure is straightforward after the fractions have been written with the same denominator.

Subtracting a fraction from a whole number Diagnostic work here includes such exercises as $3 - \frac{1}{2}$ and $7 - \frac{3}{5}$. Two approaches are available in helping students with this type of problem. One of these makes use of the familiar concept of borrowing. For example, for $3 - \frac{1}{2}$, students would borrow 1 from the 3, rewriting the 1 as $\frac{2}{2}$, so that the 3 becomes $2\frac{2}{2}$. Now the exercise is $2\frac{2}{2} - \frac{1}{2} = 2\frac{1}{2}$. In using the other approach, students would convert the 3 to $\frac{6}{2}$. The exercise then becomes $\frac{6}{2} - \frac{1}{2} = \frac{5}{2}$, or $2\frac{1}{2}$.

Subtracting a mixed number from a whole number Typical diagnostic exercises here are $4 - 1\frac{1}{3}$ and $5 - 1\frac{11}{12}$. Although textbooks show a variety of "best methods," probably the most direct one is the borrowing procedure shown earlier. For the exercise $4 - 1\frac{1}{3}$, students would convert 4 to $3\frac{3}{3}$ and subtract $1\frac{1}{3}$ to arrive at $2\frac{2}{3}$.

Subtracting one mixed number from another, like denominators Diagnosing this includes such exercises as $6\frac{7}{10} - 2\frac{1}{10}$ and $8\frac{1}{4} - 2\frac{3}{4}$. The first is quite direct because $6\frac{7}{10} - 2\frac{1}{10}$ requires nothing more than two separate operations—the whole-number part and the fractional part. Hence, students would perform the operations $\frac{7}{10} - \frac{1}{10} = \frac{6}{10}$ and $6 - 2 = 4$, resulting in a difference of $4\frac{6}{10}$. In the second case, $8\frac{1}{4} - 2\frac{3}{4}$, the expression $8\frac{1}{4}$ can be rewritten as $7\frac{5}{4}$ by borrowing. The problem now becomes $7\frac{5}{4} - 2\frac{3}{4}$, or $5\frac{2}{4}$. ($5\frac{1}{2}$ if further simplification is insisted upon).

Another approach that is sometimes used with exercises such as $8\frac{1}{4} - 2\frac{3}{4}$ is to write each as an improper fraction. Using this procedure, students would write $8\frac{1}{4}$ as $\frac{33}{4}$ and $2\frac{3}{4}$ as $\frac{11}{4}$. The solution is $\frac{33}{4} - \frac{11}{4} = \frac{22}{4}$ or $5\frac{2}{4}$ or $5\frac{1}{2}$.

Subtracting one mixed number from another, unlike denominators Typical cases for this type are $9\frac{1}{3} - 5\frac{5}{8}$ and $10\frac{5}{12} - 2\frac{7}{8}$. The concepts involved—renaming, and as required, borrowing—have already been treated. Hence, they will not be repeated here.

Multiplying fractions

Multiplication involving fractions has long been taught as a procedure. Rules covering certain cases frequently could be used to produce correct answers. However, at the risk of repeating, the best approach to the skills in this area is through an understanding of the processes.

Multiplication with a fraction and a whole number as factors
Diagnostic exercises in this phase are of the type $\frac{1}{8} \times 5$ and $16 \times \frac{1}{3}$. Some textbooks treat these differently, especially when the exercise is written vertically. However, conceptually, they are very similar.

Misconceptions can sometimes be cleared up by use of an adapted nomenclature. For example, in $\frac{1}{8} \times 5$, students could write:

$$\begin{array}{r} 1 \text{ eighth} \\ \underline{\times 5} \\ 5 \text{ eighths} \end{array}$$

The advantages of this system is that the operation now looks like that with other denominate numbers (e.g., 1 gallon $\times$ 5). In both cases, the 1 is a named number, and the product bears the name of the multiplicand.

Another approach makes use of fraction cutouts of some sort. If segments are marked "$\frac{1}{8}$," and if students take 5 of these, they continue to sum 1 eighth plus 1 eighth until they arrive at 5 eighths or $\frac{5}{8}$.

Multiplying one fraction by another, no reduction This procedure requires diagnostic work of the type $\frac{1}{4} \times \frac{1}{4}$ or $\frac{3}{8} \times \frac{1}{2}$. In many cases, the procedure has, from the first contact, been treated by the rule, "Multiply the numerator together, then multiply the denominators together." Although the rule works, it is not adequate to satisfy the curiosity of many young children. A widely used instructional procedure is to use simple geometric models as shown earlier in this chapter.

Multiplying one fraction by another, one reduction The diagnostic exercises to discover difficulties here include several of the type $\frac{1}{2} \times \frac{4}{5}$ and $\frac{2}{3} \times \frac{5}{8}$. Follow-up instruction takes two possible directions. In the first, students simply take $\frac{2}{3} \times \frac{5}{8}$ as written to get $\frac{10}{24}$. Because this is not in lowest terms, students then divide 10 and 24 by 2 to get $\frac{5}{12}$.

Another approach makes use of reduction prior to multiplication. Again, using $\frac{2}{3} \times \frac{5}{8}$, students can reduce the 2 and 8 before multiplying. The exercise then becomes:

$$\frac{\overset{1}{\cancel{2}}}{3} \times \frac{5}{\underset{4}{\cancel{8}}}$$

Multiplying in the usual way obtains the answer $\frac{5}{12}$. Reducing before multiplying results in a product in lowest terms.

Multiplying one fraction by another, two reductions Diagnostic work for this type of exercise includes examples such as $\frac{3}{5} \times \frac{5}{12}$ and $\frac{9}{10} \times \frac{2}{3}$. Instruction follows the previous type very closely. For $\frac{9}{10} \times \frac{2}{3}$, students can get $\frac{18}{30}$, then reduce by 6 to get $\frac{3}{5}$. However, many teachers prefer the reduce-before-multiply procedure. In $\frac{9}{10} \times \frac{2}{3}$, students would reduce the 9 and the 3 to get $\frac{3}{10} \times \frac{2}{1}$. After another reduction (the 10 with the 2) the exercise becomes $\frac{3}{5} \times \frac{1}{1} = \frac{3}{5}$. In a single step, the work looks like this:

$$\frac{\overset{3}{\cancel{9}}}{\underset{5}{\cancel{10}}} \times \frac{\overset{1}{\cancel{2}}}{\underset{1}{\cancel{3}}} = \frac{3}{5}$$

Multiplying a fraction by a mixed number In order to locate areas of difficulty teachers can use such exercises as $\frac{1}{3} \times 1\frac{1}{2}$ and $\frac{3}{5} \times 2\frac{1}{4}$. There are several instructional approaches that can be used here, but we will stress the most popular one, which involves simply rewriting the mixed number in the form of an improper fraction. This concept was treated earlier in this chapter. In the exercise $\frac{3}{5} \times 2\frac{1}{4}$, students convert the latter term to $\frac{9}{4}$. That results in $\frac{3}{5} \times \frac{9}{4} = \frac{27}{20} = 1\frac{7}{20}$.

Multiplying one mixed number by another mixed number Typical cases in this category are $8\frac{1}{3} \times 5\frac{1}{4}$ and $1\frac{2}{5} \times 7\frac{1}{2}$. Conceptually, these are similar to the exercises in the previous category. The most commonly used method is to rewrite both terms as improper fractions. For example, $1\frac{2}{5} \times 7\frac{1}{2}$ becomes $\frac{7}{5} \times \frac{15}{2}$. The 5 and the 15 can be reduced to get $\frac{7}{1} \times \frac{3}{2} = \frac{21}{2} = 10\frac{1}{2}$. Some other approaches can be used, but many of them become quite complicated. Hence, they are not included here.

Multiplying by use or more than two factors When several factors are involved—fractions and mixed numbers—the same procedures described earlier are used. Examples are $\frac{3}{8} \times \frac{7}{10} \times \frac{5}{6}$ or $\frac{3}{5} \times 2\frac{1}{2} \times \frac{5}{6}$. In the latter case, students could rewrite the expression as $\frac{3}{5} \times \frac{5}{2} \times \frac{5}{6}$. Without reduction, the expression becomes $(3 \times 5 \times 5)/(5 \times 2 \times 6) = 75/60 = 1\ 1/4$. By reducing before multiplying, it becomes:

$$\frac{\overset{1}{\cancel{3}}}{\underset{1}{\cancel{5}}} \times \frac{\overset{1}{\cancel{5}}}{2} \times \frac{5}{\underset{2}{\cancel{6}}} = \frac{5}{4} = 1\frac{1}{4}$$

Dividing fractions

The glibly repeated "Invert the terms of the divisor and then multiply" has long been prominent in the operation of division with fractions. There is a valid reason for use of this procedure, as has been shown earlier.

Dividing a whole number by a fraction To locate problems in this operation teachers may use exercises such as $4 \div \frac{1}{2}$ and $6 \div \frac{2}{3}$. The real meaning of this process can be shown by using the measurement concept of division. For example, to show the meaning of $4 \div \frac{1}{2}$, have students take a 4-inch strip and a set of half-inch strips, and have them match these to show that the 4-inch strip has the same length as 8 half-inch strips. This can then be related to the expression $4 \div \frac{1}{2} = 8$. This method is effective, but students prefer to use the method described below.

Dividing a fraction by a fraction Diagnostic procedures include such exercises as $\frac{3}{4} \div \frac{5}{6}$ and $\frac{8}{9} \div \frac{1}{2}$. Although the basis for the rule of division has been cited previously, a more detailed illustration might serve a useful purpose. Consider the example $\frac{3}{4} \div \frac{5}{6}$. This could be done as $(3 \div 5)/(4 \div 6)$, but that would do little to clear up the problem. The basic premise is that both dividend and divisor can be multiplied by the same number without changing the quotient. The next step is based on the fact that the identity element for division is one (i.e., dividing any number by one leaves the number unchanged). It follows from the identity property that one is the easiest of all divisors to use. Thus, in $\frac{3}{4} \div \frac{5}{6}$, if one could multiply both dividend and divisor by a quantity that would yield a divisor of 1, the problem would be simplified. To arrive at a divisor of one, a multiplier of $\frac{6}{5}$ (the reciprocal of $\frac{5}{6}$) is used. The problem now becomes $\frac{3}{4} \times \frac{6}{5} \div \frac{5}{6} \times \frac{6}{5}$ (i.e., the divisor is $\frac{30}{30}$ or 1). The problem is now rewritten as $\frac{3}{4} \times \frac{6}{5} \div 1$. Because the divisor does not enter into the further work, it is often dropped, the problem is stated $\frac{3}{4} \times \frac{6}{5}$. Note that, in this process, the new operational sign is for multiplication; also, although $\frac{5}{6}$ has seemingly been replaced by $\frac{6}{5}$, technically this is not the case.

Dividing a fraction by a whole number The diagnostic work in this area includes such exercises as $\frac{5}{8} \div 3$ and $\frac{4}{5} \div 2$. Some students find this work a bit confusing because it draws on fractional *and* whole-number concepts. One very simple procedure, also limited in its application, can be illustrated with $\frac{4}{5} \div 2$. If students write this as 4 fifths ÷ 2, the obvious result is 2 fifths. However, use of this procedure in other cases (such as in $\frac{5}{8} \div 3$) can become very confusing.

A method of more general usage in this area is a direct outgrowth of the work in the previous section. Using the "invert and multiply" procedure, $\frac{5}{8} \div 3$ becomes $\frac{5}{8} \times \frac{1}{3} = \frac{5}{24}$. In explaining the reason for inversion, the discussion above is useful.

Dividing a mixed number by a fraction Illustrative diagnostic exercises here are $3\frac{1}{3} \div \frac{5}{6}$ and $4\frac{1}{2} \div \frac{1}{2}$. The most practical method of solution is simply to rewrite the mixed number as an improper fraction. In the case of $3\frac{1}{3} \div \frac{5}{6}$, students rewrite it as $\frac{10}{3} \times \frac{6}{5} = 4$. There is no reason to avoid using the invert and multiply procedure. However, it is desirable that students understand why it works.

Dividing a mixed number by a whole number Diagnostic exercises would be of the type $4\frac{1}{2} \div 3$ and $7\frac{1}{5} \div 6$. Conceptually, this is quite similar to some of the earlier types. The usual method in cases such as $4\frac{1}{2} \div 3$ is to rewrite the mixed number as an improper fraction. The exercise would then become $\frac{9}{2} \times \frac{1}{3} = 1\frac{1}{2}$.

Dividing a mixed number by a mixed number To locate difficulties here one would use such exercises as $5\frac{1}{3} \div 3\frac{1}{3}$ or $8\frac{1}{4} \div 2\frac{2}{5}$. The concepts described earlier are again relevant. The usual procedure is to rewrite both terms as improper fractions. For the example $8\frac{1}{4} \div 2\frac{2}{5}$, students would rewrite the terms as $\frac{33}{4} \times \frac{5}{12} = \frac{55}{16} = 3\frac{7}{16}$.

Decimal fractions

12

The meaning of a fraction as part of a whole quantity is not affected by the system used to describe that part. However, because common fractions and decimal fractions do not look at all alike they are dealt with in somewhat different ways.

The decimal-fraction concept appeared on the scene in comparatively modern times. However, it is so simple and logical that it has grown very rapidly in usage. This growth will likely continue as we come to rely more and more on computers because these devices convert all fractions to the decimal form before undertaking further processing.

Students frequently encounter some inconsistency in terminology relating to decimal fractions. The word "decimal" refers to base 10. For example, the Hindu-Arabic number system is a decimal system because of its use of base 10. Some people refer to the point (as in .87) as a decimal. Others refer to the entire fractional quantity as a decimal. In this volume, an effort is made to use the longer, more descriptive terms in the latter two cases. Thus we call the point a "decimal point" and the fraction, a "decimal fraction."

Role of decimal fractions in elementary school mathematics

Most students have early, even preschool, contact with decimal fractions through our money system. However, as a formal topic of study such fractions are usually reserved for the middle grades.

There is rather general agreement that decimal fractions are easier to use than common fractions. Nevertheless, students study common fractions first. Although that may seem illogical there is a reason for our use of what might appear to be reverse sequence. As will be shown, it would be very difficult for students to comprehend the meaning of .3 unless they had prior knowledge of the meaning of $\frac{3}{10}$.

Unclear Concepts

Despite the fact that decimal fractions are simple and easy to use, they are conceptually difficult for many students. This is true for a variety of reasons.

The unseen denominator Students who understand the role of the "top number" and "bottom number" in common fractions are likely to feel somewhat confused when faced with a fraction that does not exhibit these components. A teacher may instruct students on how to apply certain rules in order to relate a number like .3 to common fractions. But even after they have been reassured continuously that .3 is three-tenths, some students still complain that they do not see a ten anywhere.

Restricted denominators In common fractions students do not encounter any forbidden values in the denominator position. Although they actually use certain denominators more frequently than others, this is a matter of convenience rather than concept. However, in decimal fractions, students are limited to ten and powers of ten in the denominator. It is much easier to envision $\frac{1}{4}$ in terms of its true meaning than it is to visualize .25.

Lack of symmetry In their work with whole numbers, students identify the last digit on the right as the ones place, the next as the tens place, and so on. But when this system is extended to include mixed numbers, as in 222.222, students find themselves in a confusing situation from the standpoint of reading the number. For example, in the case of the three places to the left of the decimal point, the largest value is hundreds; however, for the three places to the right of the decimal point, the smallest value is thousandths. This characteristic grows from our use of ten and powers of ten as follows:

10^2	10^1	10^0		10^{-1}	10^{-2}	10^{-3}
2	2	2	.	2	2	2

It is little wonder that many elementary students find this confusing. Perhaps that is why many of them (and adults as well) read 222.222 as "two two two point two two two."

Actually, the number shown above is symmetrical around the ones place. If this position is used as a point of reference, the first place to the left is tens place and the first to the right is tenths, and so on. The decimal point's only function is to show where the whole number ends and the fraction begins.

Ease of usage

After students have understood the logic and structure of decimal fractions, they are in a position to appreciate them in the operations. For example, the time-consuming task of finding a common denominator in order to rename addends disappears. All that is now required is that they adhere to the time-honored rule to "keep the decimal points in a column." Then they will automatically add like quantities.

Similar simplifications occur in most of the operations with decimal fractions. One possible exception is division, which sometimes gives trouble, mainly in the interpretation of the quotient.

Teaching the concepts

As mentioned earlier, decimal fractions differ from common fractions only in the area of notation. Hence, for students who understand common fractions, the chief problem is to adjust to the new language used in describing quantities.

In early work with decimal fractions, the teacher should try to relate the two systems, showing that .5 and $\frac{5}{10}$, for example, are two ways of describing the same quantity. Representational material such as is found in Figure 12.1 may help. There a rectangle is divided into ten equal parts, with five of them shaded. Students associate the shaded part with $\frac{1}{2}$, $\frac{5}{10}$, and .5.

The money system in use in the United States is also very helpful in teaching decimal fractions because it is, to a large degree, a decimal system. Coins that are most useful, because of the "ten-ness" of their relationships, are cents, dimes, and dollars. It is easy for most students to see in $2.57 a combination of two dollars, five dimes, and seven cents.

Widespread acceptance of the metric system of measurement will mean a continuing growth in the usage of decimal fractions. Certain measurements in this system can be written in a variety of ways. For example, a length of 25 millimeters might, on occasion,

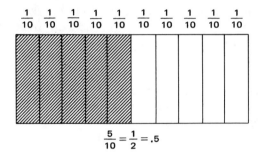

$$\frac{5}{10} = \frac{1}{2} = .5$$

Figure 12-1. Showing the equivalence
of $\frac{5}{10}$, $\frac{1}{2}$, and .5

be described as 2.5 centimeters or even .025 meters, depending on the use to be made of the results.

Most teachers' editions of textbooks provide many suggestions for the teacher in the area of decimal fractions. Teachers should make maximum use of these helps because they directly parallel the text material.

Teaching operations with decimals

Most of the operations with decimal fractions are very straightforward and are quite similar to the same operations with whole numbers.

Addition and Subtraction

In some programs the operations of addition and subtraction with decimal fractions are introduced by relating them to the same operations with common fractions. For example, .3 + .4 would be considered along with $\frac{3}{10} + \frac{4}{10}$. Students who can arrive at the common-fraction sum of $\frac{7}{10}$ should be able to see the decimal fraction sum as .7. Similarly, students who can perform $\frac{7}{10} - \frac{3}{10} = \frac{4}{10}$ should be able to handle .7 − .3 = .4.

Even the operations of carrying and borrowing fall into place quite easily with decimal fractions. Consider the following exercise:

①
$$
\begin{array}{r}
1.8 \\
+\,3.7 \\
\hline
5.5
\end{array}
$$

Students do not need to make any particular effort to "see" this as a fractional operation. It involves carrying (or borrowing) across the decimal point just as in work with whole numbers. Again, by keeping the decimal points in a column, they can eliminate any problems related to common denominators.

Incidentally, some teachers stress the importance of "keeping the decimal points straight" as though it were a basic principle. Actually, it is a convenience, a matter of housekeeping. If students can manage to add tenths to tenths, hundredths to hundredths, and so on, they will be using a correct procedure, whether or not their decimal points are in a column. But they will certainly simplify the task of adding or subtracting like quantities if the decimal points are in a column.

Multiplication

A popular method of introducing multiplication with decimal fractions is to begin with the process of addition set in a concrete problem. For example, if Henry lives 1.6 miles from school, how far does he ride his bike each day in order to make the round trip? Obviously, students can find out by adding, thus:

```
  1.6 miles
+ 1.6 miles
  3.2 miles
```

The same result, however, can be achieved by multiplying, in this fashion:

```
1.6 miles
× 2
3.2 miles
```

The placement of the decimal in the introductory phases of this work is frequently done by estimating. In the above example, the possible results (.32 miles, 3.2 miles, and 32.0 miles) might be listed for class discussion. The reasonable-answer test indicates that 3.2 miles is the only one that makes sense. From a variety of such experiences students are led to see the generalization, "Point off as many places in the product as you have pointed off in multiplier and multiplicand."

Some teachers like to relate the early phases of multiplication of decimal fractions to the comparable operation with common fractions. Thus, $1\frac{6}{10} \times 2 = 2\frac{12}{10} = 3\frac{2}{10}$ (or $3\frac{1}{5}$). This approach might clarify the process for some students.

Students frequently have difficulty multiplying two decimal

fractions. This usually is not particularly hard in decimal mixed numbers because the sensible answer usually shows rather clearly where to place the decimal point. For example, in $2.3 \times 1.1 = 2.53$, the other possible answers (.253, 25.3, or 253.0) obviously would not apply. However, consider the following:

$$\begin{array}{r} .3 \\ \times\, .3 \\ \hline .09 \end{array}$$

How does the student decide where to place the decimal point? Obviously, one way is by applying the rule, "One place in the multiplier, one place in the multiplicand, two places in the product." Students may prefer to verify their results by using common fractions: $\frac{3}{10} \times \frac{3}{10} = \frac{9}{100}$. This can also be written as .09. Only after students have had some experience with this type of multiplication does the product .09 look reasonable to them.

Division

The division of decimal fractions is essentially the same as the division of whole numbers. Some difficulty, however, is encountered in trying to make division with decimal fractions meaningful. One problem is in deciding where to place the decimal point in the quotient.

Teachers usually begin by using a whole number as the divisor. For example, $2\overline{)\,.8}$ rather obviously yields a quotient of .4. This can be verified by "multiplying back" as one should do with whole numbers: $2 \times .4 = .8$. The same kind of reasoning may be applied to a decimal mixed number as a dividend, such as $2\overline{)\,1.4} = .7$. This is the only quotient that will yield 1.4 when multiplied by 2.

Students encounter the most difficulty when both dividend and divisor are decimal fractions. Many teachers like to use the division-as-measurement idea here. For example, in $.2\overline{)\,.8}$ students can image .8 of a foot to be measured off into segments .2 of a foot in length. Obviously, the measure would be applied 4 times so that $.2\overline{)\,.8}$ yields a quotient of 4. This result can be verified by multiplying divisor and quotient to get the dividend.

Several different methods have been used to help students locate the decimal point in the quotient:

1. The traditional rule is: "The number of decimal places in the quotient equals the number of decimal places in the dividend less the number in the divisor." By this rule, $.5\overline{)\,.125}$ yields .25 because three places in the dividend less one place in the di-

visor gives two places in the quotient. Although this system works, there is a tendency to apply it in a very mechanical manner without understanding.

2. The *sensible-answer system* is one in which students carry out the division process in order to find the digits in the quotient. Then they survey the several possible decimal fractions that these digits could produce. In the preceding example 25.0, 2.5, .25, and .025 would be among the possible answers. From these, students select one that makes sense to them and place the decimal point accordingly. This procedure obviously requires a thorough understanding of the principles involved. A student who is deficient in such understanding would find this system highly unsatisfactory.

3. The *multiply-back system* is one in which students divide without regard for the placement of the decimal point in the quotient. In the example .125 ÷ .5, they arrive at a quotient of 25. They then multiply in the following fashion:

$$
\begin{array}{r}
(?)25 \\
\times\,.5 \\
\hline
.125
\end{array}
$$

Obviously, if .125 is the product, the multiplicand must be .25, and the decimal point is placed accordingly.

4. The *equal-multiplication system* multiplies both dividend and division by a multiple of 10. In the problem $.3\overline{)\,.9}$, students would find it relatively simple to multiply both numbers by 10, which would yield the simple form: $3\overline{)9} = 3$. This system is rather widely used in those cases in which the divisor is a decimal fraction. For example, $.04\overline{)2}$ may be rewritten as $4\overline{)200}$, and the placement of the point is handled as it would be when the divisor is a whole number.

5. The *caret system* is a rather mechanical application of the equal-multiplication system. For the problem .125 ÷ .5 the carets are inserted so as to make the divisor a whole number, thus:

$$
.5_\wedge\overline{)\,.1_\wedge 25}^{\,.25}
$$

The decimal point in the quotient is placed above the caret as indicated.

Doubtless there are other variations of the general procedures for locating the decimal point in the quotient. No one of them constitutes the perfect system. Generally, teachers will end up using the method that works best in their own classroom. It is well, however, to keep in mind that there are several ways of achieving the desired result.

Although division with decimal fractions and mixed numbers is almost identical with the one carried out with whole numbers, students usually, find it somewhat more difficult to visualize the operation with decimals. For some reason a divisor of 8 seems less complex than a divisor of .8. But students who really understand the meaning of division will soon realize that the processes of dividing whole numbers and decimal fractions are essentially the same.

Percent

Because "percent" is closely associated with decimal fractions, it is included as part of this chapter. The meaning of the term can be derived from associations in other contexts. The word "per" has long been associated with the concept of rate, as in miles *per* hour, feet *per* second, and many others. "Cent" means hundred and is found in such words as "century" or "centurion" and in our own system of money. Hence, the term *percent* means per hundred.

Concept

Various approaches are used to introduce the percent concept. A hundred-chart, shown in Figure 12-2, is a common method. If five squares are shaded, the squares on the chart have been shaded *at the rate of* 5 per hundred. Students can then be familiarized with the notion that the rate could be described as 5 percent. Numerous examples using the hundred-chart will help develop understanding of percent.

Another method to teach the concept of percent involves use of classroom games or school sports. Suppose that Jane won three of the ten games that were played in the classroom. Students might be asked to describe this situation in a variety of ways. Some would say that Jane won $\frac{3}{10}$ of the games. The teacher can then extend the example. If Jane's skill and luck hold out, she might be expected to win:

6 games in 20
9 games in 30
15 games in 50
30 games in 100

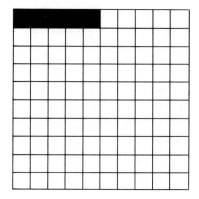

Figure 12-2. A hundred-chart illustrating
that 5 percent means 5 of 100 parts

Students should note that these are *rates* of winning. Hence, Jane won at the rate of 30 games per 100. The association of this fact with the written symbol 30% can then be made plain, and students can be asked to interpret the meaning of the percent sign.

Throughout the early phases of work with percent, a close relationship should be maintained between this system of writing fractional quantities and the two systems described earlier, that is, common fractions and decimal fractions. Hence, in the preceding illustration, the 30 per 100 idea should be written interchangeably as $\frac{30}{100}$, .30, and 30% for a time.

Usage

Although the percent concept is used in a diversity of ways, most of these usages center around the following three patterns:

1. Finding a percent of a number: 6% of 240 = ?
2. Finding what percent one number is of another: 16 is what percent of 64?
3. Finding a number when a percent of it is known: 6 = 30% of what number?

Percent means per hundred, and therefore the percent in a problem should be changed to the equivalent common or decimal fraction. To find 6 percent of 240 means the same as $\frac{6}{100}$ of 240. This, from a study of common or decimal fractions, means $\frac{6}{100} \times 240$, or .06 × 240.

The second pattern mentioned above, the ratio of two numbers may also be expressed as percent. The ratio should first be expressed as hundredths and then as a percent. For example, if a student got 32 questions correct on a 40-question quiz, the percent of correct answers would be expressed in the following way:

$$\frac{32}{40} = \frac{8}{10} = \frac{80}{100} = 80\%$$

The third usage of percent, finding the whole amount when a part and the percent are given usually causes students some difficulty, possibly because of the lack of social applications. Such examples as 6 = 30% of ____ do not have many applications. Again, the teacher must demonstrate that the direction, "find a percent of a number" means multiply. Thus:

$$6 = .30 \times \text{\_\_\_\_}$$

Using the already understood relationship of a product to its factors, students may see that

$$\text{\_\_\_\_} = 6 \div .30$$

Some writers use the generalized percentage formula for this work. The formula is usually written:

$$p = b \times r$$

where:

p = percentage or part
b = base or whole
r = rate or percent

The introduction of percents greater than 100 may come in the seventh grade. Students usually wonder how it is possible to have more than all of the whole of something. Percents greater than 100 come about in comparing two numbers or in converting their ratio to a percent. When a smaller number is compared to a larger number, the ratio is less than 1 and the percent is less than 100. When comparing a larger number to a smaller number, the reverse is true. Thus, to compare 32 to 20 results in a ratio of $\frac{32}{20}$, or $\frac{8}{5}$. To convert this to a percentage, the fraction must be expressed in terms of the base 100, thus:

$$\frac{8}{5} = \frac{160}{100} \text{ or } 160\%$$

Thus, 32 is 160 percent of 20.

Some of the uses of percent can be quite confusing to students. For example, raising the price of an item from $20 to $25 represents a 25 percent increase. But reducing the price from $25 back to the original $20 is a 20 percent decrease. That is because of the change of base in the two examples.

Most texts give the teacher a great deal of help in working with percents at the middle- and upper-elementary levels. However, this topic offers many opportunities for local applications. Instead of dealing with price discounts described in a textbook, problem situations can be drawn from the local newspaper. The same holds for problems dealing with tax rates, sports, and many others.

Diagnosis and prescription

Because decimal fractions represent an extension of the place-value concept to fractions, there is a fairly restricted amount of new learning involved in moving to decimal fractions. Consequently, our treatment of this topic will be less detailed than was the case in earlier chapters.

Decimal-fraction concepts

If students understand number structure and the basics of common fractions, they are not likely to encounter major difficulty with the introductory parts of decimal fractions. However, there are certain adjustments involved.

Decimal-fraction structure A basic point of confusion for some students in working with quantities such as .6 or .73 is that no denominator is seen. There is little to be gained by going into a detailed development of this point because our system is simply based upon a convenient practice. However, students should be able to relate .6 with $\frac{6}{10}$ and .73 with $\frac{73}{100}$. This association will demonstrate that the denominator is there but not apparent as with common fractions.

Another aspect of decimal fractions—one that many students discover on their own—is that all of the denominators are ten or powers of ten. Hence, describing a quantity like $\frac{3}{4}$ in decimal fractions requires that it be rewritten as a fraction with a denominator of 10, 100, or 1000.

A widely used diagnostic procedure to test understanding is to have students read decimal fractions aloud. The opposite procedure—having students write decimal fractions from dictation—can also help locate misconceptions. Recently a class of college juniors was asked to read the number 444.444. An amazingly large number read "four four four point four four four." Although this was probably a matter of habit, it could have reflected an actual misconception on the part of some students.

As mentioned earlier, a point of confusion that frequently

arises in work with decimal fractions has to do with a lack of symmetry in such numbers. For example, the first digit to the left of the decimal point of 33.33, is ones whereas the first digit to the right is tenths, and so on with the other digits to the left and right. Explaining that the number is symmetrical around the ones place may help some students, but it may confuse others.

Although many teachers object to the use of "this is the way it is done" in mathematics, a student who has difficulty with the points described above may well become even more confused if high-level mathematical principles are invoked. Because our decimal fraction system is essentially a matter of shifting to a new set of conventions and symbols, there is a place for "this is the way it is done" in this instance.

Associating decimal fractions with common fractions Some students tend to see decimal fractions as a totally new concept. This misconception may arise because of the confusion in terminology mentioned at the beginning of this chapter. In order to minimize confusion, the recommended procedure is to use complete terms—"decimal fraction" and "decimal point."

To locate areas of difficulty regarding the relationships between common fractions and decimal fractions examples like the following can be used:

1. Write each of the following as a common fraction:

    .7 = ‾‾‾‾
    .83 = ‾‾‾‾
    .746 = ‾‾‾‾

2. Write each of the following as a decimal fraction:

    $$\frac{4}{10} = \text{‾‾‾}$$

    $$\frac{7}{100} = \text{‾‾‾}$$

    $$\frac{243}{1000} = \text{‾‾‾}$$

Clarification of misconceptions can make use of geometric figures and related material. However, because the basic difference between $\frac{6}{10}$ and .6 is in the system of symbols used, the correctional work is essentially a matter of emphasizing the meaning of the symbols in both systems.

Renaming one type of fraction as another type Some writers consider the renaming of a common fraction as a decimal fraction (and its inverse) as an operation. However, for our purposes, we consider this process a concept.

When renaming .8 as a common fraction, students simply write it as $\frac{8}{10}$, then reduce it to $\frac{4}{5}$. However, consider the task of changing $\frac{3}{7}$ to a decimal fraction. The problem should be set up in the form of a proportion, $\frac{3}{7} = \frac{\square}{100}$. Using the algorithm for solving a proportion, students should cross-multiply to get 7 $\square$ = 300. Dividing each side of the equation by 7 results in $\square = \frac{300}{7}$, which is approximately 43. The proportion thus reads $\frac{3}{7} = \frac{43}{100}$. The second term can also be written .43 so that, by equivalence $\frac{3}{7}$ = .43. Many students will discover that the procedure really involves dividing 3 by 7 in order to get this result.

Associating decimal fractions with percents In the middle- and upper-elementary grades percent begins to get some attention. Logically, this topic is usually treated in close relationship to decimal fractions. Most students encounter little difficulty in changing .43 to 43%. A diagnostically oriented teacher needs little structured help in locating misconceptions at this point. A work-aloud procedure is usually adequate.

Operations with decimal fractions

For most students, the real "payoff" of decimal fractions, when compared to common fractions, is in the operations. Structurally the decimal-fraction system is an extension of whole-numbers and as a result, operations with decimal fractions generally follow those with whole numbers. Reasonable proficiency in whole-number operations usually means that students are likely to encounter few major difficulties when working with decimal fractions.

Addition There is no significant difference between adding whole numbers and adding decimal fractions. Even when carrying is involved, as with 3.83 + 2.79, students generally proceed as though they were dealing with whole numbers and place the decimal point at the indicated position.

A student who has trouble with the addition of decimal fractions is very likely to be deficient at some other point. Probably the best diagnostic procedure is to have the student do some work-aloud exercises. Logically, these would be exercises that have given him or her trouble. In a large majority of such cases, the difficulties are not with decimal fractions specifically but with more basic whole-number concepts and procedures.

Once the problem is located, corrective work should be undertaken immediately. It may be frustrating for the teacher to learn that work that was supposed to have been learned in the fourth grade is not known in the seventh. But, with a certain amount of practice, most students can be brought up to grade-level work rather quickly.

Subtraction To a large degree the earlier comments about addition are also applicable to subtraction. Students can proceed with the algorithm just as though they were dealing with whole numbers and then place the decimal point after arriving at the difference. Again, a work-aloud procedure can be helpful in isolating specific difficulties.

Students may wonder why, in adding or subtracting decimal fractions, they do not have to be concerned about a common denominator. Of course, in the exercise .8 − .3 they are working with a common denominator—10. To demonstrate this, the teacher should write the problem as $\frac{8}{10} - \frac{3}{10}$. Thus, the concept of common denominator is unchanged; only the system of writing is altered.

Multiplication The difference between common fractions and decimal fractions in the multiplication operation is more apparent than real. The student who is clear on multiplication with whole numbers and multiplication with common fractions is not likely to encounter any major problems with multiplication of decimal fractions.

There are at least three identifiable levels in this operation. The first is multiplying a decimal fraction by a whole number—cases such as 4 × .2. The product is obviously 8, but the question is 8 whats? This can be resolved by writing the .4 as $\frac{4}{10}$. The example can then be worked as $\frac{4}{10} \times 2 = \frac{8}{10}$, which is then written as .8.

The second level involves multiplying one decimal fraction by another, such as .3 × .4. This operation can also be seen as $\frac{3}{10} \times \frac{4}{10} = \frac{12}{100}$ or .12. Another aid to the student is the hundred-chart, mentioned earlier. It can be shown easily that the dimensions .3 and .4 bracket 12 of the 100 cells. This can be expressed as $\frac{12}{100}$ or .12 of the total area. After such exercises students should be ready to state the rule governing the placement of the decimal point in the product, namely, that the number of places "pointed off" in the product is the sum of the number of places "pointed off" in the factors.

This generalization leads logically to the third case, in which two mixed numbers are multiplied. Thus, to multiply 3.2 and 4.6, students should treat these as though they were whole numbers and then locate the decimal point with two places pointed off.

The diagnosis of difficulties in multiplying decimals does not require a structured instrument because most such difficulties are related to basic operations. However, if students miss the correct answers to exercises, and if the teacher listens carefully as the students work aloud on these exercises, the diagnosis will probably be fairly simple. Corrective work on problem areas logically follows.

Division One writer has identified eight types of exercises in division with decimal fractions. However, the points of difficulty are very similar in all these types. The biggest difficulty for most students lies in placing the decimal point in the quotient.

There are several approaches that can be used in dealing with this type of exercise. For example, $.8 \div 4$ could be written as $\frac{8}{10} \div 4$, or $\frac{8}{10} \times \frac{1}{4}$. The solution is $\frac{8}{40}$ or $\frac{1}{5}$, which can be reconverted to $\frac{2}{10}$ or $.2$. Another pattern makes use of the principle that the product of the divisor and quotient must be equal to the dividend. Hence, in $.5\overline{).45}$, the quotient must be 9. Again, the question is, 9 whats; that is, where do we place the decimal point? If, in multiplying back, the product of .5 and 9 equals .45 then the 9 must be .9.

Operationally, the use of the caret is widespread. The exercise above, using this procedure, would be rewritten as $.5\overline{).4.5}$ with quotient $.9$. This system, in effect, uses a common multiplier on dividend and divisor (in this case, 10). That procedure permits work with a whole-number divisor, with consequent simplification.

The recommended diagnostic procedure for students who have trouble in dividing decimal fractions is, again, the work-aloud method. If the student can perform the operation of division with whole numbers, the only new work is in placement of the decimal point in the quotient. Any of the systems described earlier can be used to teach that procedure.

Selected references

BLAIR, GLENN MYERS. *Diagnostic and Remedial Teaching.* New York: Macmillan, 1956.

DUMAS, ENOCH. *Math Activities for Child Development.* Boston: Allyn & Bacon, 1971.

GREEN, GEORGE F., JR. *Elementary School Mathematics.* Lexington, Mass.: Heath, 1974.

GROSSNICKLE, FOSTER, and RECKZEH, JOHN. *Discovering Meanings in Elementary School Mathematics.* New York: Holt, Rinehart and Winston, 1973.

HEDDENS, JAMES W. *Today's Mathematics.* Chicago: Science Research Associates, 1974.

JUNGST, DALE G. *Elementary Mathematics Methods: Laboratory Manual.* Boston: Allyn & Bacon, 1975.

KENNEDY, LEONARD. *Guilding Children to Mathematical Discovery.* Belmont, Calif.: Wadsworth, 1975.

SWENSEN, ESTHER J. *Teaching Mathematics to Children.* New York: Macmillan, 1973.

UNDERHILL, ROBERT. *Teaching Elementary School Mathematics.* Columbus, Ohio: Merrill, 1972.

part V

There are no recipes for solving problems. Anyone who can answer a question by applying a set procedure is not truly dealing with a problem but is, rather, performing an exercise. True problem solving requires that the solver engage in high-level thinking—the kind that does not come easily to anyone. Perhaps that is the reason many people avoid problem solving, whether it be inside or outside the school setting.

Teaching problem solving is a very demanding task, and no chapter on the topic can answer all questions about it. Perhaps some day we will have a clearer picture of the entire process. Until then, we keep trying.

problem solving

Problem solving

13

No matter how varied our aims in teaching arithmetic, the eventual end is problem solving. Although treated as a separate topic in many arithmetic-method textbooks, including this one, problem solving ought to be inherent in the development of each topic in arithmetic. All teachers at every level, including kindergarten, should teach arithmetic topics with the realization that their eventual usefulness is helping individuals solve problems encountered as students, consumers, workers, and citizens.

What is a problem?

One of the most common complaints of teachers of mathematics is that many students who can perform arithmetic calculations very well have great difficulty solving problems. This may seem to be a contradictory statement because, for many people, calculations are essentially problems. The term "problem" in mathematics generally refers to what has been called word problems, story problems, or verbal problems. A *problem* is a situation described in words requiring a quantitative answer. Further, the method or operation by which the answer is derived is not given. Hence, the solution to a problem involves (1) deciding what needs to be done and (2) doing it.

Let us contrast a problem as described and

an exercise. In the example $23 \times 37 = \square$, there are no decisions to be made; the operation is quite clear. Hence, this is an exercise. However, if students are asked how much money they would have if they earned 23 cents one day and 37 cents the next day, they must decide which operation will yield the answer. Therefore, this is a problem.

Why does problem solving give trouble?

Whatever they are called, problems seem to be a mystery to many students. Why do students, many of whom seem to have little difficulty performing arithmetic or algebraic calculations, become bogged down with problems involving these same operations?

There are probably several reasons why problem solving is more difficult than a simple exercise for many students. Problem solving requires complex mental processes involving imagination, abstraction, and association of ideas. One must be capable of developing original schemes because a pattern that solves one problem is not likely to solve many others. Developing original schemes requires quantitative thinking, something many students find rather difficult. Such students would be happy to settle for semiquantitative descriptions, such as large or small, and depend upon others to go beyond this point. Hence, one of the tasks of teachers is to convince students that this unique type of thinking is essential. The best approach seems to be bringing the students into repeated contact with real problem situations that require a quantitative approach.

Abilities needed in problem solving

One strange feature of problem solving is that this ability does not seem to follow any pattern. Some students of outstanding abilities in other areas have great difficulty with problem solving; others of seemingly lesser ability take it in their stride.

Intelligence

Problem solving seems to require a high level of thinking, so that intelligence certainly is of importance. It is generally accepted that there are many factors of intelligence, one of which is quantitative in nature. Thus, it would not be impossible (indeed it is a fairly common occurrence) for a person who has a high level of ability in verbal factors of intelligence to rank considerably lower on non-verbal, or quantitative, factors. Problem solving requires that a student have not only intelligence, but a particular kind of intelligence. What happens if a student is lacking in this respect? Teachers must still attempt to bring him or her to the highest possible level of achievement through skillful, patient teaching.

Reading

Another requirement for solving "word problems" is the ability to read. Paradoxically, many students who are considered good readers have difficulty with problems. This situation arises because there are many types of reading, most of which do not require that a course of action be based upon what is read. Problem solving requires careful, analytical reading that leads to a decision as to what should be done. Some students become quite adept at finding cue words to help them make the decisions (detecting that "at" means "to multiply," for example). Such practices should be discouraged because they defeat the real purpose of problem solving and frequently steer students into errors.

Basic skills

After analyzing a problem situation and deciding what is to be done, there remains the matter of manipulating the numbers involved to arrive at the correct results. Hence, students need to know the fundamental operations. This, however, is usually the easiest part of problem work. One youngster who was a bit confused on terminology complained, "I can solve the problem if someone will tell me what to do."

Teaching problem solving at the primary level

The fact that problem solving requires creative thinking does not mean that the teacher simply assigns problems and leaves students to "sink or swim." Teachers may not actually be able to instruct a student to think logically and creatively, but the methods used in teaching problem solving may lay the groundwork for original thinking. The attitude of the teacher may produce an atmosphere conducive to creativity.

Doubtless many teachers and students would find it convenient to reduce problem solving to a fixed set of steps. Such a procedure, however, would remove the prime ingredient of problem solving. Still, there are certain procedures that aid in problem solving and that can be taught. The approaches suggested below should help youngsters develop the critical thinking necessary in problem solving.

Looking for details

In the primary grades children should be taught to look for important details in pictures and stories. Suppose, for example, that the teacher shows the class a picture in which the central subject is a mother hen tugging at an earthworm while her three baby chicks look on in eager anticipation. There will probably be other items in the picture, but the children should be encouraged to look for important details that help tell the story. The teacher may show the picture, then, placing it out of view, ask such questions as, "What did you see in the picture?" "What was the hen doing?" "What were the chicks doing?" "How many hens were there in the picture?" "How many chicks were there in the picture?" When students learn to write, they may be asked to write a story telling what they saw in the picture. Then, by a reverse procedure, students may be asked to draw a picture depicting the main ideas of a story as told to them by the teacher or one of the students. Not only do students generally enjoy such activities but they also learn to be observant in what they see and hear.

Problems without numbers

Working with problems without numbers enables students to practice making decisions on what is to be done without getting into computation. Such activities can serve to focus attention on the process to be used. The teacher may ask students to react to a story that he or she or one of the other students tells. For example, the teacher may say, "There were several turtles sitting on a log. Some other turtles came and sat on the log with them. Now, how many turtles are on the log?" Reactions will probably range from a puzzled shrug to wild guesses of huge numbers. Eventually students should say that there are simply more turtles after the second group joins the first group. The idea of "more" is one of the objectives. Then the teacher may say, "Yes, this is true, there are more. But, how *many* are there altogether?" Then, with luck, students will say, "We don't know, but if you will tell us how many were on the log in the beginning and how many came and sat by them, we can tell you how many turtles are now on the log." Next question, "How would you find out?" The desired answer is, "We would add." This type of reaction is desirable because it shows that students know what operation is to be performed in this particular case.

Problems without questions

Many teachers use problems without questions as brain teasers. The idea, of course, is to help the student who seems to have difficulty deciding which operation is called for in a given problem. Suppose the teacher writes this problem on the chalkboard: "Jim and Tom went fishing. Jim caught six fish and Tom caught four fish." That's all. Students will no doubt ask, "What is the problem?" The teacher may say, "You ask a question that makes it a problem." Or, the teacher may instruct students to ask a question that makes an addition problem or a subtraction problem of the situation. Such exercises help students develop the habit of analyzing each situation rather than trying to fit every situation to a set pattern.

Problems with superfluous data

Statements containing data that are not a part of the problem may be an aid in helping students at all levels develop the habit of looking for pertinent information. Such problems may begin at the primary level, where the superfluous information may be nothing more than descriptive in nature, such as the colors of items involved in addition or subtraction problems. For example, "Two blue birds and three red birds were perched on a limb. How many birds were on the limb?" A more complex version might be, "Two blue birds and three red birds were perched on a limb. Four black birds were sitting on the fence. How many birds were on the limb?" Now students must select the data appropriate to the question asked.

Teaching problem solving in the middle grades

Problem-solving techniques do not change essentially from grade to grade, only the complexity of the problem encountered. As students learn to solve simple algebraic equations, they gain a new tool for solving problems. A smooth merger of solving equations and problems will give students a reason for studying algebraic equations.

Discussion of the problem

One procedure is "talking through" a problem in order to arrive at a plan for finding a solution. Such strategies usually center around finding appropriate answers to the following questions:

1. What is the question—what is asked for?
2. What data are given?
3. How can the given data be used to find a solution?

The teacher should be an active participant in all discussions of problem solving. However, he or she must not yield to the temptation to tell students how to work the problem. Rather, by asking a sequence of questions, the teacher should help students break down larger concepts into smaller steps. The type of questioning that will help steer students to formulate their own schemes for finding solutions requires a great deal of preparation and patience.

Similar problems

In the search for a solution to a rather difficult problem, analogous but simple problems may be posed as a means of developing a line of thought. This technique is particularly useful at the upper-elementary levels, where problems of increasing complexity are presented.

Drawing a diagram

Many students find that drawing a diagram is helpful in establishing meaningful relationships between variables in certain types of problems. Diagrams are particularly helpful in identifying the role of data in problems involving perimeters, areas, rate, time, and distance.

Translating word phrases into mathematical phrases

In today's elementary schools mathematical equations are introduced very early. At the lower levels, however, the term "sentence" is used instead of "equation." For instance, $3 + 4 = 7$ is called a *sentence,* and $3 + 4 = \square$ is an *open sentence.* In the middle grades (sometimes earlier), the $\square$ may be replaced by a letter such as n or x, resulting in sentences such as $3 + 4 = x$, $3 + x = 7$, or $x + 4 = 7$. Because a sentence must express a complete thought (including a subject and a predicate), $3 + 4$ is not a sentence but a *mathematical phrase.* The ability to translate word phrases into mathematical phrases is an important prerequisite to the solution of certain types of problems. Translation of phrases involving two or more operations may become rather complex. However, certain word phrases may be translated by many pupils in the lower grades. A few examples are:

Word Phrase	Mathematical phrase
Five plus three	$5 + 3$
Eight minus four	$8 - 4$
Three less than nine	$9 - 3$
Five added to four	$4 + 5$
Three times two	3×2
A certain number increased by five	$n + 5$
Four less than a certain number	$n - 4$
Three times a certain number	$3x$
A certain number divided by four	$\dfrac{x}{4}$

Translating such phrases can be fun, and the exercise is a necessary warm-up for translating number sentences into mathematical sentences.

Finding rules

Another approach that has been found helpful in teaching children to solve problems is finding a general statement or rule that expresses the relationship between two sets of numbers. Such exercises can begin in the lower grades if they are kept to an appropriate level of difficulty. An example would be the following:

First number	Second number
2	4
3	6
4	8
n	10
6	n

The question asked with this set of numbers is, "What is done to the first number to get the second number?" It is important that students learn to look for a pattern. In the first line 4 could be 2 + 2, but the next line does not fit this rule of adding two because 3 + 2 is 5 not 6. Consequently, the student must look for another rule. The rule "multiply by 2" obviously applies because $2 \times 2 = 4$, $3 \times 2 = 6$, and $4 \times 2 = 8$. The next step is to think $2 \times n = 10$. What number multiplied by 2 is 10? In the lower grades n may be found intuitively, whereas students in the upper grades may be encouraged to solve such equations as $2 \times n = 10$ by "undoing" what has been done to the "unknown" n. (NOTE: Many authors prefer the term "variable" rather than "unknown.")

Translating problem situations into mathematical sentences

Formulating mathematical sentences of problem situations is very much like translating phrases as described in the previous section. It may be necessary, however, to remind students of the meaning of the phrase "is equal to." In a mathematical sentence the symbol "=" means that the quantity expressed in the phrase preceding the symbol is the same as the quantity coming after the symbol. Students not totally clear on this point are almost sure to have difficulties in translation.

Translating from word sentences to mathematical sentences requires analysis of the situation in terms of the three questions discussed earlier: (1) What is given? (2) What is asked for? and (3) How are the data used to find the answer? Once the pertinent facts are isolated and the question is stated, students must further determine the relationship between the given data and the unknown. As examples, consider the following:

1. Tom had 3 marbles. Maryann gave him 4 more. How many marbles did Tom then have?

    The data given are 3 and 4 marbles.
    The question is, "What is the total?"
    The operation is addition.
    The first phrase is 3 + 4.
    The sentence is $3 + 4 = \boxed{}$.

2. Jack had 10 marbles. He gave Maryann 4 of them. How many marbles did Jack then have?

    The data given are 10 and 4 marbles.
    The question is, "How many are left after 4 are removed?"
    The operation is subtraction.
    The first phrase is 10 − 4.
    The sentence is $10 - 4 = \boxed{}$.

Problems of these types should be introduced by the talking-through technique discussed earlier. Then, with the students working individually, the teacher assigns one problem at a time so that the efforts of each student can be observed as he or she searches for a solution. Letting the students write word sentences from mathematical sentences may also prove to be a valuable exercise. They may profit from making up their own problems and solving them.

Some diagnostic procedures

Although it is impossible to establish a simple diagnostic process for use in problem solving, there are some steps that are available for use in identifying difficulties in this area. Most of these procedures require that the teacher work with an individual student.

Reading

The teacher should start with a problem that would be considered quite easy for the student's age level. The student should be asked to read and explain the problem. Because vocabulary is a common stumbling block, special attention might be given to that area.

Listening

In certain types of problem work listening is of major importance. The same type of problem would be used as was mentioned earlier. The teacher reads the problem to the student. Then, they discuss the content in order to see if the student has "heard" the problem. Again, vocabulary is important.

The question

Discussion in this area would center around what is being sought. The problems used for this purpose should be simple but not completely obvious.

The procedure

Some teachers like to use problem situations without numbers in diagnosing procedural problems. The idea is to focus the student's full attention on the procedure itself. The discussion might include such directions as, "Read this story carefully, think it over, and tell me what you would do first." Probably this method will need to be used a number of times in order to get the student working comfortably with it. The teacher should refrain from asking very many questions while the student is at work on his or her analysis. Such questions constitute a disruption and can also provide useful clues. If the student desires to think aloud during this phase, the teacher should listen carefully. Useful information about the student's thought patterns may emerge.

Classifying data

As a further check on whether the student has developed a usable procedure, a teacher may sometimes use problems with excessive or insufficient data. These can serve a useful purpose but should not be overemphasized. Again, if the student wishes to work aloud, the teacher should give careful attention to what is said. The work-aloud method has real merit in this phase of diagnosis.

Carrying out a procedure

Once the student decides how the problem should be solved, much of the remaining work is in the skills area. The teacher should never assume that this area is "under control" because there is an ever-present danger of retrogression. Hence, the teacher should observe all phases of the operations in problem solving.

Evaluating the result

After the student arrives at a solution, the teacher should discuss with him or her such matters as, "Does this answer make sense?" and "Would you be willing to pay this much for a bike?" If the problem is one that yields a denominate number (8 dollars, 20 pounds, 10 gallons), the student should be clear as to what the units are.

Some remediation methods

There is no "complete" list of remedial procedures for students who have trouble with problem solving. However, some teachers have had a certain degree of success with each of the following:

1. The problems asked of students should be meaningful to those students. Community-based problems are most helpful in this regard. Also, allowing students to write some problems rather than having them work exclusively on the problems written by others stimulates interest.

2. For students who are having difficulty, the simplest possible problems should be used as a start. This means, of course, that grade-level problems would be much too difficult. Student self-confidence is important, and success on an easy problem is much better than failure on a grade-level problem.
3. Regarding the above, the motivating influence of success is well established. Along with this, a word of commendation from the teacher is a valued reward. However, compliments should be used *only* when genuine commendation has been merited. Unearned compliments are self-defeating.
4. As is true of the diagnostic approach generally, remedial work is most effective if it is on target. Hence, it is important that, through use of the procedures described here and others that might be devised, the teacher start remediation after he or she has gained as much information as possible regarding the specific areas of difficulty.

Selected references

COPELAND, RICHARD W. *Mathematics and the Elementary Teacher*. Philadelphia: Saunders, 1976.

HIGGINS, JON L. *A Metric Handbook for Teachers*. Washington, D. C.: National Council of Teachers of Mathematics.

LEFFIN, WALTER W. *Going Metric*. Washington, D. C.: National Council of Teachers of Mathematics, 1975.

OSTERGARD, SUSAN, SILVIER, EVELYN, and WHEELER, BRANDON. *The Metric World: A Survival Guide*. New York: West, 1975.

SCHMINKE, C. W., and ARNOLD, WILLIAM R. *Mathematics Is a Verb*. New York: Dryden Press, 1971.

part VI

measurement and geometry

The heading for this section might seem repetitive because the "metry" in the term "geometry" refers to measurement. However, many types of measurement today, including 5 dollars and 10 kilograms, are not based on geometric concepts.

On the other hand, many concepts of measurement are geometrical—distance, area, and volume among them. Also, many geometric concepts are not necessarily related in any specific way to measuring things.

In this section, again, an effort is made to achieve a degree of balance between methods of teaching and the specific techniques of diagnosis and prescription.

Measurement 14

The process of measurement is vital to us—commercially, scientifically, and personally. Indeed, human progress generally closely parallels the development of systems of measurement. Students who are interested in history can find many fascinating facts related to measurement through the centuries.

Meaning of measurement

A measurement is essentially a description. Indeed, it would be difficult to write a description of an object without the use of quantitative terms. True, such characteristics as color or texture might be described qualitatively, but problems would arise in dealing with size, weight, and certain other traits. Hence, measurement is generally associated with a quantitative description.

Use of standards

Because standards mean little in early childhood, statements such as "I'm bigger than you" are quite adequate. Indeed, in some of the earlier phases of civilization adults used systems that were almost this crude. But trade between neighboring villages became feasible only as systems of measures in these villages became reconciled.

Over a period of many centuries, then,

people developed standards of measurement to meet their needs. There is no reason to believe that this process is complete. Indeed, many units of measurement—the nanosecond, the square micron, and the megahertz among them—are relatively new.

How many units of measurement do we need? Young children need very few, but maturity brings people in contact with an ever-growing assortment of them. For example, measurement of distance for children may involve only the concept of blocks, but as they mature they have to deal with such measures as area, volume, velocity, and others.

Measurement as a process

Three second-grade students set out to measure the width of a desk by using a yardstick. Each measured it in turn, and they came up with widely divergent results. The problem was that not one of the three matched the end of the yardstick with the edge of the desk; the amount of "overhang" varied from three to ten inches. As a mark of misplaced self-confidence, the students got into a noisy argument as to whose results were most accurate. It should be pointed out that this was a perfectly good yardstick; the error was in the way it was used.

Basically, measurement is a process of comparing a known quantity to an unknown quantity. The motive is to arrive at information about the unknown.

The case of the three students illustrates that there are two components that vitally affect the accuracy of a measurement: (1) the accuracy of the measuring instrument and (2) the skill of the persons using the instrument. Human scientific and technological progress has closely paralleled the improvement of instruments and the development of skills in the use of these instruments.

The end product of measurement

Most measures lead to results that are described as denominate numbers. The term "denominate" means "to name," a *denominate number* is thus a named number, or a number associated with a unit. Some examples of denominate numbers are 4 liters, 17 centimeters, and 5 dollars.

Denominate numbers can take on strange characteristics. For example, what is the product of $4 and $3? Some students blithely accept $12 as the answer—until they think about it. It is simply not possible to multiply $4 by $3 and arrive at a meaningful answer.

However, $4 can be multiplied by 3, as in: If you had 3 sets each consisting of $4, how much money would you have? Note that the 3 is sets, not dollars.

On the other hand, it is perfectly feasible to multiply 4 feet by 3 feet, the result being 12 square feet. However, the new unit, square feet, is used to measure area, whereas feet are used to measure distance. Hence, the new unit measures something quite different from that measured by the "parent" units.

To some degree, this same logic applies to division. It is possible to divide $25 by $5 (the measurement situation), but the quotient is 5, not $5. Basically, this answers the question: How many sets, each containing $5, can be taken from $25?

Generally, in operations with denominate numbers, the criterion as to what can—and cannot—be done is: Does the answer make sense? In some cases, as in 4 feet × 3 feet = 12 square feet, the answer does make sense. But, in $4 × $3, can you imagine 12 square dollars?

Teaching measurement

With young children, learning measurement involves a great deal of activity—comparing, estimating, and others. Certainly these youngsters have little interest in the technical aspects of measurement, and there would be no purpose served in having them memorize structure or conversions. Indeed, at this level there is much use of simple comparative terms such as, "Which is the longer pencil?" or "Which of these books is heavier?" Such activities do not lead to a numerical description, but they are quite adequate in the lives of young children. At a higher level the task might be to take a set of sticks and put them in a prescribed order—shortest to longest, for example.

As a special application of rudimentary measurement, many activities can be built around informal measurements using non-standard units. For example, the class might settle on an eraser as their unit and use it in measuring other items within the room.

Systems used

The English system of measures, long dominant in the United States, is not notably logical. For example, in converting from one unit of length to another, conversions of 12 (inches to feet), 3 (feet to yards), 5280 (feet to miles) and other equally difficult units are used. While the rest of the world moved toward a more logical system, namely metrics, the United States clung to the English units. However, legislation at the national level as well as pressure from businesses that are tired of our being "an island in a metric world" are moving us toward the metric system at a fairly rapid rate.

Which system should be taught? The conversion from the English to the metric system will probably require years, even decades. So, for a while, teachers must instruct students in both. However, the systems should be taught as parallel ways of doing the same thing. Little time should be spent on converting from one system to the other.

The feature about the metric system that makes it especially useful is the ease of conversions. For example, the prefix *kilo* means 1000. Thus, a kilogram is 1000 grams. Likewise, a kilometer is 1000 meters. The same holds for all the other prefixes—*milli* meaning one-thousandth, *centi* meaning one-hundredth, and so forth.

Specific measurements

Obviously, developing concepts and skills in measurement is a growth process that extends over a period of time. During that period students move toward (1) more sophisticated types of measures and (2) greater accuracy in measurement.

Distance or length This is probably the simplest of the measurement concepts because students can see what is being measured. The instruments are simple and easy to use as well. Hence, this is often the starting point for work on measurement.

Most of the elementary-mathematics programs provide guidance in a logical and sequential development of distance measures, both metric and English. However, if this work is to be meaningful, it must be developed around activities in which students measure things. Many teachers urge students to estimate distances before they measure them. Certainly students who can arrive at a reasonable estimate of the width of a room before measuring it are demonstrating a high degree of understanding.

Some teachers use student heights as an interesting point of departure in measurement—an activity that certainly arouses student interest. Results can be recorded in both inches and centimeters. Also, because of the rapid growth of young children, the entire cycle can be repeated at regular intervals.

Area Although considerable work in distance measurement precedes the introduction of area, the two concepts are closely related. Many teachers make use of floor tiles, ceiling tiles, and various types of cutouts as teaching materials to try to give meaning to the area concept. For example, a 2-inch square can be covered with four 1-inch squares. Activities of this type also contribute to an understanding of denominate numbers. One youngster, working with the material cited above, discovered that 2 inches × 2 inches = 4 square inches. She pointed out with much excitement that "I multiplied the numbers, then I multiplied the names." Although some technical objections might be raised as to the logic here, she had made a meaningful observation.

Volume The sequence of length-area-volume is a straightforward one. Again, the key to comprehension of volume seems to be activity, that is, having students work with volume measures. Many teachers keep a variety of containers on hand for this purpose, often beginning with the half-pint milk carton from the lunchroom. Again, the English units are difficult to learn because of the irregular conversion factors. However, by beginning with the cubic centimeter and building from it, the units are logical and easy.

Temperature The work on temperature goes as logically with science as with mathematics. The Fahrenheit scale is still widely used, with its reference points at 32° and 212°, so that the freezing point of water and its boiling point are separated by 180°. The centigrade, or Celsius, scale uses 0° and 100° to describe these reference points. Many teachers prefer the term "centigrade" because the prefix *centi* describes the division of the scale into 100 parts. However, the usage "Celsius" is also common.

Again, students should work with some thermometers in their study of temperature. This is much more effective than to have the students look at pictures of thermometers in a textbook or just read about them. Also, students should not be burdened with the tedious task of making extensive conversions of readings from one scale to the other.

Time Many students have trouble in their work in time measurement. One reason doubtless lies in the fact that time is abstract, especially when compared to concepts such as length. Further, young children see little reason for adults' concern regarding time-related matters. To add to the difficulty, our system of time measurement is quite complex (utilizing such terms as A.M. and P.M., time zones, daylight time, and others). The system makes major use of 60 as a conversion factor until one reaches the hours of the day and the days of the year. The fact that months vary in length is confusing. Perhaps widespread usage of digital clocks and watches will help in the mechanics of reading time, but the concepts are still difficult.

It is important that teachers bring students into frequent contact with time measurement. Many activities are feasible. For example, in most communities students love to bring nonoperating alarm clocks from home to use in class games. Also, rubber stamps for producing clock dials are available from supply houses. Perhaps of equal importance is the simple matter of time consciousness —the time until lunch, a 10-minute visit, getting to school on time, and other matters of this sort.

Weight In some schools, student height and weight are entered on records and reports. Many teachers make the compiling of this information a major teaching–learning experience.

Weight measures are fairly easy to conceptualize, but again, the English system is complex because of the conversion process. In the metric system the usual set of prefixes is used, this time combined with grams. The best known measures are the kilogram (1000 grams) and the milligram ($\frac{1}{1000}$ gram).

Many teachers make use of simple balances, often improvised, to add meaning to the measurement process. In fact, so simple a mechanism as a wire coat hanger can serve fairly well, and a small-scale version of the seesaw is even better. Again, the most effective way for a student to learn the measurement of weight is to work with it.

Others There are many other types of measurement-related work in elementary schools. For example, our system of money involves understanding equivalencies (1 dime = 10 cents, for example). However, inflation has proved that there is nothing absolute about a dollar.

Some derived units are encountered in elementary-mathematics programs. These might include speed, density, and others. However, such units do not represent anything that is basically new or different and thus give little trouble to those students who are clear on the components. For example, 50 miles per hour is not likely to cause trouble for the student who understands miles and hours.

Diagnosis in measurement

Although work in measurement does not break down into a clear-cut set of components, there is still a place for the diagnostic approach. Two phases of student work are actually involved in this area: (1) compiling data through use of a sequenced set of activities and (2) interpreting the data. To a considerable degree, these parallel the combination of performance and product.

The activity phase

When students are working at the task of measurement, there are several areas of observation by means of which the teacher can locate problems.

Are they Inaccurate? If students engaged in measurement consistently arrive at results that are grossly inaccurate, they are almost certainly doing something wrong. There is no limit to the number of possibilities. However, the observant teacher can usually determine the difficulty by close attention to students at work.

Do they frequently fumble? Anyone is likely to be inefficient upon first contact, but this should be a transitional phase. Often, students who fumble a great deal in carrying out a measurement are stalling in the hope that the teacher will go elsewhere. This, in turn, probably means a lack of understanding of the process involved.

Are they satisfied with unreasonable results? One student recorded the length of a classroom table as 150 meters—and insisted he was right! Actually, the table was 150 centimeters (1.5 meters) in length. Obviously he had a complete misconception as to the length of a meter.

Can they explain results? Students who are clear as to what they are doing should be able to explain it to others. The inability to do so indicates a problem area.

The interpretation phase

Meaningful measurement usually starts with activity but leads into seat work. There are several symptoms of difficulty observable in this phase.

Can they supply units in their answer? A student once measured a book cover as 5″ × 8″. Then she multiplied to get the area, which she listed simply as 40. She got quite disturbed when the teacher told her the answer was incomplete. A few minutes of in-

194 Measurement and Geometry

struction concentrating on the problem area cleared up the difficulty.

Do they try impossible combinations? One student measured a rectangle to find its perimeter. He came up with readings of 1½ feet plus 1½ feet plus 10 inches plus 10 inches, for a perimeter of 23, no unit of measurement specified. Through careful questioning, the teacher led this student to see the fallacy of the procedure used. However, until this was done, the student was quite content with his answer.

Do they accept impossible results? This problem is quite similar to the earlier ones. Even college students occasionally accept measurement data or computations based on such data that fall far short in terms of logic. The student who multiplied $5 by $4 to get a product of $20 is a case in point.

Basically, the diagnostic process in measurement centers around the same approaches that apply in many other phases of work. Students should be given a variety of tasks, and they should be observed closely as they work. Teachers should then give careful scrutiny to the products (papers, reports, and others) of their work and, having located difficulties, make an effort to correct them.

Geometry

Geometry is one of the oldest studies in mathematics. For thousands of years people have studied the characteristics and properties of geometric figures in order to make them more useful and more beautiful. Arranging geometric figures to make patterns pleasing to the eye is an age-old practice in the arts. Using models of figures to achieve strength in structures is probably as old as designing. One has only to view the pyramids of Egypt to realize that 5000 years ago the study of geometric design was fairly well developed.

Until a very short time ago geometry was generally considered to be a high-school topic, usually taught at the tenth- or eleventh-grade level. With the introduction of the new math in the early 1960s, many geometry topics began to be included in elementary-school textbooks. Even the curricula of the primary grades include geometry topics of a very informal nature.

There are several reasons for the introduction of geometry in the elementary-school curriculum. The study of geometric ideas allows pupils to analyze the physical world around them. Also, it provides an opportunity for a change of pace that may generate a new interest in the study of mathematics. Geometry is a new field of mathematics for primary-grade pupils. It can, with a little effort and imagination on the part of the teacher, be made very exciting for the young.

Early exposure to geometry can provide a

foundation for basic concepts and vocabulary necessary for the continued study of mathematics. Equally as true geometry in the elementary school can be as practical for the pupils who may drop out of school as for those who plan to go on to college.

At one time geometry meant earth measurement. Indeed the necessity of locating boundaries that had been obliterated by flooding probably was the mother of the study of geometry. Today, however, the study of geometry has a much broader meaning. *Geometry* may be defined as the study of the ideas of points, lines, curves, planes, and space. Although this statement is probably an oversimplification, it at least gives us a point of departure for discussion.

When geometry is closely associated with the process of measurement, it is called *metric geometry*. In this study pupils compute the perimeters, areas, and volumes of certain geometric figures. The approach can be very practical for pupils interested in almost any pursuit and is thus fairly common in the curricula of the middle and upper grades.

Geometry may be treated as a *deductive science*, which refers to a study built on a series of theorems based on undefined terms and unproved axioms. This very formal approach is found in the high-school curriculum, very often as an elective for pupils planning further study in the field of mathematics.

Neither of these approaches should be found in the primary grades. At this level attention should be directed to selected geometric properties of objects familiar to the student—properties that do *not* depend on measurement or a formal deductive system. This is not to say that logical thinking is to be omitted; on the contrary, logical thinking about the ideas presented is encouraged. The study of geometry at the primary level provides a marvelous opportunity for pupils to explore, experiment, and discover new ideas. At the same time they are encouraged to formulate reasonably precise statements and logical conclusions.

Building on preschool concepts

Children develop many ideas concerning geometry during their preschool years. From a very early age most children have experiences involving concepts of lines, angles, shapes, inside versus outside, similarity, and many other geometric ideas. For example, children understand the idea that a ball is round and that their toy train goes around the track. They see that the building blocks with which they construct things have sharp corners and edges. They see, too, that square objects such as blocks "fit together" better than balls or marbles. Many children learn very early that structures made of sticks must touch the floor at a minimum of three points in order to stand up, and that three straight sticks of similar length, when tied together at the top, will furnish the skeleton for a tepee (the tripod principle).

These preschool ideas form the basis for building geometric ideas at an early age. The idea of play can continue to some degree while at the same time proper terminology and principles are being introduced. In modern classrooms children can be taught a great deal of geometric terminology incidentally by using various models of geometric figures to represent sets and space holders. Figure 15.1 provides an example of one such model.

To establish a one-to-one correspondence between set A and set B, the triangles in sets A and B have been located in the regions bounded by the rectangles. Referring to the figures by their proper names helps pupils develop an association between the figures and their names. At this early stage no reference is made to properties of the figures. This comes later. Another example is seen in the use of models in arithmetic sentences such as $3 + 4 = \square$, $4 + \square = 7$, $\square + 5 = 8$. The space holders can be referred to by name (as squares or rectangles), thus establishing an association between the figure and its name.

Picture puzzles may be developed into vehicles for teaching the names of shapes and ideas about congruence. The pieces to be placed in the proper cutouts are in the shape of various geometric figures—triangles, rectangles, circles, squares, and others. By writing the names of the figures in the spaces where the shapes are to be fitted, pupils associate names and shapes. Ideas of congruence may also develop out of students' efforts to match like shapes as they fit pieces to fill out the picture. Almost all children enjoy piecing together picture puzzles. Thus, motivation is built into the activity automatically. Puzzles of this type may be constructed by cutting the various geometric figures from a picture that would be of interest to children. The pieces formed are then traced on a piece

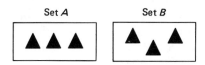

Figure 15-1. Sets in
one-to-one correspondence

of cardboard, which acts as a map to which the pieces must be fitted. Each piece has a proper place on the carboard, which can be inscribed at the proper place with the name of the figure that fits.

Another activity usually enjoyable to children is that of identifying shapes by the feel of models that cannot be seen by them. This may be accomplished in several ways. The child may wear a blindfold, reach into a box, or have the models placed in his or her hands from behind. This activity has a further advantage in that it helps the pupil develop concepts through another sense—that of touch.

Basic concepts

The study of geometry, as noted above, is generally built on ideas of point, line, plane, space, and curves. These ideas are abstract in that they cannot be seen, felt, or in any way experienced directly through any of the usual five senses. Ideas are developed, however, through studying models of these concepts—models that are concrete and common objects that students see or feel in their everyday experiences. These experiences are the building blocks of geometric knowledge. Abstract ideas should be developed as they are needed for further study of a formal nature.

Point

Abstractly, a *point* is a position in space, although it occupies no space and thus has no dimensions. It is an abstraction of a fixed position. In a formal study no attempt is made to define point; it is simply accepted as an undefined entity. The dot made by a pencil or a piece of chalk represents a point and may be called a point. It is not necessary to belabor the notion that a point cannot actually be seen. Young children need the idea of point as a basis for discussion of further topics, but they are not yet mature enough to properly grasp abstract ideas of things unseen.

Most children have, by the time they reach the upper-elementary grades, matured mathematically to the stage where abstract ideas have some meaning. At that stage, teachers may say that the idea of a point in geometry is merely "suggested" by the dot on a piece of paper or on the chalkboard. A dot represents a point in that it indicates approximately a location in space.

Pupils should be encouraged to represent points. An interesting exercise for primary-school children is that of diminishing the size of the dot that represents a point. The idea, of course, is to show that even the smallest dot is big enough to represent several points. By doing this, children gradually get the idea that a point actually has no size but is instead an abstract thing.

Line

Geometric lines, like points, are abstract entities. These abstract ideas are not for children in the primary grades. For very young children important properties of lines may be discussed without getting into deep discussions of abstract ideas. Certainly teachers should not try to define or describe lines in any detail. Lines may be discussed as they are represented by the intersection of the ceiling and a wall of the room, the edge of a table or block, the cracks between floor tiles, or simply a "line" drawn on the board.

A line, as discussed in the primary grades, is understood to be straight and of a definite length. Little is accomplished by continually reminding children that the line extends indefinitely because they probably do not understand the meaning of indefinite. The idea of straight, which is probably somewhat nebulous even among adults, can be discussed with young children by employing line segments. One way is to mark two spots on the floor and ask pupils to walk along a path that represents the shortest distance. Two points marked on the chalkboard may furnish an even better model because they are probably more visible. One game to play with this model is to ask pupils to draw the shortest path and some longer paths. The teacher may eventually tell students that the shortest path lies along a line and that the line between the two points, including the points, is called a *line segment*. Although some mathematicians may be offended, it is probably easier and more expedient to study line segments before considering lines.

Another exercise that demonstrates certain properties of the line segment is that of stretching a string from one point to another. The string is attached at point A and draped loosely between points A and B on the chalkboard or felt board. Pulling the string taut makes it lie along a "straight line." It can also be pointed out that there is some string beyond point B, demonstrating that the straight path is shorter than another path. The question then to be considered is: "Is it the shortest path between A and B?"

One other representation of a line segment is the mark drawn along a ruler's edge between two points on paper or chalkboard (see Figure 15-2). Two points A and B may be connected by placing a ruler so that both points touch an edge. The chalk or pencil mark drawn along the edge from point A to point B describes the line segment AB. Pupils in the middle and upper grades may under-

Figure 15-2. Line segment

stand that the line segment exists independently of the chalk mark. If the mark were erased, the segment would remain. The segment includes both points A and B and is said to be "determined" by A and B. By repeating the exercises done in earlier grades (stretching string and determining the path of shortest distance between two points), the teacher may conclude that two points determine a line segment (or line). The symbol for the line segment determined by the points A and B is $\overline{AB}$. Care should be taken to refer to *the* line segment $\overline{AB}$, which implies that there is only one such segment.

If the segment $\overline{AB}$ is extended indefinitely in both directions, the result is a straight line, as is shown in Figure 15-3. Its symbol is $\overleftrightarrow{AB}$. To make the distinction between a line segment and a line the mark is extended slightly beyond each of the points A and B, as it is done in Figure 15-3, and an arrow is drawn indicating that the extensions never stop. The *line* is an infinite set of points that can never be wholly represented in a drawing because of the drawing's limited nature. At this point in the development of the concept, pupils must use their imagination, which, as will be indicated by open discussion, is itself rather unlimited. Such discussions often include remarks such as, "But everything must end somewhere." To the sophisticated teacher, the statement may sound somewhat immature, but further reflection may reveal that it is actually an astute observation. In the students' physical world everything seems to have an end. The teacher may help pupils develop some insight into the unlimited nature of abstract ideas by asking, "Is there a greatest counting number?" There is, of course, no greatest counting number, for any such imagined number increased by one yields a still greater number. The same may be said of a line. Any line segment drawn may be extended by simply continuing the mark representing the line.

Figure 15-3. Line

After students have learned these basic concepts, certain properties of points and lines may be developed. Consider point A in Figure 15-4. Students may be asked, "How many lines can be drawn through point A?" Pupils enjoy such challenges. Some of the

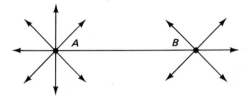

Figure 15-4. Two points determine a line

more enthusiastic will continue drawing lines until the area sur-
rounding the dot (point) is penciled in solidly. Others will conclude
much earlier that there is no limit to the number of lines containing
the point A.

The exercise can be extended by considering two points A and
B, and asking the question, "How many lines can be drawn that
pass through both points A and B?" Obviously, many lines can be
drawn through A and many lines can be drawn through B, but only
one line can be drawn through both A and B. This exercise teaches
students two very important properties of lines: (1) that any two
lines intersect at exactly one point, or, that the intersection of two
lines determines a point; and (2) that if two distinct points are
given, one and only one line contains both points.

Ray

A *ray* is the part of a line from any given point in one direction from
that point. Figure 15-5 represents a ray. Using the labels on this figure, its symbol is $\overrightarrow{AB}$. There is one and only one end point, in this
case, the point A. In the symbol $\overrightarrow{AB}$ the first letter designates the
end point of the ray and the second letter designates the direction.
Many rays may be considered to be contained in one line. For ex-
ample, in Figure 15-5 there are $\overrightarrow{AB}$ and $\overrightarrow{BC}$ among others. One
method of developing ideas concerning designation of rays is to
name several points on a given line and have the pupils name as
many rays as possible relative to the name points.

Rays are probably not as familiar to the pupil as points and
lines, but they are necessary when discussing angles. One everyday illustration of rays can be seen in light rays emanating from a
source such as a flashlight or the sun.

Figure 15-5. A ray

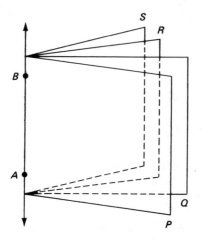

Figure 15-6. A line in several planes

Planes

Another geometric concept that, in its first presentation, need not be explained abstractly is the plane. Any flat surface may serve as a model of the plane. Within the classroom there are desk tops, chalk-boards, walls, floor, ceiling, and window panes. In the primary grades the limitation of these models should not cause objections. In the upper grades, however, it should be pointed out that only a small portion of the plane is represented by any model.

The infinite nature of lines will probably have already been taken up prior to the discussion of the infinite nature of planes. Teachers may therefore point out that if any portion of a line is con-tained in a plane, the entire line is contained in the plane. They may also note that even though we speak of a line in a plane, a line may be thought of as being in many planes. Figure 15-6 illustrates this. Line $\overleftrightarrow{AB}$ obviously lies in planes P, Q, R, and S. In fact, many students will discover that $\overleftrightarrow{AB}$ represents the intersection of the planes P, Q, R, and S. In a crude manner, the pages of an open book represent intersecting planes. A model of intersecting planes may be constructed of poster paper or construction paper.

Curves

A *plane curve* is any figure that can be represented by a mark beginning at a certain point and proceeding to another point without picking up the marking instrument. The path thus described may cross and recross itself, wandering about at the pleasure of the designer.

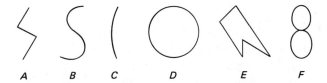

Figure 15–7. Plane curves

Several types of curves are represented in Figure 15-7. The important distinction students must learn is that between open curves and closed curves. A *closed curve* is a plane curve represented by a figure that can be drawn without retracing and with the marking instrument stopping at the same point from which it started. An open curve, of course, does not fulfill these two conditions.

Some closed curves are called "simple closed curves." A *simple closed curve* divides a plane into two distinct regions—interior and an exterior. Students should be able to pick out points that are interior and points that are exterior, that is, points that are on the inside and those that are on the outside. Curves A, B, D, and F in Figure 15-8 are simple closed curves. Each of these figures divides the plane into two distinct regions. Curves C and E do not divide the plane into two distinct regions and are thus not considered simple closed curves. A simple closed curve never crosses itself anywhere. Thus, the interior of a simple closed curve may be colored in without crossing the curve at any point with a crayon.

There are many interesting exercises that may help pupils make the distinction between simple closed curves and closed curves not so classified. One such exercise begins with a sheet of paper on which are drawn several simple and nonsimple closed curves. Pupils must color the simple closed curves. In another exercise, pupils draw and label both types of closed curves. Once their drawings are completed, selected specimens may be shown and explanations given as to why each curve is classified as simple or nonsimple. Polygons and circles are the simple closed curves most familiar to elementary pupils.

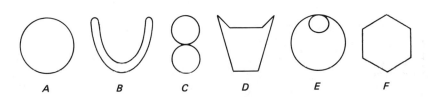

Figure 15–8. Simple and nonsimple closed curves

Polygons

If a simple closed curve is the union of three or more line segments, it is called a *polygon.* Polygons are named according to the number of segments involved. Those polygons having three segments are called *triangles,* and those with four segments are called *quadrilaterals.* Names for all other polygons are made up from the Greek word for the number of segments followed by the suffix "gon." Thus, a polygon of five segments is called a *pentagon,* one of six a *hexagon,* and one of eight an *octagon.* These are the more common polygons, but names for many more may be found in a good glossary of geometric terms.

Having pupils classify polygons just for the sake of classification serves little purpose. In the study of metric geometry, however, such knowledge may be very useful. Classification may be made more palatable if the approach is on an informal basis. A case in point is quadrilaterals. Instead of beginning with a taxonomy to be memorized, teachers can choose two quadrilaterals, such as those shown in Figure 15-9, and ask students such questions as:

In what ways are Figures *A* and *B* alike?
In what ways are Figures *A* and *B* different?
What generalization may be made?

Each student should have a chance to discover differences and similarities and perhaps make some generalization as to the relationship between the two figures.

Metrics of polygons Metric geometry, as noted above, involves measuring the distance around plane figures, the surface of plane figures, and the volume of space figures. The study has a twofold purpose. First, it is a practical study in that almost everyone, at one time or another, has a need for such knowledge. Second, it furnishes a vehicle for practice in arithmetic. In elementary mathematics the concepts of a polygon's perimeter and its area are studied.

The distance around a plane figure is called its *perimeter,* and it is expressed in linear measure. Commonly, students begin the study of perimeters with rectangles and triangles. The perimeter is

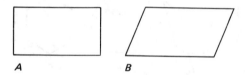

A   *B*

Figure 15-9. Two quadrilaterals

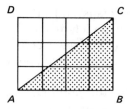

Figure 15–10. Finding the
areas of polygons

the sum of the measures of the sides of a polygon. Students should *not* be given a formula for finding this measurement but should be led, instead, to discover that any two or more sides of equal lengths in a figure may call for multiplication as a shortcut to addition. Such discovery is part of the rationale for the study of geometric figures in the elementary school. Also, the introduction of formulas for perimeters and areas often leads to confusion as to which formula applies in a given situation.

The measurement of the surface of a plane figure is called its *area*. This is a rather difficult concept for many elementary students. In the lower grades it is a good idea to make use of unstandardized units. For example, students could find how many small squares it takes to cover a given rectangle. If each small square is 1 inch on each side, it is called a *square inch*. This is a new type of measurement which can be very exciting for young students. Finding the number of squares in a rectangle such as the one in Figure 15-10 gives students a new motive for multiplication and is an excellent way of demonstrating the fact that multiplication is indeed a shortcut to addition.

It is not particularly difficult to demonstrate the method for finding the area of a triangle. Consider the triangle ABC in Figure 15-10. It can be shown that there are exactly half as many small square units in triangle ABC as in the rectangle $ABCD$, which has the same length and width as the triangle. The area of the rectangle $ABCD$ is 4×3; therefore, the area of the triangle ABC is $\frac{1}{2}(4 \times 3)$, or $\frac{1}{2}(12)$. Again, it is a good idea to be very slow about giving the students formulas. Ideally, they would discover generalizations deductively.

The circle

The circle is one of the more interesting examples of the simple closed curve. Because of its beautiful symmetry and interesting properties, the circle has intrigued mathematicians and artisans throughout the ages. The circle is a plane figure, which means that all points of a circle are in a common plane. In set language a *circle* is defined as a set of points in a plane equidistant from a given point called the center.

The circle in Figure 15-11 has as its center the point O. Any line segment having the point O as one end point and any point on the circle as its other end point is called a *radius*. All radii of any given circle are of equal length, thus satisfying the condition set forth in the definition. In Figure 15-11, $\overline{OA}$, $\overline{OC}$, and $\overline{OB}$ are radii of the circle.

Any line segment that has end points as points on a circle and that has the center of the circle as a point is called a *diameter*. In Figure 15-11, $\overline{CA}$ is a diameter of the circle. The length of the diameter is twice that of a radius and determines the size of the circle. Thus, the longer the diameter, the larger the circle.

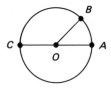

Figure 15–11. A circle

When students begin the study of the properties of circles, they should be encouraged to draw and measure many diameters of given circles. The objective of this exercise is to underscore two facts: (1) that there is no limit to the number of diameters that may be drawn in a given circle; and (2) that all diameters of the given circle are of equal length. A similar exercise may be carried out with radii.

Constructing circles using the compass is another useful exercise in showing that all radii of a given circle are equal. Students should discover that the distance between the point on the compass and the point that describes the circle is constant because the compass is held rigid. If there is not a chalkboard compass available, a piece of string tied to a piece of chalk makes an excellent compass and has an advantage in that the piece of string represents the line segment (the radius) visibly.

Metrics of the circle There are many properties of the circle, but the circumference and perhaps area are the ones usually studied at the elementary level. Like the perimeter of a polygon, the *circumference of a circle* is the distance around the figure. One of the most interesting properties of the circle is the relationship between the circumference and the diameter, expressed as a constant called *pi*. This property should be discovered by pupils in an inductive manner. One way to begin this study is with a piece of string and a round can or other circular object. The children should measure the distance around the can using the string or measuring tape. The diameter is then measured and the two measures compared. The procedure should then be repeated using a larger or smaller can. By keeping a record of such measures, students will have the necessary data to demonstrate to themselves that the circumference of a circle—any circle—divided by its diameter yields pi as a fixed value.

Angles

In the language of sets an *angle* may be defined as the union of two rays that have a common end point but that are not parts of the same line. In Figure 15-12, $\overrightarrow{BA}$ and $\overrightarrow{BC}$ have end point B in common and thus may be defined as an angle. The common end point is called the *vertex* of the angle. The symbol for angle is $\angle$, which is itself an angle. Angles are named by using the names of three points on the angle, one point on each ray and the vertex. The letter naming the vertex is placed between the names of the points on the rays. For example, in Figure 15-12, the angle may be named angle *ABC* or angle *CBA*, but not angle *BAC* or *CAB*.

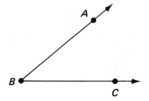

Figure 15-12. An angle

An angle divides a plane into two regions, referred to as the interior and exterior of the angle. In Figure 15-13, point *D* is in the interior of angle *ABC*, and point *E* is in the exterior. Sometimes it is not clear which region should be considered the interior of a given angle. There are, after all, two possibilities for designating interiors and exteriors of the angle *ABC*. For elementary pupils this point should not be emphasized, but it does present a good opportunity

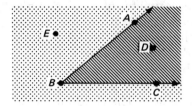

Figure 15-13. Designating an interior
and exterior angle

for some work in exploration. The teacher may ask pupils to try to discover ways of defining angle *ABC* so there could be no question of intent. Some authors draw a curved arrow from one ray to the other designating the interior of the angle. Another method of designation is that of shading the interior or exterior of the angle (or both as is done in our illustration).

Students should be encouraged to locate angles in the classroom. The teacher should pay particular attention to angles that are special examples, such as right angles and obtuse angles.

Angles are compared according to magnitude, which is also, in a sense, the shape of the angle. This is a difficult concept for many pupils. One method for developing the concept begins with an illustration like the one in Figure 15-14. An extensive series of activities (identifying the smallest angle, largest angle, and others) can be built around this figure.

Another method of showing angle shapes is to let the edges of scissors be models for the two sides of an angle. Different angles can be shown by opening and closing the scissors. Another good model may be found in a chalkboard compass. Pupils should draw several angles and compare them as to magnitude.

One method for laying the groundwork for measurement of angles begins with four right angles drawn on a piece of poster

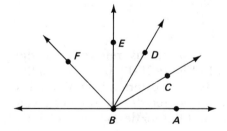

Figure 15-14. Comparing angles

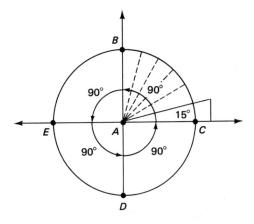

Figure 15-15. Measuring angles

paper. Models of a portion of the interior of an angle of 15° should be cut from a piece of cardboard and used as units for measurement. Students can then explore the question, "How many of these models would it take of fill the region that is the interior of angle *BAC*?" By placing six such models as shown in Figure 15-15, the interior of angle *BAC* is filled. Students can then be asked how many models it would take to fill the four angles *BAC, CAD, DAE,* and *EAB.* If they seem agreeable, students might also try making models of different sizes and determining how many are needed to fill the regions. Although the original units of measure should be the students' own, later work can show that one such unit which is used as a standard is $\frac{1}{90}$ of the region *BAC* and $\frac{1}{360}$ of the total region. The term degree and its symbol can then be introduced, and pupils can begin learning to use a protractor to find the measure of angles. After some general class instruction, each pupil should practice measuring angles at his or her own desk. This work should be very closely observed by the teacher to ascertain that each pupil is making proper use of the protractor with a certain degree of accuracy. This is still another application of the diagnostic point of view.

Some special angles Angles, as noted above, are classified according to magnitude. Such classification is very useful in both formal studies and everyday conversation. In Figure 15-16 angle *BAC* is a right angle. The measure of angle *BAE* is obviously less than that of the right angle *BAC.* Any angle having $\overrightarrow{AB}$ as one of its sides, *A* as its vertex, and another side with a point that falls in the

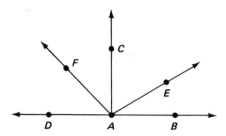

Figure 15–16. Special angles

interior of *BAC* is an angle that measures less than 90° and greater than 0°. Such angles are called *acute angles*. After drawing several such angles themselves, students might then be asked, "How many such angles may be drawn?" Many children will name some number that they consider to be of great magnitude such as 100, 1000, or 1,000,000. It should be pointed out that if 100 are drawn then 101, 102, 103, and so forth could surely be drawn, by using a pencil having an increasingly finer point. Such questioning will help pupils develop some ideas concerning things that are not finite.

Figure 15-16 is also useful in bringing angles like *BAF* to students' attention. Obviously, angle *BAF* is greater in measure than the right angle *BAC*. Such an angle is called *obtuse* because its measure is greater than 90° but less than 180°.

Students should have some practice in identifying and drawing all of these types of angles. Again, a "diagnostic eye" should be sharply focused on their work.

Congruence

Until a few years ago "congruence" was a term used in high-school geometry to describe an equivalence relationship that may exist between two polygons, usually triangles. In modern classrooms *congruence* is used in much the same way that "is equal to" was used a few years ago, namely, to describe an equivalence relationship between two line segments, two angles, or any two figures.

Two line segments are said to be congruent if they have equal measures. Any two polygons are congruent if they are of equal size and have the same shape. In the elementary grades congruence is best demonstrated by cutout models of figures being compared. For example, two triangles are congruent if, when one is placed on top of the other, corresponding vertices and sides coincide.

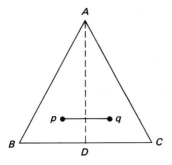

Figure 15-17. Symmetry

Symmetry

A figure exhibits *symmetry* if it has two matching halves that are mirror images of each other. Lines, points, or planes may be said to be symmetrical. The idea of symmetry may be demonstrated by folding an isosceles triangle so that the crease forms a line segment between the vertex A and midpoint D of the base BC, as shown in Figure 15-17. The triangle ABC is symmetrical with respect to the line segment $\overline{AD}$. It can be shown that for any point p in triangle ACD, there is a point q in triangle ABD such that $\overline{pq}$ is perpendicular to $\overline{AD}$ and the distances from p to $\overline{AD}$ and q to $\overline{AD}$ are equal.

Elementary students will usually develop their own description of symmetry such as, "It looks the same on each side of a line." They should be encouraged to try the folding technique with figures such as squares, rectangles, and circles.

Similarity

Many very practical principles of mathematics are based upon the idea of similarity. Figures are *similar* if they have like shapes. Thus, all circles are similar, all squares are similar, and all equilateral triangles are similar. There are many ways of demonstrating similarity. The concentric circles and triangles shown in Figure 15-18 are one way.

Figure 15-18. Similar figures

Film projectors are marvelous instruments for demonstrating similarity. For this demonstration the screen should be a piece of poster paper or other material that may be marked. With the projector and screen at a given distance apart, a figure (preferably a geometric figure) can be projected upon the screen and the outline of it marked with a crayon-type pencil. By changing the distance between the screen and the projector, figures of varying size but the same shape as our original one may be outlined.

Perpendicular lines

Two lines are *perpendicular* if their intersection forms adjacent angles that are of equal measure (congruent).

In Figure 15-19 angle *BOC* and angle *AOC* are equivalent angles. Earlier in the discussion it was indicated that a complete revolution encompassed 360°. It can be shown that one-half of that, or angle *BOA*, is 180°. If angle *BOC* + angle *AOC* = 180°, and if angle *BOC* is equal in measure to angle *AOC*, then angle *BOC* = 90° and angle *AOC* = 90°. An angle that measures 90° is a *right angle*. Also, $\overline{CD}$ is said to be perpendicular to $\overline{AB}$.

A very rewarding experience can sometimes begin with the teacher challenging pupils to describe the manner in which $\overline{CD}$ intersects $\overline{AB}$. Some of the comments that may be heard are: "They meet squarely," "They meet at square corners," or "They form squares." Most of the comments coming from elementary children concerning perpendicular lines do involve the word "square." Although the term as applied to perpendicular lines is not mathematically sound, it does seem to describe the relationship rather aptly. And, most dictionary definitions indicate that perpendicular means "that which meets to form square corners."

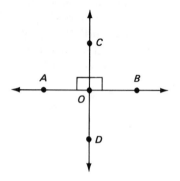

Figure 15-19. Perpendicular lines

Pupils should attempt to draw lines that are perpendicular. Also, the identification of perpendicular lines in the classroom or on the playground can be a good activity.

Parallel lines

Parallelism is a very important concept in the study of geometry. There are many ways of defining parallel lines, depending upon the level of sophistication. Younger students will find acceptable the time-honored definition, of *parallel lines* as "two lines in a plane that never intersect." In discussing the concept, teachers may bring out the fact that at any point the distance between the two lines, measured on a line perpendicular to the lines, is equal to that at any other point.

There are many models of parallel lines that students see every day. Among the more familiar models are lines on ruled paper, curbs on a street, and seams in the floor tile. It is interesting to have students construct parallel lines and observe the manner in which they go about it. Some will draw one line and then the other by sight. Others may draw one line and then try to find two points of equal distance from the line that will determine a parallel. The latter method, of course, indicates some understanding of parallelism.

Space figures

Space figures, sometimes called "solid figures," are those that are three dimensional. Reviewing the major concepts discussed up to this time, the following hold true:

1. A point has no dimensions.
2. A line has one dimension: length.
3. A plane has two dimensions: lengths and width.
4. A space figure has three dimensions: length, width, and depth.

In the language of sets, space is the set of all points.

There are many examples of space figures. However, the more common ones, shown in Figure 15-20, are the triangular prism, cube pyramids (triangular and rectangular), the cylinder, and the cone.

A term that has become very familiar in modern mathematics classes is "polyhedron." *Polyhedrons* are space figures formed by portions of plane surfaces called "faces." The two general types of polyhedrons studied in the elementary grades are prisms and pyramids. *Prisms* are polyhedrons having two parallel and congruent

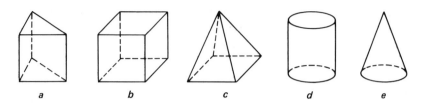

Figure 15–20. Space figures

faces, or bases. These bases may be triangles, rectangles, and so on. The shape of the base gives the prism its name. For instance if the bases are triangles, the figure is a triangular prism; if they are squares, it is a square prism; and so on. In Figure 15-20, *a* is a triangular prism, whereas the cube in Figure 15-20*b* is a square prism.

Pyramids and cones intrigue some elementary students because of their historical and modern references—the pyramids of Egypt and cones from the ice-cream parlor. Students can see that pyramids have bases that are some type of polygon and faces that are always triangles. The cone always has a circular base. Inspection of these figures by sight and feel accompanied by a group discussion is probably one of the most worthwhile activities. Further study may be done through actual construction to demonstrate certain properties. It is doubtful that a study of the metrics of such figures should be made in the elementary grades except for the advanced student.

Diagnosis

Teaching geometry in the elementary grades differs from teaching arithmetic in several respects. Because geometry as it is taught in the elementary schools is generally intuitive, there is no prescribed set of rules or skills analogous to those necessary in arithmetic. It would be very difficult to classify components of geometry according to any sort of hierarchy. Yet learning certain phases of geometry depends upon knowledge of other phases.

Matching shapes

Students in the lower grades should be able to match shapes such as triangles, rectangles, squares, and circles. For example, if one set of figures contains four figures and another set contains only three of the four figures, students should indicate which figure is missing. The ability to do this indicates that students can associate like shapes.

Recognition

The main thrust in the lower grades is toward building vocabulary and association of names with shapes. Consequently, activities calling for these abilities are necessary tools for diagnosing. Such activities may begin very early. Students who do not yet read well may be able to associate words and shapes. Given a set of shapes such as a square, circle, rectangle, and triangle, a student may be asked to point to the figure named by the teacher. For students who read, a simple matching exercise works quite well. Figures are placed in one column and names of the figures in another column. The students' task is to draw a line from each figure to its name. Of course, more advanced students should match more complex figures and their names.

Concepts

The ability to distinguish between models of basic geometric ideas such as points, lines, line segments, and rays may be measured in several ways. In one method a student points to or otherwise indicates that he or she can distinguish between lines and line segments or line segments and rays. Similar activities may be used to measure students' ability to distinguish between parallel lines and perpendicular lines, diameters and radii, cones and pyramids, and many other figures.

Point of view

Even though geometry does not lend itself to the detailed diagnostic procedures that are used in some other fields of mathematics, a diagnostic point of view on the part of the teacher is important. For example, observing that a young student who matches triangles with squares, or an upper-elementary student who is satisfied with triangles the sums of whose angles exceed 180° tells a teacher that remedial steps must be taken to clear up basic misconceptions.

In short, it is important in teaching geometry that the teacher continuously observe students as they work and that written material be carefully examined for patterns of errors. This means, in effect, that in geometry, as in other phases of mathematics, the point of view of the teacher is the prime ingredient in the diagnostic process.

Selected references

DUTTON, WILBUR H. *Evaluating Pupils' Understanding of Arithmetic.* Englewood Cliffs, N.J.: Prentice-Hall, 1964.

FEHR, HOWARD F., and PHILLIPS, JO MCKEEBY. *Teaching Modern Mathematics in the Elementary School.* Reading, Mass.: Addison-Wesley, 1972.

KIDD, KENNETH P., MYERS, SHIRLEY B., and CILLEY, DAVID M. *The Laboratory Approach to Mathematics.* Chicago: Science Research Associates, 1970.

National Council of Teachers of Mathematics. *The Slow Learner in Mathematics.* Thirty-fifth Yearbook. Washington, D. C.: National Council of Teachers of Mathematics, 1972.

OTTO, WAYNE, and MCMENEMY, RICHARD A. *Corrective and Remedial Teaching.* Boston: Houghton Mifflin, 1966.

part VII

some advanced topics

The decision as to what curriculum is to be taught students and when is a fairly complex matter. Moreover, topics in mathematics have a way of moving around.

Some of the topics touched upon in this chapter were once introduced at the secondary-school level. However, they have been relocated in recent years and are now found in many textbooks at the middle- and upper-elementary levels.

Opinions differ as to which level, lower or upper elementary, requires more attention to methodology. However, teachers generally recognize that there is *no* level at which learning occurs in a totally spontaneous manner. Hence, there is a need for attention to ways of teaching, or methodology, at any level.

Special topics in elementary mathematics

16

Experienced teachers are aware of the fact that students do not all achieve at equal or even near-equal rates. There are many students who, because of intelligence, interest, or other reasons, seem to master general goals in a much shorter period of time than the majority of students. It is essential that these high-performance students be challenged. They should be given an opportunity to investigate topics that will not only serve as challenges but will prepare them for further study in the fields of mathematics and science.

Many topics can enrich the curriculum for students who have the interest and incentive to explore such topics. It is generally recommended that enrichment be horizontal rather than vertical: it should be designed to broaden the base of topics being studied rather than to introduce completely new topics.

This chapter is devoted to a few of the more common areas that may be considered enrichment material. Both subject matter and methodology will be covered as well as some diagnostic techniques when working in this area.

Content

Students in the elementary grades can be exposed to a wide range of other than standard topics. Considered below are only the most common areas—the number system, graphs, and some elementary statistics.

Extending our number system

One of the most practical enrichment topics for students is work with the real numbers. In fact, study of the real-number system is a part of the general curriculum in the seventh and eighth grades of many programs.

Work on the set of real numbers should begin with a review of the sets of numbers studied previously, their fundamental properties, and other basic concepts. This is a necessary part of the study because each of the sets of numbers—the natural numbers, the whole numbers, the integers, and the rational numbers—is a subset of the set of real numbers. Every property of these subsets belongs to the set of real numbers. The set of real numbers is thus a challenging extension of our number system. A review is in order because recognition of the existence of irrational numbers (the extension of rational numbers) requires an acute awareness of the properties of those sets of numbers previously studied.

Natural numbers   The set of *natural numbers* (sometimes called counting numbers) is the set {1, 2, 3, 4, 5, 6, 7, 8, 9, 10, 11, 12, . . .}. Parenthetically, it should be noted that there is not total agreement as to the definition of natural numbers. Some authors include zero as a member of the set of counting numbers.

Properties of the natural numbers that should be investigated in an introduction of the real numbers are:

1. *Uniqueness:* The sum or product of two natural numbers exists and is unique.

2. *Commutativity:* Addition and multiplication of natural numbers are commutative operations. Thus, if a and b are natural numbers, then:

    $a + b = b + a$
    $a \times b = b \times a$

3. *Associativity:* Addition and multiplication of natural numbers are associative operations. Thus, if a, b, and c are natural numbers, then:

    $a + (b + c) = (a + b) + c$
    $a \times (b \times c) = (a \times b) \times c$

4. *Distributivity:* Multiplication of natural numbers distributes over addition. Thus, if a, b, and c are natural numbers, then:

    $a(b + c) = a \cdot b + a \cdot c$

5. *Identity:* There exists in the natural numbers a multiplicative identity element. Thus, if a is a natural number, then there exists a natural number 1 such that:

$a \cdot 1 = a$

6. *Closure:* The set of natural numbers is closed under the operations of addition and multiplication. Thus if a and b are natural numbers, and $a + b = c$, then c is a natural number. And, if a and b are natural numbers, and $a \times b = c$, then c is a natural number.

Properties that do not belong to the set of natural numbers should also be investigated in reviewing the properties of the natural numbers. For example, such questions as, "Is there an identity element for addition in the set of natural numbers?" and "Is the set of natural numbers closed under the operations of subtraction and division?" can lead to very searching discussions. It is important that students discover how the number system can be extended by the inclusion of a single number. Such is the case with whole numbers.

Whole numbers The union of the set of natural numbers and zero is the set of *whole numbers*. The set of whole numbers is {0, 1, 2, 3, 4, 5, 6, 7, 8, 9, 10, 11, 12, . . .}.

Obviously the only element contained in the set of whole numbers not contained in the set of natural numbers is 0. The properties of the natural numbers belong to the set of whole numbers. The number 0 gives the set of whole numbers an additional property:

7. *Identity:* There exists in the set of whole numbers an additive identity element. Thus, if a is a natural number, there exists a number 0, such that:

$a + 0 = a$

The identity element for addition of whole numbers, zero, may not appear to be very important. However, it is a necessary and interesting property, particularly in certain proofs.

Integers The set of *integers* includes positive and negative numbers. The set of integers is the union of the set of whole numbers and the negatives of all the positive whole numbers and zero. The set of integers is {. . . -5, -4, -3, -2, -1, 0, 1, 2, 3, 4, . . .}.

In addition to the properties of whole numbers, all of which apply to the integers, there is an additional property:

8. *The additive inverse:* Every element in the set of integers has

an additive inverse. Thus, if a is an integer, there exists another integer $-a$ such that:

$a + (-a) = 0$

An interesting point is that negative numbers were not dealt with in operations to any extent until the seventeenth century. Even the great philosopher and mathematician René Descartes (1596–1650) considered a negative number of greater absolute value larger than one of smaller absolute value; to him -6 was greater than -3. Although many ancient Babylonian, Greek, and Hindu scholars played around with ideas of zero and negative numbers, solutions involving such numbers were considered meaningless.

To elementary students it may seem inconceivable that there can be less than "none" of something. It should be explained that this is not what is meant by negative numbers. The set of negative numbers is not a means of counting or enumerating but is used to describe another quality of a number, namely, direction. Students at the middle- and upper-elementary levels have probably played games in which points can be lost as well as gained; they know something of earning and spending money, distances above and below sea level, or temperatures above and below zero. Therefore, they should be able to comprehend that for certain quantities there are other quantities that are oppositely directed. In fact, most modern elementary-arithmetic books refer to integers as directed numbers.

In order to relate the concept of directed numbers to everyday problems, the game of football serves as a good example. Students might consider the following problem. Suppose that the football is on the 20 yard line. On the first play the halfback gains 5 yards, and on the second play he loses 5 yards. Where is the football now located, and what was the net gain? The answer, of course, is that in two plays there is no net gain and the football is on the 20 yard line—where it was at the beginning. The problem could then be extended to include a third play in which the halfback loses 5 yards, and students would be asked the same questions. Terminology could then be introduced expressing a gain as a "+" and a loss as a "−".

Another familiar example is seen in reading thermometers. When asked the question, "If the temperature is 4°F and drops 6° what will be the new reading?" Some students may say that the temperature is 2° below zero. With guidance they can be made to see how this can be expressed using directed numbers.

Use of a number line can be helpful as a visual material. The

number line can be extended to include points corresponding to
negative numbers in the following manner:

Just as points on the line were assigned to correspond with the
whole numbers, points on the line corresponding to the opposite of
each of the whole numbers can be assigned. Thus opposite the
number 1 and at an equal distance from 0, there is a point designated as − 1. The same can be said for 2 and − 2, 3 and − 3, and so
on. A scale is thus constructed where 0 corresponds to a point from
which it is possible to make measurements in either direction.

In some cases it may be feasible to perform operations with
directed numbers in the upper-elementary grades. Such algebraic
operations should probably begin with the number line. For example, the addition of $^+2 + ^+3$ may be shown as follows:

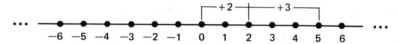

This type of illustration may be drawn on the chalkboard, showing
first the bar representing 2; then, to indicate the positive direction
for addition the chalk should be moved three more spaces to the
right, thus extending the bar to $^+5$. The sum $^+2 + ^+3$ is $^+5$.

Addition of a positive and a negative number may be illustrated in a like manner:

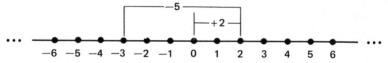

The sum $^+2 + ^-5$ is shown to be $^-3$. Efforts should be directed
toward building concepts, not learning rules.

Rational numbers   A *rational number* is a number that can be
expressed as the quotient of two integers, as long as division by 0 is
not involved. If a and b are integers, $b \neq 0$, then a/b is a rational
number. Students are likely to suggest at this point that rational
numbers are fractions. Although fractions make up the set of
numbers adjoined to the integers to form the set of rational
numbers, each integer is also a rational number. It would be appropriate to have students examine the properties of integers as they
relate to the rational numbers and determine whether each property of the integers applies to the rationals. Each student should

also try to discover the new property inherent to the rational numbers, namely: multiplicative inverse.

9. *The multiplicative inverse:* Every element in the set of rational numbers, except zero, has a multiplicative inverse. Thus, if *a* is a rational number, there exists another rational number 1/*a* such that

$$a \cdot \frac{1}{a} = 1$$

This is a most useful property in proofs and explanations.

Exponents   As a matter of logical sequencing, irrationals could be introduced at this point. However, before considering irrational numbers, certain basic concepts of exponents and radicals should be examined.

In the expression $2 \times 2 \times 2 \times 2 \times 2$, the number 2 is a factor 5 times. This may be written as 2^5, in which 2 is the *base* and 5 is the *exponent*. The exponent expresses the power of the base, that is how many times the base is a factor. The power of the base is usually expressed in ordinal form. For instance, 2^4 is read "two to the fourth" and 3^6 is read "three to the sixth." There are two exceptions to this practice; the second power is usually referred to as the square of the base and the third power as the cube. Thus, 3^2 is read "three squared" and 2^3 is read "two cubed."

Although computation with exponents is not usually a part of the general curriculum, questions that may be raised by students require that teachers be familiar with basic operations.

Multiplication and division are the basic two operations to be considered. Because addition of numbers with exponents requires multiplication before addition, there is no way to cut short the operation. Thus, to add 10^2 and 10^3, one must perform the following:

$$
\begin{aligned}
10^2 + 10^3 &= (10 \times 10) + (10 \times 10 \times 10) \\
&= 100 + 1000 \\
&= 1100
\end{aligned}
$$

In multiplication, however, there is a shortcut. The expression $10^2 \times 10^3$ is equivalent to $(10 \times 10) \times (10 \times 10 \times 10)$. Because the product has 10 as a factor 5 times, it may be expressed 10^5. Again, $2^5 \times 2^3$ is equivalent to $(2 \times 2 \times 2 \times 2 \times 2) \times (2 \times 2 \times 2)$, an expression with 8 factors. This may be written 2^8. Working several simple exercises of this type should lead students to the conclusion that the exponent of the product of two or more exponential numbers having the same number as a base is the sum of the exponents. The general statement for this is:

$$x^a \cdot x^b = x^{a+b}$$

Division of numbers expressed in exponential form may be explained in like manner. Consider the expression $10^5 \div 10^2$. Because $10^5 = 10 \times 10 \times 10 \times 10 \times 10$ and $10^2 = 10 \times 10$, the expression $10^5 \div 10^2$ may be written as $(10 \times 10 \times 10 \times 10 \times 10) \div (10 \times 10)$, or:

$$\frac{10 \times 10 \times 10 \times 10 \times 10}{10 \times 10} = 10^3$$

Further investigation leads to the conclusion that the exponent of the quotient obtained by dividing numbers with like bases is obtained by subtracting the exponent of the divisor from the exponent of the dividend. Thus $10^5 \div 10^2 = 10^{5-2}$. A general statement is:

$$x^a \div x^b = x^{a-b}$$

This investigation leads to the discussion of a phenomenon that, although strange to students, is perfectly logical and necessary to the development of many important ideas in mathematics. The statement $x^a \div x^b = x^{a-b}$ seems to be logical if a is greater than b, but what happens if a equals b? The result, of course, is x^0. The meaning of this expression is best arrived at by considering an example such as $10^5 \div 10^5$:

$$\frac{10^5}{10^5} = 10^{5-5}$$
$$= 10^0$$

But students know from their work with division that $10^5 \div 10^5 = 1$ because any number divided by itself (except 0) is 1. Logically, then, it follows that $10^0 = 1$. Stated formally, in all cases, except when $x = 0$:

$$x^a \div x^a = x^0 = 1$$

Square roots The inverse operation of squaring a number is *finding the square root*. In the preceding section it was shown that raising a number to the second power, such as 3^2, requires multiplying 3×3. Thus, $3 \times 3 = 9$ or $3^2 = 9$. Suppose it is required to find the square root of 9. This means that a number must be found that, when multiplied by itself, is equal to 9. Since $3 \times 3 = 9$, then 3 is a square root of 9. Notice the statement that 3 is *a* square root of 9. There may be another. Since $^-3$, $\times^-3 = 9$, -3 fulfills the requirement stated for a square root. However, the symbol $\sqrt{}$, by agreement among mathematicians, indicates the positive square root. Thus, $\sqrt{9} = 3$, $\sqrt{16} = 4$, and so on. The positive square root is called the "principal" square root. The negative square root may be indicated by preceding the radical with a minus sign. The negative square root of 9 is written $-\sqrt{9} = -3$.

Irrational numbers One of the interesting properties of rational numbers, the density property, was discussed in the section on rational numbers. *Density* means that between any two numbers in a set there is a third number of the set. If the numbers of the set are associated with points on a line, then between any two rational points there is a third rational point. Although it might seem that all points on the line correspond to rational numbers, this is not the case.

It can be shown that points do exist on the number line that cannot be associated with rational numbers. Consider the right triangle in Figure 16-1, in which the sides a and b are each 1 unit in length. Let the hypotenuse c be a segment of a number line. By the Pythagorean Theorem, $a^2 + b^2 = c^2$. Thus, substituting the values $a = 1$ and $b = 1$:

$$1^2 + 1^2 = c^2$$
$$1 + 1 = c^2$$
$$2 = c^2$$
$$c^2 = 2$$
$$c = \sqrt{2}$$

Thus, c is a segment whose length is $\sqrt{2}$. If B is considered to be the zero point on the number line, then A is a point corresponding to $\sqrt{2}$. It can be shown that $\sqrt{2}$ is not a rational number, but the proof is rather difficult and is not recommended for elementary students. However, if there are students who may profit from such an investigation, good treatments of the topic are to be found in many high-school textbooks.

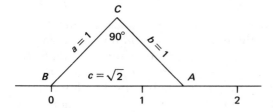

Figure 16-1. $\sqrt{2}$ on a number line

Real numbers The preceding discussion has demonstrated how the number system has been extended to include *irrational numbers*, those to which no rational number can be assigned on the number line. The union of the set of rational numbers and the set of irrational numbers is called the set of *real numbers*. Every real number corresponds to a point on the number line, and every point on the number line corresponds to a real number. This is a very important principle. There is now a completeness in our number system that was not present without the irrational numbers. Although the above discussion demonstrated that only one point on the line does not correspond to a rational number, students should be made aware that there are many such points. To give them some idea of the boundless nature of the set of irrational numbers, they might be shown that the product of $\sqrt{2}$ and any rational number is an irrational number. The same can be shown for other irrational numbers such as $\sqrt{5}$, $\sqrt{7}$, and $\sqrt{11}$.

Work with graphs

Many children enjoy studying graphs. The study begins with the number line. Number-line graphs help students think about important sets of numbers such as the natural numbers, integers, rational numbers, and real numbers. Other graphs present pictorial representations of relationships existing between sets of variables. The relationships between two sets of numbers seem to become more vivid when represented graphically. Besides number lines, there are three important types of graphs to which students can be exposed—the bar graph, the line graph, and the circle graph.

The *bar graph* is a very effective means of comparing amounts such as sales, profits, and so on. Either vertical or horizontal bar graphs can be used to present vivid displays of data. For example, the graph in Figure 16-2 indicates a steady increase in attendance of basketball games.

A second type of graph, the *line graph*, is an excellent means of showing the fluctuation of data. The reference lines, one vertical and one horizontal, are labeled by the two sets of data the graph compares. Care must be exercised in selecting a scale for the line graph that will present the data in the best way.

The graph in Figure 16-3 shows the same data as Figure 16-2. The study of such graphs should help students learn how to see and predict trends. Learning to read and construct line graphs is very practical for youngsters in today's world.

One final type of graph, the *circle graph*, is an excellent method of showing a clear picture of the comparative size of a unit's

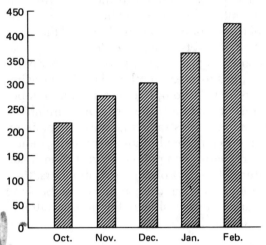

Figure 16-2. Bar graph

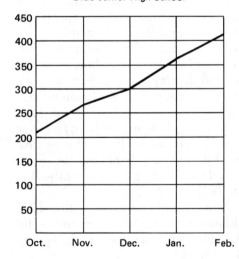

Figure 16-3. Line graph

Party Expenses for Fair Park
Sixth Grade

Figure 16-4. Circle graph

components. The sectors of the circle are in proportion to the size of the components they represent. Students studying this kind of graph should already be acquainted with ratios, proportions, and angular measure. Circle graphs are often used in budget preparation, as Figure 16-4 shows.

Measures of central tendency

Another practical topic that students often enjoy studying is averages. Numerical data that have been organized tend to cluster, to some degree, about a point. This clustering is called the data's *central tendency,* or *average.* There are three common measures of central tendency—the mean, the median, and the mode.

When the term "average" is used, people often have in mind the mean. The *mean* of a set of data is determined by dividing the sum of the data by the number of observations. For example, the mean of a student's test scores is derived by adding the scores and dividing by the number of tests. Thus if a student took 4 tests on which the scores were 90, 85, 80, 75, the mean is (90 + 85 + 80 + 75) ÷ 4, or 82.5. This number, of course, becomes very meaningful to students since evaluation is usually on the basis of the mean.

If a set of data is arranged in order of size, the *median* is the point below which half the scores fall. For example in the set of scores 6, 7, 8, 9, 10, the median is 8. In the set of scores 6, 7, 8, 9, 10, and 11, the median is found by adding the two middle scores and dividing by 2. Thus the median is (8 + 9) ÷ 2, or 8.5. There are circumstances in which the median is more meaningful than the mean. When extreme scores are involved, the mean may become distorted. In such cases the median may be a better average to consider. Students should discuss other ways in which statistics may be used to distort rather than clarify.

The *mode* is the measure that occurs most in a set of measures. Thus if the set consists of 3, 4, 4, 5, 6, 7, 7, 7, 8, and 9, the mode is 7. Obviously, a set of data may not have a mode.

Probability

Young students are generally intrigued by games of chance, so that it is usually not very difficult to generate interest in probability. The easiest way to introduce the topic is to toss a coin a number of times and have students observe the incidence of heads and tails. The question, "What is the probability of a head?" is sure to bring a number of answers. Collecting data and computing the probability is a good exercise. The discussion can be enlivened by tossing two coins. Students can then collect data, compute chances of matches, show how many ways there are of getting two heads or two tails, and find the probability mathematically.

A die has six faces. Therefore, the probability of rolling a die and having a one come up is 1 in 6. The same is true for any of the other five numbers. One problem that can generate a great deal of mathematical discussion is to calculate the probability of seven being the total of the dots when two dice are rolled. Students should be encouraged to work the problem themselves. A few leading questions may help them develop a scheme. For example, students may be asked, "How many ways can seven occur?" The answer is 6, one way of which is to roll a four on one die and a three on the other. If students elicit that answer, the teacher can then ask what the probability of four is and after that what the probability of three is. Such discussions can become quite involved and interesting.

Methods

The first point relative to methodology in work on material described in this chapter involves a point of common sense: Do not expect each student to cover each page in a textbook. The topics described here and other similar topics can be interesting and challenging to some students; to others, however, the only possible outcome if they try to work in these areas is frustration and defeat.

Even high-performance students do not automatically rise to the challenge in this type of work. For one thing, it should be presented as an opportunity, not an assignment leading to a test on the content. Another feature is that work of this type should supplement, not replace, work on the basic program. If this is not kept in mind, a teacher may produce a group of top performers in abstract content who have not mastered the multiplication facts. A final challenge to the teacher is to give merited recognition to the student who performs well in, for example, irrational numbers without setting him or her apart as an object of envy and rejection for peers.

While the high performance students are working on special topics, what is happening to the other students? They should be working on other topics in keeping with their own needs. To repeat an earlier position, a teacher who has all students working on the same thing at the same time and at the same rate of speed is not likely to be reaching all students. This principle is as applicable at the upper-elementary level as it is at any other level.

Diagnosis

There are a number of reasons why teachers should be concerned about diagnosis when working with accelerated students on enrichment material. One is that misconceptions are not limited to any one level of performance so that they can easily develop among such students. The accelerated student has as much right to expect assistance in this situation as does any other student. Another reason for the diagnostic approach in this situation is that poor work habits can develop at any performance level. The sloppy worker, the sprawler, the mumbler can be found almost anywhere, and such habits need to be corrected as early as possible.

It is impossible to anticipate specific points at which diagnosis could serve a useful purpose. Hence, the diagnostic teacher at this level must continuously observe the two broad areas of performance and product. Of course, as has been pointed out earlier, the information gained by the diagnostic teacher is helpful only to the extent that it is used to benefit the student.

appendices

Some useful materials

Tests

1. The Adston Diagnostic Series. This consists of (1) diagnostic tests in readiness for operations, (2) diagnostic tests in whole-number operations, and (3) prescriptive sets in whole-number operations. Other tests are in the process of development. Distributed by Adston Educational Enterprises, Inc., Drawer 18430B, University Station, Baton Rouge, La. 70803.
2. Allyn & Bacon. This company's *Handbook in Diagnostic Teaching* contains a section on arithmetic, including diagnostic material. The primary emphasis is on learning disabilities. Distributed by Allyn & Bacon, Inc., Longwood Division, Link Drive, Rockleigh, N.J. 07647.
3. CTB/McGraw-Hill. This publisher has several types of material available. First, they have the classic *Diagnostic Tests and Self-Helps in Arithmetic*, by Leo Brueckner. Then they have an elaborate series of *Prescriptive Mathematics Inventory* material. Distributed by CTB/McGraw-Hill, Del Monte Research Park, Monterey, Calif., 93940.
4. Houghton Mifflin. This publisher has diagnostic tests as part of their *Mathematics for Individual Achievement* material. Distributed by Houghton Mifflin Company, 110 Tremont Street, Boston, Mass. 02107.

5. Harcourt Brace Jovanovich. The Stanford Diagnostic Arithmetic Test is designed to pinpoint a student's needs, with guides to indicated follow-up instruction. Distributed by Harcourt Brace Jovanovich, Inc., 757 Third Avenue, New York, N.Y. 10017.

Books

1. BRUECKNER, LEO, and BOND, GUY L. *The Diagnosis and Treatment of Learning Difficulties*. Englewood Cliffs, N.J.: Prentice-Hall, 1955.
2. National Council of Teachers of Mathematics. *The Slow Learner in Mathematics*. Washington, D.C.: National Council of Teachers of Mathematics, 1972.
3. OTTO, WAYNE, and MCMENEMY, RICHARD A. *Corrective and Remedial Teaching*. Boston: Houghton Mifflin, 1966.
4. REISMAN, FREDRICKA. *A Guide to the Diagnostic Teaching of Arithmetic*. Columbus, Ohio: Merrill, 1972.
5. SMITH, ROBERT M. *Teacher Diagnosis of Educational Difficulties*. Columbus, Ohio: Merrill, 1969.

A diagnostic survey in a school system

A person who has not had teaching experience, or a teacher whose work has been with high-performance students, might well wonder if the diagnostic approach as presented here deals with a real situation. Frequently such persons ask, "How could that give trouble?" or "Didn't you draw on your imagination to set up such difficulties?"

In order to add a further touch of reality, therefore, we are presenting, in summary form, the data that resulted when a diagnostic survey was made in a specific school system. The system used is essentially rural but is near a major industrial area.

The public schools in the system had, at the time of the survey, a total enrollment of about 10,000 students. However, the survey was restricted to students enrolled in the sixth grade, which included 690 students. The diagnostic testing was carried out during the last month of the school year.

The survey data are presented in table form and with essentially no elaboration because the table entries seem largely self-explanatory. Since percentages are rounded to whole numbers, columns do not total 100 in all cases.

As can be observed from Table 1, the greatest sources of difficulty in addition were lack of mastery of the addition facts, inability to carry properly, and inability to handle column

Table 1 Analysis of errors on addition tests

Type of error	Frequency	Percentage of total errors
Combinations		
Incorrect combination	218	24
Zero in combination	33	4
TOTAL	**251**	**28**
Carrying		
Did not carry and add number to next column	108	12
Recorded tens and carried ones	35	4
Did not carry—recorded two digits in one place	34	4
Carried wrong number	10	1
Carried unnecessarily	3	—
TOTAL	**190**	**21**
Procedure		
Added ones to both ones and tens in horizontal examples	41	5
Performed wrong operation	26	3
Recorded only one digit of two-digit sum	24	3
Combined two operations	22	3
Skipped column with only zeros	18	2
Did not bridge to next decade in horizontal examples	12	1
Reversed digits in recording sum	1	—
TOTAL	**144**	**16**
Miscellaneous		
Inability to handle column addition	302	34
Incomplete	15	2
Undetermined	10	1
TOTAL	**327**	**37**
GRAND TOTAL	**912**	**100**

addition. Specific difficulties can be isolated only in a work-aloud procedure, and this was not feasible with the group under study.

It should be noted in Table 2 that the group under study made more than twice as many errors in subtraction than in addition despite the fact that the subtraction test was shorter. This serves to verify the opinion of many teachers as to the relative difficulty of the two operations.

Again, zero was the great offender. Also, borrowing gave a great deal of trouble. A major procedural error was to subtract the minuend from the subtrahend when the minuend was smaller. This

Table 2 Analysis of errors on subtraction tests

Type of error	Frequency	Percentage of total errors
Combinations		
Incorrect combination	182	7
Incorrect combination when minuend and subtrahend were identical	77	3
TOTAL	**259**	**10**
Zero		
Recorded zero when minuend was zero	280	11
Recorded subtrahend when minuend was zero	259	10
Recorded zero when subtrahend was zero	90	4
Disregarded column with zero in minuend and subtrahend	40	2
Recorded zero when subtrahend was larger than minuend	33	1
TOTAL	**702**	**28**
Procedure		
Subtracted minuend from subtrahend when minuend was smaller	632	26
Recorded subtrahend when subtrahend was larger than minuend	36	1
Recorded minuend when minuend was larger than subtrahend	16	1
Subtracted minuend from subtrahend regardless of relative size	3	—
TOTAL	**687**	**28**
Renaming		
Did not deduct from minuend after renaming	435	18
Distributed renamed quantity incorrectly throughout minuend	87	4
Renamed largest place in minuend more than one time	75	3
Renamed unnecessarily	43	2
Renamed thousands as ten ones	25	1
TOTAL	**665**	**28**
Miscellaneous		
Undetermined	117	5
Wrong operation	21	1
Incomplete	18	1
Two operations combined	8	—
TOTAL	**164**	**7**
GRAND TOTAL	**2477**	**100**

is an error related to borrowing in that the student uses this procedure because it makes borrowing unnecessary. Many students resort to this completely erroneous procedure.

In the phase of the survey dealing with multiplication by one-digit multipliers, the greatest source of errors, as can be seen from Table 3, was lack of mastery of the basic facts. Carrying was also a source of errors, though significantly fewer. The category classed as "undetermined" included difficulties that could be classified only through use of a work-aloud procedure.

Table 4 indicates that the procedures used in multiplication problems with multi-digit multipliers are somewhat more sophisticated than those of earlier operations. For example, many errors

Table 3 Analysis of errors on multiplication exercises using one-digit multipliers

Type of error	Frequency	Percentage of total errors
Combinations		
Incorrect combination	538	43
Incorrect zero combination	61	5
TOTAL	**599**	**48**
Carrying or renaming		
Carried incorrect number	113	9
Did not carry after renaming	98	8
Skipped place with zero when carrying	8	1
TOTAL	**219**	**18**
Procedure		
Added carried number and multiplier when multiplicand was zero	52	4
Added carried number to multiplicand before multiplying	45	4
Recorded two digits in one place	43	4
Multiplied carried number and added multiplicand	14	1
TOTAL	**154**	**13**
Miscellaneous		
Undetermined	184	15
Two operations combined	29	2
Incomplete	25	2
Digits reversed when recording	18	2
Wrong operation	10	1
TOTAL	**266**	**22**
GRAND TOTAL	**1238**	**100**

Table 4 Analysis of errors on multiplication exercises using multi-digit multipliers

Type of error	Frequency	Percentage of total errors
Combinations		
Incorrect combination	641	31
Incorrect zero combination	79	3
TOTAL	**720**	**34**
Carrying or renaming		
Did not carry or add to next column	133	6
Carried incorrect number or added carried number incorrectly	98	5
Carried unnecessarily	9	—
TOTAL	**240**	**11**
Procedure		
Added partial products	270	13
Aligned columns of partial products incorrectly	225	11
Multiplied each column independently	183	9
Skipped zero in multiplicand	40	2
Added carried number and multiplier when multiplicand was zero	39	2
Added carried number to multiplicand before multiplying	10	1
TOTAL	**767**	**38**
Miscellaneous		
Undetermined	190	9
Incomplete	121	6
Two operations combined	27	1
Digits reversed when recording	11	1
Two digits recorded in one place	1	—
TOTAL	**350**	**17**
GRAND TOTAL	**2077**	**100**

were made in work with partial products. However, a close competitor was errors caused by lack of mastery of the basic facts.

The survey of errors in division with one-digit divisors, reported in Table 5, indicates that students were still having trouble—quite predictably—with the multiplication and division facts. Also, numerous procedural errors arose, especially with regard to zero in the quotient. Some of the students in the survey group were operating at such a low level in division that they really could not be considered as participants in this phase.

Table 5 Analysis of errors on division exercises using one-digit divisors

Type of error	Frequency	Percentage of total errors
Related operations		
Multiplication and division combinations	210	21
Subtraction	79	8
Addition	10	1
TOTAL	**299**	**30**
Procedure		
Omitted zeros in quotient	147	15
Did not divide all digits in dividend	95	10
Did not divide zeros in dividend	94	10
Underestimated quotient	56	6
Carried operation extra step	48	5
Overestimated quotient	27	3
Eliminated partial remainder before bringing down number	8	1
Brought down incorrect number	8	1
TOTAL	**483**	**51**
Miscellaneous		
Undetermined	185	19
Quotient recorded incorrectly	13	1
Remainder recorded incorrectly	8	1
Partial quotient and divisor reversed	5	1
TOTAL	**211**	**22**
GRAND TOTAL	**993**	**100**

All of the outcomes in the final phase of the survey dealing with division using multi-digit divisors were fairly predictable. As Table 6 shows, almost half of the total number of errors (49 percent) were in related operations. This leads to the logical conclusion that many of the problems in division stem from those areas that are outside the field of division but figure into the division process, such as multiplication and subtraction.

After reviewing the results recorded above, one might well agree with a participating teacher in the survey. She said that if her students could (1) achieve mastery of the basic facts in the four operations and (2) become clear on the role of zero in the operations, most of their deficiencies would be cleared up. If she had added to her list the basics of carrying and borrowing, her position would have been even more defensible.

Table 6 Analysis of errors on division exercises using
multi-digit divisors

Type of error	Frequency	Percentage of total errors
Related Operations		
Multiplication	272	19
Subtraction	260	18
Multiplication and division combinations	165	11
Addition	21	1
TOTAL	**718**	**49**
Procedure		
Underestimated quotient	189	13
Omitted zero in quotient	139	9
Did not divide all digits in dividend	89	6
Overestimated quotient	34	2
Divided remainder before bringing down	20	1
Brought down incorrect number	6	—
Eliminated partial remainder	3	—
TOTAL	**480**	**32**
Miscellaneous		
Undetermined	252	17
Quotient recorded incorrectly	8	1
Remainder recorded incorrectly	4	—
Partial quotient and divisor reversed	3	—
TOTAL	**267**	**18**
GRAND TOTAL	**1465**	**100**

Two
case studies

In the use of an approach such as the one we have examined here, it is seldom adequate merely to study *about* it. A person needs to work with it over a period of time. However, working with an entire class is a massive task and not ideal for trying out the procedures. Hence, the authors and their colleagues have made extensive use of a case-study procedure, in which a college student works in a one-to-one situation with an elementary student. As a culmination to this phase the college student prepares a written report summarizing that work with the student, with special attention to diagnosis and remediation.

The two case studies that follow are essentially as they were originally written except that some background material on the student has been omitted in order to conserve space. The first study was prepared by Helen Grant; the second, by Frances Ferguson.

John

A small, slight boy with tousled hair and an unkempt appearance, John presented himself at the initial session as eager to learn. He freely expressed his need for help in mathematics and recounted his present difficulties in that subject area. According to his description of the classroom situation, the students work individually on assigned pages in the text and are tested at the conclusion of the assignment. He states there is no group instruction and that he does not ask for explanations from his teacher.

Diagnosis

The first ten minutes of his work on the Adston Survey were interrupted by frequent comments and attempts at conversation. This talkativeness betrayed John's nervousness, as did two trips to the bathroom within twenty minutes. Once he settled down, John worked quickly and quietly through the addition and subtraction sections. His pace noticeably slackened in the multiplication and division sections, however. He remarked that he could not remember how to work exercises dealing with zero. He attributed this to the lengthy time he had been studying fractions at school.

John completed the survey instrument in a total of 45 minutes. Scoring the test revealed that the addition and subtraction sections were without error. Fewer than half of the multiplication exercises, however, were correct. Half of the division exercises were also in error.

Having no need for further testing in addition and subtraction, John moved on to the Diagnostic Instrument of Multiplication Facts. All seven incorrect answers given here were zero facts. John's errors resulted from using zero as if it had a value of one. For example, these facts were among those missed: $0 \times 9 = 9$ and $9 \times 0 = 9$. This misconception was pointed out to John while scoring the section.

At the second session John was observably more at ease. He told of asking his teacher for help with three problems he did not understand and expressed confidence in his ability to pass a level test scheduled for the following day. He had failed this test two weeks earlier.

The test battery was completed at this session by the administration of the Diagnostic Instruments in Multiplication and Division Operations. John set to work purposively and finished the 63 exercises within 40 minutes. Examination of the multiplication exercises showed that the testing of the previous session had proven to be a learning situation. John had made no further errors in multiplying with zero. In fact, his three mistakes were careless ones and not operational in nature. Moreover, in the interpretation of the division exercises, no operational pattern of error could be perceived. Of the four problems missed, however, each error involved a zero in a different way. In one the quotient was expressed as 199 r 3, rather than 200. In another, a zero was omitted in writing the quotient as 470 *r* 2, rather than 4070 *r* 2. This error may be attributed to carelessness because the sequence of multiplication and subtraction steps was properly done. The remaining errors were also careless ones: 6 × 67 = 382 rather than 402 and 237 − 217 = 27 rather than 20.

Remedial teaching

The concluding level of the fifth-year Houghton Mifflin text in use includes review of the major learning tasks incorporated within the book. The only topic to be introduced at this level is computation with decimal fractions. Despite John's persistent difficulties with common fractions, decimal fractions posed no problems for him. Their conversion from common fractions and vice versa was quickly mastered, as were operations employing them. In fact, John did not request any assistance with this aspect of the program. He asserted that decimal fractions were easy, and selected examples worked with him verified his competence.

Division of whole numbers The review of long division posed special problems for John. The year and a half he had spent on fractions had offered few opportunities to practice previously acquired skills. With regard to the task of dividing a six-place dividend by a two-place divisor, for example, the technique of rounding off the divisor had to be retaught. By beginning with a four-place dividend and the partial-quotient method, John soon became proficient. His tendency to be sloppy and careless in his written work was discouraged by turning note paper sideways and using the lines to guide placement of the digits in columns.

A short form of division that required intense concentration confirmed that John is not inherently lacking in arithmetical ability. The method, illustrated below, was accomplished by John within minutes of its demonstration.

$$\begin{array}{r} 3668 \ r \ 4 \\ \hline 7)25680 \\ 4466 \end{array}$$

To make practical application of long division, John used a monthly milk bill to compute the price per quart and half gallon. Word problems were composed using a major automotive company's annual report. For example, the shipping weights of compact and intermediate-size cars were found by dividing the weight of each shipment by the number of cars shipped.

Another method that provided both variety and entertainment was a practice sheet of problems for which the quotients had been recorded on the back in Egyptian notation. Rather than check his work with the usual multiplication, John converted his quotients to the Egyptian system to verify the answers.

Common fractions   When the review of common fractions commenced, John's interest waned. He was neglectful of assignments and classwork and inattentive in tutoring sessions. Because his long siege of fractions probably had led to the development of a negative attitude, work was centered around unfamiliar materials. Concrete objects enabled John to acquire a clearer idea of the nature of fractions and how they work. Fraction labs were set up in which building blocks illustrated wholes, halves, and fourths. The same blocks were used to work addition and subtraction problems. These manipulations were of assistance in work on the lowest-common-denominator concept, a continuing difficulty for John.

Other exercises required John to discover some fractional part of a group of objects. For example, eight golf balls were displayed. Two were marked "Titlist." John was asked what fractional part of the set of balls was represented by that brand. Ten movie-film cans were arranged in stacks of six and four. John was asked what fractional part of the group was in each stack. Overlays illustrative of the interpretation of "×" and "of" gave new meaning to the multiplication of fractions.

Although some of the lab exercises seemed rather elementary, John relished them and enjoyed devising his own problems. His pleasure in these activities was understandable after so many months devoted exclusively to textbook assignments.

Initially, division of fractions posed a problem because John had difficulty remembering to invert and multiply. He would invert and divide or fail to invert and multiply. Supervised practice finally eliminated this tendency.

When John had completed representative portions of the text section designated as level 35, a trial test was devised for review. Although only 80 percent of the trial-test exercises were done correctly, it was considered advisable for John to attempt the next level test. John passed this examination with a score of 88 percent.

Conclusions

When tutoring sessions began, it was difficult to understand how as intelligent a child as John could have fallen so far behind in the mathematics program. Working with him for three months has indicated what many of his problems are. Some of these are unique to John's emotional and physical makeup. Others are an outgrowth of circumstances currently prevalent in many schools.

Despite his problems, or perhaps because of them, John responded well to the tutoring relationship. On the whole, he was an apt and eager pupil whose innate abilities were demonstrated time and again. The difficulties revealed by the Adston Diagnostic Instruments were readily corrected, and John went on to make more progress in two months than he had in as many years. He advanced two levels and started work with the sixth-year text. He now seeks the classroom assistance of his teacher. His math grade has risen from D to C. During the second semester his absentee record has been reduced by more than half.

These are but a few of the positive indications that John's interest in math in particular and school in general has increased. Equally important, his self-confidence has been bolstered and a positive self-image promoted.

Sherri

Sherri, a very contradictory and sometimes obstreperous young lady of eight, became this writer's client. The first impression of Sherri will be long remembered. She chewed gum quite vigorously, tossed her head, and gestured often to avoid a direct reply. When her answers were given, they were curt and almost shockingly negative. She stated that she did not have any hobbies, that she did not like anyone or anything, that she did not have any friends, and that she did not know why she was even in the tutoring session in the first place! One of her first remarks was, "I've already finished the fourth-grade math book. Are you going to put me in the fifth-grade math book?" This question received the reply that there would be no textbook to "put her in," and that we were merely going to see how well she could do and help her if there was any indication that she needed help. This seemed to satisfy her temporarily, and she agreed to take the diagnostic test that had been brought to the first session.

During the weeks that Sherri attended the tutoring session, it was discovered that she has mastered the art of impression management.

Initial diagnosis

The Adston Diagnostic Instruments used in the survey testing were completed in the first two days of the tutoring session. During the test Sherri began to count on the fingers of one hand. She looked up at intervals to detect whether or not she was being observed. As she grew more confident, and as she apparently began to feel more secure in the use of a crutch in the presence of a tutor, she began to use both hands as well as the pencil to touch one finger after the other. With more difficult problems she worked more slowly and became more obviously dependent on the counting procedures.

In addition, Sherri missed problems 7, 8, and 10 as well as the horizontal addition problem number 12. She was successful with one-, two-, and three-digit numerals and with single-column addition as long as the problems were fairly simple. But when she reached the three-column addition problems containing four sets of numerals, she was unsuccessful and showed her frustration by rushing through, by not bothering to check her answers in any way, and by not seeming to be aware that her answers were totally unrealistic.

The types of mistakes Sherri made were easily discernible. For example, in recording her answers in addition she reversed the order of the numerals and placed in the ones column the numeral that should have been carried to the tens column. Then she did not add the hundreds column correctly. Her computations were as follows:

678	401
954	308
321	506
+ 107	+ 809
242	342

These samples taken from her survey test seemed to indicate a need for further study of place value because she was getting the correct answer but was recording the answer incorrectly. It was also clear that she needed to master the facts before she would ever feel comfortable working addition problems. In the horizontal addition problem that Sherri missed it was only a matter of miscounting her fingers! Her answer was: $17 + 8 = 24$. On the day that she was requested to tell how she had arrived at this answer, she counted on her fingers and came up with 25.

In the subtraction operations, Sherri missed the last five out of eight problems for various reasons. First, she had not mastered the subtraction facts. Second, she did not know when or how to borrow whenever the problem was larger than two digits. And finally, the zeros in subtraction problems seemed to be a signal for her to either give up or put down anything to occupy space. Her subtraction computations were as follows:

$$
\begin{array}{ccccc}
\overset{\overset{(0)}{}}{7\cancel{1}\cancel{5}^{(15)}} & 60 & 9060 & \overset{(12)}{7\cancel{8}\cancel{4}\cancel{3}\cancel{2}^{(12)}} & 8000 \\
-518 & -34 & -4200 & -1947 & -6329 \\
\hline
206 & 30 & 4060 & 685 & 2000 \\
\end{array}
$$

When she reached the first problem above, she asked if she was supposed to borrow. The answer given was, "Can you take 8 from 5?" She didn't reply but immediately marked through the 5, made it a 15, and subtracted to get 6. Again she ignored the zeros in several problems. The fourth problem was accompanied by audible grunts, sighing, looking about, and somehow getting lost when she reached the hundreds column.

Sherri was unable to complete the multiplication and division sections. Possibly at the third-grade level these operations had not been emphasized. She did complete the first three multiplication problems correctly, however, which means that she had been exposed to the multiplication concept, but again, that she had not mastered the necessary facts.

Later, in working with Sherri, it was found that she knew that multiplication was another way to add. She completed most of the facts sheet using the repeated-addition approach. The division section of the Adston Survey Instrument was temporarily put to one side, however. Sherri just filled spaces by placing single-digit numerals for all quotients in Division 1 problems and a minimum of two-digit numerals for quotients in the Division 2 section. She said she could not work those problems.

Prescriptive teaching

Careful checking of the completed survey revealed that priority should be given to remedial work in addition and subtraction facts and in addition and subtraction whole-number computations. Sherri is going into the fourth grade. She needs a stronger working knowledge of the skills mentioned, and it was felt that for 30 minutes a day, over a period of about 3½ weeks, it would be better to focus on the two aforementioned specific areas in the hope of helping her establish a firmer foundation.

Sherri's daily routine during the first phase of the in-depth study consisted of:

1. Looking at the addition facts and saying the answers aloud
2. Working an average of six different types of problems daily, using the addition facts that continued to cause difficulty
3. Using the place-value chart while she was learning how to carry and reinforcing it by writing the problems and their

answers on paper (a practice that was alternated with that of placing the counters in the pockets and having her write the problem on a piece of paper)

One amusing note: Sherri was completely lost every time 7 + 5 appeared. Her frustration was so obvious that for three days she was called Miss 7 + 5. She graciously played the game by answering, "Yes, that's my name, but I like to be called Miss 12 better!" This dialog occurred at intervals during the tutoring session, and the fact appeared almost daily in some of the problems she was to work. At last, one day during the solving of a subtraction problem she saw 12 − 7 and remarked immediately, "Well, I guess here that I'd be called Miss 5!" It is difficult to describe the satisfaction that one gathers from such occurrences.

In a relatively short period of time Sherri became much more adept at accurately saying her addition facts, and in approximately 1½ weeks she seemed much more sure of her carrying and place-value concepts. Her finger counting began to diminish. In fact, there were times when she worked rapidly and accurately without hesitation. She was highly praised when she did well. When she began to experience a fairly high percentage of success, it was decided that the time had come to concentrate on subtraction. Sherri's daily routine changed only slightly. It consisted of:

1. Looking–saying the subtraction facts
2. Working with the place-value chart to better understand the "why's" and the "how's" of borrowing
3. Writing down number problems that corresponded to the story problems she had "maneuvered" on the place-value chart
4. Her talking about how to proceed when a zero appeared in the subtrahend, in the minuend, or in both, and then working some problems explaining aloud what she was doing
5. Working problems not using the pocket chart while she explained, or talked about, the steps

Samples of errors

Sherri first worked with the problems she had missed on the test. Later, work was extended to problems reflecting the same operations.

In column addition she explained that she combined some of the numerals in her head. When asked how she avoided leaving out some of them, she said that she placed a small mark beside each one as she combined it. For example Sherri was given the following example:

```
   8
   4
   1
 + 7
```

She explained that she added the top 8 to the 7 + 1 (8) to get 16, and then added in the 4 to get the final sum of 20. After performing each of these operations, she placed a mark next to those numbers already worked with. It was found during class time, however, that Sherri often forgot to mark numerals; consequently, she left out a numeral or two and made mistakes. In the brief time available, no all-out effort was made to induce her to change this approach. She was alerted to the fact, however, that carelessness produces wrong answers and that it is very important not to leave out *any* numerals. Some examples of her carelessness are recorded below

```
  ⓪
①6̷78     Sherri added the ones column correctly but recorded
  954     the answer incorrectly.
  321
 +107
 2,062
```

```
  218     This was really an off day for Sherri. When she
 +586     worked aloud and explained the process, she saw
71114     her own mistake and corrected it. At this time, she
          was still working with the place-value chart.
```

In subtraction, Sherri had difficulty being consistent, as the following examples show:

```
   9      Sherri described this problem as meaning "9 take
  -2      away 2."
```

```
  43      However, in this problem, Sherri said "8 take
 -18      away 3." She was referred to her explanation of the
          first subtraction example, and she said she guessed
          that she would have to borrow. She did and got the
          correct answer.
```

```
   ⑩
③4̷0̷2̷⑫    Sherri called the 2 a "12," the 0 a "10," and the 4
 -167     a "3." She arrived at the answer "245." She then
  245     used the place-value chart, set up the problem,
          manipulated the markers, and arrived at the
          answer.
```

$$
\begin{array}{r}
\text{⑤①①①} \\
\cancel{\$}00\cancel{0} \\
-6329 \\
\hline
781
\end{array}
$$

Sherri called the first three 0s tens, and then said the thousand had "been borrowed down to 5." She added, "That isn't right!" The place-value chart was used again, the markers were manipulated, and she wrote the problem as she worked it. The correct answer and accompanying praise brought a broad smile.

Conclusions

The tutoring program for Sherri evidently produced minute but definite benefits. Not only did Sherri improve in specific mathematical skills, her posttest results showed, but most important of all, her attitude changed dramatically. After the third day gum was graciously offered to her tutor and she settled down to work with less effort, began to communicate more freely, and seemed to be less on the defensive when she made mistakes. She stopped complaining when requested to talk about a problem. On her own, she made a small place-value chart with counters of red construction paper and proudly announced that she had been using it to "solve problems." Her efforts to shock the tutor were dropped, and she settled down to the business of mathematics.

Throughout the tutoring session, Sherri displayed signs of nervousness, but they, as well as the finger counting, slowly diminished as the tutoring progressed.

index